OMAHA
HIGH-LOW

OMAHA
HIGH-LOW

BILL BOSTON

CARDOZA
PUBLISHING

Cardoza Publishing is the foremost gaming publisher in the world, with a library of over 175 up-to-date and easy-to-read books and strategies. These authoritative works are written by the top experts in their fields and with more than 8,500,000 books in print, represent the best-selling and most popular gaming books anywhere.

FIRST EDITION

Copyright © 2006 by Bill Boston
- All Rights Reserved -

Library of Congress Catalog Card No: 2005920564
ISBN: 1-58042-175-X

Visit our web site—www.cardozapub.com—or write for a full list of books and computer strategies.

CARDOZA PUBLISHING
P.O. Box 1500, Cooper Station, New York, NY 10276
Phone (800) 577-WINS
email: cardozapub@aol.com
www.cardozapub.com

TABLE OF CONTENTS

ACKNOWLEDGEMENTS

Several people have been instrumental in assuring the publication and success of this book. I thank Bob Wilson, owner of Wilson Software, for his assistance in the design of the statistical charts. He patiently answered my questions during our numerous telephone conversations. I also appreciate the advice of Shane Smith, who assisted me in refining several of my strategy points. And to June, my wife of 30 years, I give my heartfelt thanks for her patience and endurance in helping me edit the stats charts. I couldn't have done it without her. It is my pleasure to wish you the best of luck, and I hope to meet you in the winners' circle.

To find out more about the author, go to www.cardozapub.com and select "Bill Boston" from the list of authors.

▪1▪
INTRODUCTION

I first became addicted to Omaha high-low in 1985 while vacationing in Las Vegas. When I walked into the Horseshoe Casino, an Omaha high-low tournament was about to begin. I'd never heard of this strange game with its split pots and only-two-from-your-hand rule. You could even use the same cards for both ends of the pot, and the ace was so powerful that you could use it for high and low. "I've gotta try this game," I thought. "If I can't win high, I can win low — and if I really get lucky, maybe I'll win both."

Seven-card stud was my main game and I'd never played a tournament, but I didn't let that bother me. I signed up for my first-ever poker tournament, and that's when the fun began. It didn't take me long to forget the two-card rule, but I was reminded of it when I played three cards from my hand for a full house and lost to a straight. My memory was good for the next thirty minutes — until I used four cards from the board for a nut straight and lost to a smaller straight. Fortunately I had learned patience from my years as a stud player, and decided to play very few hands while I observed and learned what cards to play. My skills were missing but my luck was good enough to take me to the final table where I finished third and won just over $13,000 for a $110 buy-in. I've been stuck on Omaha high-low ever since.

Over the next few years I recorded every hand I played in Omaha high-low tournaments and live action, and I read several books, but I knew there was still more that I needed to learn. Nowhere could I find a set of reliable statistics on the relative values of the wide spectrum of possible starting hands for Omaha high-low. Finally I purchased Turbo Omaha High-Low Split by Wilson Software and spent several hundred hours generating statistics that have answered many of my questions about the value of various starting hands. The result of that research is the meat of this book.

Since my first Omaha high-low tournament more than twenty years ago, I have played in several hundred tournaments as well as live-action games. With knowledge that I have gained from statistical information and much practice, my results in tournament and live-action games have been rewarding.

It is my intention to share with you many things I have learned about this exciting game. If you have read other books on Omaha high-low, you are going to discover that my recommendations on playing the game differs from other authors, under certain conditions. There will be no poker stories in this book. I will attempt to keep it simple and try not to bore you with unnecessary reading. I also promise that you will find information in this book that you will not find in any other publication.

▪2▪
RESEARCH METHODOLOGY

Using the hand analysis function of Wilson Software's Turbo Omaha High-Low Split, I ran at least 100,000 simulations per starting hand, and as many as 2,000,000 simulations on hands with an ace (A-x-x-x). The player type that I selected was "tight," meaning it would select only the best starting hands in a nine-handed $10/$20 game.

The statistics in this book are based on 5,278 commonly dealt hands that are played in Omaha high-low. You can switch the suits and change the order of the cards in these hands to make 270,725 combinations. The stats are based on hands that are double-suited, suited and non-suited. Since it is possible to make a flush in only one suit, discussing all four suits is not necessary. Every hand dealt in Omaha high-low can be found in this publication, along with its relative ranking and hand value.

These results are based on games in which players have high starting-hand requirements and are aggressive with good hands after the flop. I realize that few Omaha high-low games will be composed entirely of tight players, so it's possible for you to improve upon these statistical results if you are in a game with several loose players. And after 50 million hand simulations, there's only one thing I can say for sure: you will lose money if you fail to consistently play hands that have a positive profit potential.

In the chapter, "Establishing Hand Value," we will eliminate approximately seventy-five percent of all hands dealt in Omaha high-low, making this game much easier to play. I will discuss various hands that are profitable or unprofitable to play, and give my opinions about them, showing you the stats that back up my reasoning. For example, double-suited hands are much more profitable to play than non-suited ones. In fact some hands are twenty times more profitable when double-suited.

■3■
SOME COMMENTS ON THE STATISTICS

While there are only 45,000 possible hands in Texas hold'em, an astounding 270,725 hand combinations are possible in Omaha high-low. Sure makes it easy to find something to play in Omaha high-low, doesn't it? Especially in many low-limit games, where few players know the game well. In nine- and ten-handed $4/$8 or $10/$20 games, generally only two or three good players have advanced skills. (Note that this is going to change in the next few years due to the good strategy books and computer practice programs available.) It is not my intent to berate players who don't play the game well, but rather to point out that Omaha high-low is so complex that it is tough to learn everything you need to know to play it properly. In my opinion, your best learning tool is hand-analysis statistics.

The statistical charts in the back of the book will indicate the percentage of times that a particular hand will win high, win low, or scoop the pot. The charts are also a good reference for hand ranking. This is a great learning tool, and I strongly recommend that you spend some time studying it. These are the tools you need to master the art/science of hand selection.

You may notice that most negative-value hands have similar negative values. The reason most negative hands have -$1 or -$2 value is that they are not played unless in the blind in an unraised pot. If a "miracle flop" happens, they win, but this may happen 2% of the time or less.

In the last row of the charts I gave every hand in Omaha high-low a grade. I selected the hand with the best performance (A-A-2-3, double-suited), and gave it a "Hand Grade" of 100. Then I compared it to the results of all other hands.

■4■
IS OMAHA HIGH-LOW A HIGH OR A LOW GAME?

To help us answer this question, let's look at the best hand that you can be dealt in Omaha high-low, the top ranking hand in all the statistical charts: A♥ A♣ 2♥ 3♣ (A-A-2-3 double-suited in any two suits). The A-A-2-3 double-suited has the best winning percentage of any Omaha high-low hand and wins more money than any other hand.

It is expected to win high 5%, win low 9%, and scoop the entire pot 28% of hands played. In total, the A-A-2-3 double-suited is expected to win part or all of the pot 42% of hands played. This is the best hand in Omaha high-low—and yet it is going to lose about 58% of all hands played!

Many players think that Omaha high-low is a low game, while others believe that it is a high game. The correct answer is that Omaha high-low is a combination of high and low. To be successful at this game, it is necessary to play four connecting cards that work together and can scoop the entire pot. We must also keep in mind that not every hand produces a low.

Based on the 5,278 hands listed in the stats section, the high hand wins 26%, the low hand wins 21%, and scoop hands win 53% of all hands played. When one person wins the entire pot, it is considered a scoop. When pots are split between high and low, high receives 50% of the credit, and low receives 50% of the credit.

∎5∎
OMAHA HIGH-LOW
8-OR-BETTER REVIEW

For those that are new to the game or need practice, I will insert a few hands for your review. Omaha high-low is a flop game with betting structures similar to hold'em. There is a single bet pre flop and on the flop, and then the bets double on the turn and river. Some casinos allow one bet with three raises, and some poker rooms have four raises.

All players are dealt four cards face-down, of which two must be played from his hand and three must be played from the five community cards. To qualify for low, you must use two cards from your hand and three from the board that are unpaired. The highest of the five cards must be eight or lower to qualify for low. You must remember that it takes five cards to make a complete hand; two from your hand and three from the board.

High-hand qualification is the same: two cards from your hand and three cards from the board. You may use one or both cards from your hand for low and/or high. The ace is played as the lowest card in the low hand and the highest card in high hands. You may use the ace for low and high in the same hand.

For practice, compare the hands below and evaluate the strength of each as if you were playing it before the flop, then on the flop, turn and river. We will assume there has been no raise before the flop and only three players are in the hand.

Of course in the real world we will not have the privilege of viewing the hands of other players. We show them here to demonstrate how the value of any hand can change on the turn of one card. Second-best hands often win in other games, but in Omaha high-low, any hand less than the nuts can be very costly. You will see how easy it is to lose money with hands that look strong after the flop and turn. The best hand may become the worst on the river, and terrible hands may become scoopers. This game is not complete until the river card is dealt.

We are going to play the same hands several times with a different river card to emphasize the importance of that one make-or-break card.

YOUR HAND

HAND TWO

BIG BLIND HAND

FLOP	TURN	RIVER

Your hand looked great, double-suited with an ace-deuce. The flop made you a nut low and a king-high spade-flush drawing hand.

After the flop, you must ask yourself one question: is it possible that a better hand than yours can be made? The answer is yes, because there is a straight possibility on the flop. After the flop, you must understand that you may be playing for half the pot unless you make a club flush with a card that doesn't pair the board. Any time there is a pair on the board, a full-house is possible, and if you make a flush with a card pairing the board, it is wise to check your hand.

In the above hand, after the flop your opponent had a second-nut low, three sevens, and an ace-high spade flush draw. If the board had paired he would have made a full-house. The turn card made your hand's high prospects much better, with four clubs to an ace-high flush, and you already had the A-2-nut low hand.

But you became counterfeited on the river. One opponent won low for half of the pot, and the player holding the blind hand won high with a straight. Had the river card been any club that didn't pair the board, you would have scooped the entire pot. The blind hand was lucky that his straight won any part of the pot. If the river card had been any spade, your opponent would have won high with a spade flush, and you would have won low and split the pot.

When reading two hands for low, start with the highest card first and then the next lowest usable card. If two hands are identical, then the low will be split, and each player will receive one-fourth of the pot. This is referred to as being quartered.

YOUR HAND

OPPONENT'S HAND (LOW)

BLIND HAND

These hands were very close for low, but the opponent's hand nudged you out with his 7-6-3, which was lower than your 7-6-4. When the two of diamonds was dealt on the river, counterfeiting your two, you were forced to use the A-4 from your hand combined with the 2-6-7 from the board. Your opponent used the A-3 from his hand with the same board cards you used for a nut low that won half of the pot. Suppose the river card was different!

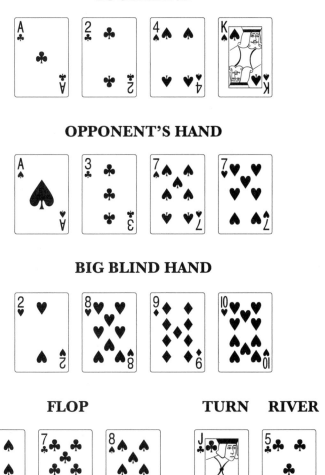

YOUR HAND

OPPONENT'S HAND

BIG BLIND HAND

FLOP   TURN   RIVER

The flop looked very good for both hands, but the turn and river cards changed everything when you made an ace-high flush, giving you a double-nut hand.

The above scenario is not uncommon in Omaha high-low, and if you have played this game for any length of time, it has probably happened to you on more than one occasion. That's what this book is about. We will cover playing A-2-x-x hands, starting hands, trap hands, non-profitable hands, and much more.

If you are new to Omaha high-low or don't have a lot of experience or self-confidence, I highly recommend that you establish an online poker account. You may open an account on many different sites and play for free. After you gain experience and confidence in your abilities, you may play live action for as low as 2¢ to 4¢ bets. One advantage you will have playing on the Internet is that your four cards are dealt face-up, which gives you extra time to figure out what you have. In live-action, your cards are dealt down. You can also view the stats in your book and check the hand value and ranking of the four cards you are holding.

It is important to know if the hand you are playing ranks one or 1,000. The stats section in this book will show the hand ranking of every hand you will ever play and indicate if it has a positive or negative expectation. This information is very important and will help you master the concepts of Omaha high-low hand values.

These poker sites also have small tournaments that you can play very cheaply. You can play one table or multi-table tournaments for a buy-in as low as $1.10. They are great for practice, require little investment, and are very enjoyable to play. Good luck and have fun.

Aloha Quilt

The
Aloha Quilt

An Elm Creek Quilts Novel

Jennifer Chiaverini

SIMON & SCHUSTER

NEW YORK   LONDON   TORONTO   SYDNEY

Simon & Schuster
1230 Avenue of the Americas
New York, NY 10020

First Simon & Schuster hardcover edition April 2010

SIMON & SCHUSTER and colophon are registered trademarks
of Simon & Schuster, Inc.

For information about special discounts for bulk purchases,
please contact Simon & Schuster Special Sales at 1-866-506-1949 or
business@simonandschuster.com.

The Simon & Schuster Speakers Bureau can bring authors to
your live event. For more information or to book an event contact the
Simon & Schuster Speakers Bureau at 1-866-248-3049 or
visit our website at www.simonspeakers.com.

Endpaper designs by Melanie Marder Parks

Designed by Kyoko Watanabe

Manufactured in the United States of America

10 9 8 7 6 5 4 3 2 1

Library of Congress Cataloging-in-Publication Data
Chiaverini, Jennifer.
The aloha quilt : an Elm Creek Quilts novel / Jennifer Chiaverini.
p. cm.
1. Compson, Sylvia (Fictitious character)—Fiction. 2. Quilting—Fiction.
3. Quiltmakers—Fiction. 4. Quilts—Fiction. 5. Divorce—Fiction.
6. Hawaii—Fiction. 7. Domestic fiction. I. Title.
PS3553.H473A79   2010
813'.54—dc22
2009027951

ISBN 978-1-4165-3318-4

To Denise Roy

aloha and *mahalo*

Acknowledgments

I am grateful to Denise Roy, Maria Massie, Kate Ankofski, Kimberly Cowser, Mara Lurie, Kate Lapin, and Melanie Parks for their contributions to *The Aloha Quilt* and their ongoing support of the Elm Creek Quilts series.

Thanks also to Tara Shaughnessy, who helped care for my sons during the time I wrote this book, and to my teammates from Just For Kicks, Oh-Thirty, and Más Cervesas for providing me with great workouts, camaraderie, and stress relief.

I offer a heartfelt *mahalo* to the people of Hawaii who generously shared their stories with me and showed me the true meaning of the *aloha* spirit, especially Dan and Amy Martin, my hosts at Hoʻoilo House in Lahaina; Suzanne Ayers of the Baldwin House for her informative and intriguing discussions of Lahaina's history; Hōkūao Pellegrino of the Kamehameha Schools Enrichment Department for help with the Hawaiian language; Eva Humphrey and Peter Delapinia of Mele Ukulele for their suggestions, demonstrations, and a delightful concert; and Mandy Kaili of the Maui Historical Society for answering my questions about *kapa* cloth.

I offer hugs and thanks to the friends and family who never fail to support and encourage me, especially Geraldine Neidenbach, Heather Neidenbach, Nic Neidenbach, Leonard and Marlene Chiaverini, Brian Grover, and my boys, Marty, Nicholas, and Michael Chiaverini. *Aloha!*

The
Aloha Quilt

Chapter One

From the bedroom doorway, Sylvia Bergstrom Compson Cooper regarded the taped and labeled cartons Bonnie had stacked against the walls, leaving only a narrow aisle between the bed and the bureau. "It might feel more like home sweet home if you unpacked."

"I don't have time," said Bonnie, shoving a box of sweaters under the bed for storage. Though it was October, she wouldn't need them where she was going. "I have too much to do before my flight."

Sylvia picked her way through the clutter to the center of the room and studied the mess, frowning thoughtfully over the tops of her glasses, which hung from a silver chain around her neck. "If you like, I can unpack for you while you're away."

"Oh, no, Sylvia. Please don't go to all that trouble."

"It's no trouble. I'll enlist a few of the other Elm Creek Quilters to help and we'll spread the work over a few days."

Sylvia didn't need to add that they would have lots of time to finish the job before Bonnie's return—too much time, thought Bonnie's friends, who agreed that she needed a getaway but perhaps not one of such long duration.

"I'll take care of it when I get back." Bonnie smiled to take the sting out of her refusal. "I'm not moving in permanently, remember?"

"The invitation stands if you change your mind," Sylvia assured her. "You'll always have a home at Elm Creek Manor, even if you only want it long enough to get back on your feet."

Bonnie thanked her, wondering which of her friends would next offer to take her in. The apartment in Grangerville had never been a real home, just a wayside between the condo she had once shared with her now-estranged husband, Craig, and wherever she might settle after her return to Pennsylvania in the spring. Sylvia had convinced her that it made no sense to keep renting an apartment for her belongings when she could store them at Elm Creek Manor for free, so Bonnie had cancelled her month-to-month lease. She had needed no more than a day to pack up the apartment, not only because the Elm Creek Quilters helped her, but also because after moving out of the condo, she had unpacked only the necessities and left everything else in boxes.

Somehow she must have known that she was not meant to stay.

"I might decide to make the manor my home," Bonnie said, stacking a laundry basket full of quilt fabric on top of a carton of old photo albums. "I honestly haven't thought it through. I've had too much on my mind and I can't plan so many steps ahead."

"A change of scenery and new challenges will do you good," said Sylvia.

"I'm counting on that." Bonnie shoved a box out of the way with her foot and sat down on the bed, absently patting the Windblown Square quilt for comfort. A few years before, she had been blindsided when she caught Craig carrying on a cyber-affair with a younger woman, but after recovering from her shock, she had fought to save her marriage. She had thrown herself into an exercise program, lost twenty pounds, had her dark curls trimmed into a flattering new style, and had endured fellow Elm Creek Quilter Diane's coaching about the best clothes for her curvy frame and makeup for her ruddy complexion. According to her friends, she looked better than she had in years—younger, fitter, more attractive—but even then she had known that a successful makeover alone wouldn't be enough to rekindle Craig's affection.

Through marriage counseling and countless date nights, Craig had led her to believe they were reconciling and rebuilding, but all the while he was secretly hiding his assets for the divorce only he had known was inevitable. To make matters worse, he had told their children that she had abandoned him, that the divorce was her idea, that he was as confused and distraught as they were, that he deserved their sympathy and Bonnie their anger. C.J., their eldest son, knew their father too well to believe it, their daughter, Tammy, refused to take sides, and their youngest son, Barry, was far too credulous where his father was concerned. Bonnie didn't push it. The very thought of engaging in a battle for the hearts and minds of their three grown children exhausted her. She didn't have the energy to persuade her kids that Craig was wrong and she was right. Now that she had accepted that her marriage was over, all she wanted was to put the whole ugly situation behind her and to move on.

To feel good again. To return to the happy, contented woman she had once been and now only vaguely remembered. But how could she heal when even the protective walls of Elm Creek Manor triggered so many painful memories?

She had despaired of ever doing so until her old friend

Claire phoned with an invitation as wonderful as it was unexpected. Bonnie rarely saw her former college roommate except at college reunions, but Claire kept in touch with chatty letters mailed from military bases in different foreign countries as she followed her officer husband from post to post. When he had retired from the service, they settled in Hawaii, having fallen in love with the island paradise while Eric had been stationed in Oahu earlier in his career. For the past several years, Claire had run a quilt shop on Maui, and when an opportunity came to expand the business, Claire contacted the long-time friend who had introduced her to quilting to enlist her help.

"A quilter's retreat in Hawaii," Claire had said. "What could be more perfect? And who knows more about setting up a quilt camp than you?"

"Sylvia Cooper, for one," Bonnie had said, but before she could reel off the names of the other Elm Creek Quilters who were far more qualified to tackle the project, Claire had accused her of her old fault of excessive self-deprecation and insisted that only Bonnie possessed the perfect combination of knowledge, experience, and trustworthiness that Claire needed to launch her new business venture. She offered to hire Bonnie as a consultant, and in exchange for Bonnie's expertise, she would provide a modest stipend, room and board in Maui for the winter, and a guaranteed room at Aloha Quilt Camp whenever Bonnie desired.

Bonnie felt as if her old friend had thrown open doors and windows to let fresh air and sunshine into a room too long shuttered and neglected. Elm Creek Quilt Camp closed for the winter, so why not spend the off-season in Hawaii? She couldn't sit at home counting the days until her divorce, as if on the day it was final, her disappointment and anger would magically vanish. Where better to begin building a new life for herself than in Hawaii, where she would be soothed by balmy breezes and lulled to sleep by the pounding surf, where she could help a beloved friend launch an exciting new business, where everything was unfamiliar and nothing would remind her of what she had lost?

◈

Bonnie slept better that first night in Elm Creek Manor than she had all summer long in the apartment. She woke refreshed, dug her walking shoes and sweats out of her suitcase, and went on a long, brisk walk around the estate, lingering in the apple orchard to savor the fragrance of ripe apples and to chat about the harvest with Matt, the estate's caretaker. She couldn't resist plucking a shiny, red Jonathon for herself and munching it as she crossed the bridge over Elm Creek on her way to the back entrance of the manor. She stretched on the stairs, enjoying the cool, gentle winds that sent fallen scarlet, yellow, and brown leaves dancing across the parking lot. The wind carried a faint whiff of wood smoke and a hint of cinnamon that told her someone had left the kitchen window open a crack.

Inside, she found several of the manor's permanent residents sipping coffee at the kitchen table: Sylvia, of course; Sarah, the cofounder of Elm Creek Quilt Camp; Sylvia's husband, Andrew; the newest Elm Creek Quilter, Gretchen; and Gretchen's husband, Joe. The plates before them were empty except for crumbs, but a platter in the center of the table was stacked with waffles, and a place was set for Bonnie at the end.

"It's Anna's cinnamon-apple waffle recipe," said Sarah as Bonnie seated herself. "I'm happy popping the frozen kind in the toaster, but she convinced me that I didn't have to be a professional chef like her to make them from scratch." She patted her tummy as if to assure her unborn twins that their mother wasn't such a bad cook after all.

"Delicious," Bonnie declared, savoring the first mouthful. Sarah rose to pour her a cup of coffee. "Sarah, sit down. I can get that."

"It's no big deal." Sarah pressed a hand to the small of her back as she crossed the kitchen, but something in her expression told Bonnie that more than the twins weighed her down. "Cream and sugar?"

"Black with two sugars, please, the usual." Bonnie looked around the circle of friends. "All right. What's up?"

Sylvia's sympathetic frown prepared Bonnie for the worst. "Craig called while you were out."

Bonnie dropped her fork to the table with a clatter. "He called the manor? How does he know I'm here?"

"Maybe he planted a tracking device in your sewing machine," said Sarah, setting the steaming cup of coffee before Bonnie. She didn't seem to be joking.

Bonnie should have known that he would find another way to reach her after she blocked his emails and stopped answering his calls on her cell phone. "Did you remind him that all communication must go through my lawyer?"

"I did indeed," said Sylvia, "but he didn't seem to hear me, so I gave the phone to Sarah."

"You could have hung up on him." Bonnie steeled herself. "What did he want?"

Sylvia and Sarah exchanged a glance. "He started off by complaining that Craig Jr. won't return his phone calls," said Sarah.

"I never told C.J. not to speak to his father," Bonnie protested. "C.J.'s angry. He needs time."

"Craig seems to think there's a conspiracy to cut him off

from his kids," said Andrew, scowling as he always did when Craig came up in the conversation. He had no patience for any man who shirked his responsibilities to his wife and children.

"Nonsense," said Sylvia. "Bonnie would never put her children in that position."

Of course it was nonsense. Bonnie wouldn't hurt her children by demanding they take sides. As badly as Craig treated her, he was still their children's father. She knew she couldn't speak disparagingly about him without hurting them. "What else?"

Reluctantly, Sarah said, "He said this divorce is a contest you won't win, and then he hung up."

Joe muttered something under his breath and drained his coffee cup. "What a horrid man," said Gretchen.

"Are you sure that's what he said?" asked Bonnie. "Were those his exact words?"

Sarah hesitated. "I'm paraphrasing a bit. He was ranting and it was hard to catch everything."

"Is it possible—" Bonnie had to force the question out. "Could he have said that he won't go along with the uncontested divorce anymore?"

Sarah blanched and eased herself back into her chair. "I don't think so," she said. "I guess . . . I guess it's possible."

"Oh, no." Bonnie's appetite fled. "I'd better call my lawyer."

When she went upstairs for her cell phone, her heart sank to discover a voicemail waiting from Darren Taylor. Though his request for her to return his call at her earliest convenience betrayed no reason for concern, Bonnie knew her lawyer was well practiced in concealing his emotions, so his cordial tone did nothing to ease her worries.

His secretary put her call right through. "Good morning, Bonnie," he greeted her. "Sorry to call so early, but I spoke with your husband's attorney this morning and I'm afraid we've run into a snag."

Bonnie paced the narrow aisle between the stacks of cartons pushed against the walls. "A snag like when you catch your fingernail on your sweater or a snag like being run over by a truck?"

Darren let out a dry chuckle. "Keep that sense of humor. You're going to need it."

"Oh, dear Lord." Bonnie sat down hard on the edge of the bed. "Okay. Tell me."

"Your husband has changed his mind about agreeing to a no-fault divorce."

"Why? He doesn't want to stay married to me. Why not get it over with?"

"Simply put, money. The marital estate is now worth much more than it was when you originally filed for a no contest."

"Only because Agnes discovered Craig's hidden assets." For years, unbeknownst to Bonnie, Craig had been siphoning off money from their joint accounts to buy expensive antiques to furnish his office. On those rare occasions when Bonnie had visited him on campus, she had never suspected the furniture's true worth, or had even known that it belonged to Craig rather than the college. Dear, faithful, curious Agnes had discovered the truth and had used her late husband's contacts in the antiques market to arrange for an auction—an astonishingly profitable auction.

Apparently Craig had decided he wanted a greater share of the windfall.

"We agreed on a fifty-fifty split of the sale of the furniture," said Bonnie. "That's more than he deserves considering that he bought those antiques with *our* money, not just his, without my knowledge, and he never declared them as assets on any of those mountains of forms we had to fill out. Shouldn't he be punished for that?"

"Believe me, the judge won't look favorably upon it," Darren assured her. "But now Craig wants to play hardball. He knows you want to resolve this as soon as possible—"

"Absolutely. Doesn't he?"

"Not as much as he wants a greater share of the money. I'm afraid he intends to use your eagerness for a quick resolution against you. This morning his attorney informed me that Craig wants to reconcile."

"What?" Bonnie exclaimed. "He doesn't want to fix our marriage, and even if he did, it's beyond saving."

"Craig knows that. This is a tactical move, nothing more. He'll proceed with a no-fault, non-contested divorce as long as you relinquish your claim upon the profits from the auction, on the grounds that he purchased the furniture with his own funds for his own professional use and they were never any part of the marital estate."

"It was only 'for his professional use' because if he had bought furniture for the condo, I would have known about it," said Bonnie, incredulous. "Either way, the money he used to buy it was as much mine as his!"

"I understand, Bonnie. You're absolutely right, and a judge would surely rule in your favor if you contested his claim. But Craig is gambling that you won't. Property disputes can drag things out for months, perhaps even years. Your husband believes you'd rather take the financial loss in exchange for finalizing the divorce as originally planned."

"I want it to be over, but the money he spent on those antiques was equally mine. He stole it from me. I can't let him get away with it. Not even if it meant the divorce could be over tomorrow. I can't."

"Then you should prepare yourself for a long, hard fight."

Her heart plummeted. "How long?"

"He can't keep you married to him against your will forever. The court can grant you a no-fault divorce if they determine that you and your husband have lived apart for two years and that the marriage is irretrievably broken."

"Two years?" Bonnie fell back upon the bed, cell phone pressed to her ear. Two years before she could put the whole mess behind her. Two years before she could get on with her life. "I can't wait two years. I don't think I can take it."

Darren fell silent, and she heard the rustle of papers in the background. "There are other alternatives, but they'd require more time before the court."

Anger surged through her. Her flight to Maui was in two days! Leave it to Craig to ruin her plans to spend the winter in Hawaii. But if she had no other choice . . . "What alternatives?"

"We could argue for mental cruelty, but given Craig's history . . ." Darren paused. "You've told me about Internet dalliances. Is it possible that he's committed adultery?"

"It's possible." Perhaps Bonnie should ask Agnes to tail Craig again. Agnes knew how to be discreet, and she seemed to have a talent for ferreting out Craig's dirty little secrets. She pictured Agnes bursting in upon Craig in a cheap motel room, a sleazy woman yawning from boredom on the bed, Craig fumbling to yank up his boxer shorts. It was cartoonish and ridiculous and far too plausible.

"It's not enough to suspect adultery," Darren warned. "We have to prove it. You either have to catch him in the act—"

"Delightful thought," Bonnie muttered.

"Or you have to show that he had the opportunity and the disposition to commit adultery. Say, for example, that you can video him entering his lover's home in the evening and not leaving until the following morning. The services of a private detective are usually called for in these circumstances, because you can hardly put your life on hold to follow him around with a camera."

"What about a few years back when he went to meet his Internet girlfriend at the Penn State football game?" Bonnie reminded him. "They would have shared a hotel room if I hadn't discovered their plans and tagged along on the trip. He certainly had the disposition to cheat then."

"I'm afraid that incident doesn't count," said Darren. "I assume you resumed marital relations with your husband afterward?"

"Well . . . yes. We were trying to work things out, or so I thought."

"In that case, since you continued to live with your husband and engage in marital relations, the court would say that you had forgiven him, or condoned the act. You can't use it to support your claim of adultery now. You can use only a newly discovered affair."

"That's unfair. I never condoned it. I tried to forgive him to save the marriage, but I was never okay with it."

"I'm sorry, Bonnie, but it's the law. I warn you, following this course could get messy. If a paramour is named, she can be required to testify. If she's married also—"

Then her secret would be out and her marriage could end up in divorce court too. So what? "Forgive me if I lack sympathy for this hypothetical other woman."

"Understandably, but we have to be sure we're right. It would be disastrous to accuse an innocent person. Her reputation would be ruined, her husband and children put through a terrible ordeal, all without cause."

Bonnie inhaled deeply and sat up. "Then we'll be sure that

we're sure. Beyond a reasonable doubt. That's the appropriate standard, right? Let's hire the detective for . . . a month. If the detective can't turn up anything against Craig within that time, I'll assume there isn't anything to turn up."

Darren agreed to take care of the arrangements, so after promising to inform him if she discovered anything on her own, Bonnie hung up and stared into space, sick at heart. Despite everything, she would not have thought Craig willing to drag things out and bicker over minutia, all for the sake of money. And now she found herself in the unimaginable position of hoping he had committed adultery and praying he had not.

Could he really have started up another affair after she spoiled his first?

Had it indeed been his first?

The thought of what she might find if she searched the shadowed corners of Craig's life frayed her every nerve, and yet, if he had cheated on her, she needed to know. She had her own health to consider. And if proof of his infidelity was what she needed to extricate herself from their failed marriage, she would be a fool not to look for it.

It was possible, she told herself with a faint glimmer of hope, that the detective would find nothing to implicate him.

Bonnie showered and dressed, preparing herself for a day that was already off to a bad start. Tucking her cell phone into her sweater pocket, she went downstairs to the library on the second floor, where Sarah and Sylvia conducted the official business of Elm Creek Quilts. The double doors opened into a room spanning the entire width of the south wing. Autumn sunshine spilled in through tall diamond-paned windows on the east wall, casting long rectangles of light on the rugs and hardwood floors. Comfortable chairs and sofas formed a square in the center of the room. Oak bookcases lined the walls, their shelves bowing slightly from the weight of leather-bound volumes and framed sepia-toned photographs of Sylvia's ancestors.

Fresh logs had been stacked in the stone fireplace on the south wall, with two armchairs drawn up to the hearth as if in anticipation of a crackling blaze when the evening grew cool. To the left of the mantel hung a scrap Castle Wall quilt, a memorial to Sylvia's first husband; to the right hung seven sections of nine composing the Winding Ways quilt Sylvia had made for her friends. She had chosen fabrics that represented each of her friends' unique qualities, and the mosaic of overlapping circles and intertwining curves, the careful balance of dark and light hues, the unexpected harmony of the disparate fabrics and colors evoked the sense of many winding paths meeting, intersecting, parting, creating the illusion that the separate sections formed a single quilt.

Two missing sections belonging to absent Elm Creek Quilters broke the continuity of the circles, and when Bonnie left for Hawaii, she would take her section with her too. When she returned to Elm Creek Manor, she would restore her portion of the quilt to its proper place. The empty spaces would remind those left behind that their absent friends would return one day and the circle of quilters would be made whole. As Sylvia often said, "Once an Elm Creek Quilter, always an Elm Creek Quilter." Bonnie hoped her friends would remember that no matter how far they traveled. She knew she always would, now that it would soon be her turn to set off on a journey.

Sarah sat at the large oak desk typing on the computer, but she looked up when Bonnie entered. "Did you reach your lawyer? Everything okay?"

"As far from okay as it could possibly be," said Bonnie. "May I borrow your computer? I need to go online and see if Craig's cheating on me."

Sarah's eyebrows rose. "Oh. Okay. Just let me save this." A few keystrokes later, Sarah closed her document, opened the web browser, hauled herself out of the leather armchair, and offered it to Bonnie. "How are you planning to catch him, exactly?"

"Last time I caught him by accidentally checking his email. I thought I'd see what happens when I check it on purpose."

"If he hasn't changed his password."

Bonnie hadn't considered that, but Craig surely would have known better than to leave his account unprotected and risk discovery the same way twice. Sure enough, when she tried to log on to the Waterford College system, his old password failed.

"Try some variations," Sarah suggested, but after a dozen such attempts, Bonnie realized it was futile. It was always so easy on television, where a clever computer expert could deftly fuse together the name of an enemy's childhood pet and his favorite candy bar and instantly gain access to every detail of his personal life.

"He's not going to make this easy for me," she said, thinking aloud.

"Of course not," said Sarah. "This is Craig we're talking about."

True enough, but Bonnie wouldn't allow Craig and his ridiculous stalling tactics to ruin her plans. She would have to wait and give the detective time to do his work, but she wouldn't wait at Elm Creek Manor. She intended to be relaxing on a white, sandy beach on Maui when Darren called with the detective's report—and the news that would be both welcome and dreadful, whatever it was.

Chapter Two

On a cold, drizzly morning, Bonnie stood outside the terminal entrance shivering in her thin jacket as Matt unloaded her suitcase from the Elm Creek Quilts minivan and set it on the curb. "You sure you're okay?" he asked, studying her. "I can stick around until you're through security."

"I'm fine," she assured him, adjusting the strap of her carry-on over her shoulder. She was lying, but she figured Matt knew that. Sarah had surely told her husband about Craig's latest antics. How could anyone in Bonnie's situation claim to be fine?

"Well, have a good flight. Take care of yourself." The big man, his back and shoulders hard and muscled from years of laboring outdoors, nearly squeezed the breath out of her with a heartfelt bear hug. Bonnie had to laugh, though tears sprang to her eyes. Matt was so kind, and Sarah, so lucky. This was a man a wife could trust. She hoped Sarah would never take that for granted, not one single day.

Bonnie passed through check-in and security in the same fog of exhaustion and latent anger she had sunk into since Darren's call. Her flight was called; she boarded the plane. She gazed out the window throughout the forty-minute flight to Philadelphia, but she dozed off on the second leg of her journey, waking with a start when the plane touched down in Phoenix. As she walked to her gate, she found herself hungry for the first time in days, so she bought a sandwich and a large bottle of water and ate as she waited for her row number to be called. On board the 737, the female flight attendants wore flower *leis* over their uniforms, and one had tucked a pink hibiscus behind her left ear. "Aloha," she greeted Bonnie pleasantly as she stepped onto the jet. "Welcome aboard."

"Aloha," Bonnie replied automatically, without putting any real feeling into the word. She knew from her travel guides that "Aloha" could mean *hello, goodbye,* or *I love you.* She needed no guide to remind her that only the first two meanings would ever apply to her.

She found her seat four rows from the back of the plane in a section that appeared to have been reserved for families traveling with small children, although that surely must have been a coincidence. But Bonnie had come prepared with earplugs and a night mask, and still making up for several nights of insomnia, she fell asleep before takeoff.

She woke to a touch on her arm and shifted groggily in her seat. "Sorry," said the passenger beside her, a large woman with a huge knot of graying brown hair. She was knitting busily, as if she hoped to finish her project before touchdown. "Didn't mean to bump you. Almost dropped a stitch when we hit that turbulence."

"That's all right." Bonnie checked her watch and discovered that she had slept five hours straight.

"Wish I could sleep as soundly as you," the woman remarked in a drawl that made Bonnie think of Texas. "I can't keep my eyes shut more than ten minutes on a plane. What's your secret? Drugs?"

"Months of little sleep thanks to a miserable soon-to-be ex-husband."

"Oh, I've had a few of those." The woman twisted her needles deftly and added a new color to the garment she was knitting. It appeared to be a brown-and-orange striped sweater for a very small person with arms and legs in odd places. "For my dachshund," she explained, noting Bonnie's scrutiny. "When does your soon-to-be ex become your official ex?"

"Not soon enough."

"I hear you. You know, it's never too soon to start lining up a few new fellas, one to marry and a couple others to fall back on."

"Not me," Bonnie declared. "I'm done with all that. I couldn't ever go through this heartbreak again."

"Why, sugar, if you pick the right man you won't need to go through this again. You'll pick one to keep forever."

"That's what I thought I did the first time."

The woman scrutinized her. "What did you know way back then? You were just a girl."

In spite of herself, Bonnie smiled. "How do you know?"

"You have the look of someone who's been unhappily married a very long time."

"It wasn't always unhappy."

"Then never say never to new love." The woman returned her full attention to her knitting, though her fingers had never stopped flicking yarn over needles even when her eyes were on Bonnie. "The islands are the most romantic place on earth. You might meet someone special."

"I'm coming to work and to relax, not to hunt down a new man."

"Well, hunting a man is work, and enjoying the ones you catch can be relaxing."

Bonnie laughed.

"A genuine laugh," the woman cried, triumphant. "I knew you had it in you, despite your long face."

For the rest of the flight they chatted intermittently. Bonnie leafed through the in-flight magazine and gazed out the window. At last the plane began to descend, and Bonnie eagerly awaited her first glimpse of Hawaii.

First she saw only the vast expanse of turquoise ocean, then steep, rugged mountains of emerald green. Awestruck, she drew in a breath and craned her neck to take in as much of the view as the small window allowed.

Beside her, the woman chuckled as she packed up her knitting. "First time?"

"Is it that obvious?" Bonnie replied, smiling. "The view is simply breathtaking. It's so much more beautiful than any photograph."

"Wait 'til you see it up close and personal. Take a helicopter tour if you have the stomach for it." Then the woman frowned slightly. "Someone meeting you here, hon? Tour group, maybe? It's not good to be alone with a broken heart, what with all the beautiful scenery and the honeymooners making a single gal feel like the only cup without a saucer."

Bonnie assured her that an old friend was waiting for her in the terminal, most likely scanning the monitors and coming as close to their arrival gate as possible without violating any TSA regulations. In fact, unless Claire had mellowed with age, she was probably scheming to persuade the security personnel to let her through even though she wasn't a ticketed passenger. It wouldn't be the first time Claire decided the rules didn't apply to her, but Bonnie hoped that today of all days, Claire would act sensibly. An arrest would ruin their reunion.

They touched down at Kahului Airport on the northern

shore of Maui, and as Bonnie was gathering her things and waiting for the seat belt sign to turn off so she could leap from her seat, it occurred to her that she had not felt so enthusiastic for anything in ages.

Already Hawaii was working its magic upon her.

She glimpsed Claire just beyond the security gate, fiddling with her purse strap, eyeing the TSA agents as if contemplating whether they would bother pursuing a harmless middle-aged woman just because she ignored the huge DO NOT ENTER signs and bypassed security to meet a dear friend. Claire probably could have outrun them if they did. Though she was Bonnie's age, fifty-six, she could easily pass for ten years younger. Petite and slender, with a girlish, unlined face and wheat-brown hair that brushed her shoulders, she had obviously kept up with the long-distance running that she had enjoyed as the darling of the Penn State cross-country team. Bonnie broke into a grin as she approached her old friend, marveling at how little the years had changed her. If it was something in the Hawaiian air, Bonnie hoped it would have a rejuvenating effect on her, too.

At that moment Claire caught sight of her and her green eyes lit up with delight. "Bonnie," she cried, waving her arm in the air. "Over here!" Claire prudently waited for Bonnie to leave the secure area before flinging her arms around her. "It's so good to see you! You look fantastic—exactly the same as you did the day after graduation, when we moved out of our apartment on Atherton Street."

"You're a liar," Bonnie scoffed, but she was touched that Claire had picked an occasion marked by Craig's absence rather than mentioning any number of the more recent occasions when the two couples had met at Penn State for class reunions or football games.

"Let's get your bags," Claire said, tucking her arm through

Bonnie's and leading her to baggage claim. While they waited, they chatted about their kids—Claire's daughters were both on the mainland, the eldest married and the youngest away at college—and old friends from Penn State who still kept in touch. When Bonnie hefted a single large suitcase from the baggage carousel, Claire exclaimed, "That's all you brought for five months?"

"I assumed you'd let me do laundry at your place," Bonnie said, wheeling the suitcase after her as Claire led the way to the parking lot.

"We'll go shopping," Claire promised, pressing the fob on her key chain. Nearby, the trunk to a blue convertible popped open. "You'll need some island wear."

"Nothing too daring," said Bonnie, eyeing Claire's bright pink and green floral blouse. "Or too bright."

Claire merely laughed.

They drove with the top down, wind whipping their hair, shouting to converse, laughing at the impossibility of under-standing each other. Bonnie put on her sunglasses and soaked in the sunshine and the scenery as they drove southwest across the island past fields of sugarcane and rugged green moun-tains. The air was fragrant with flowers, the mountains glori-ous in their beauty. They passed through a tunnel, and on the other side the ocean appeared before them, endless and blue. Overcome, Bonnie could not speak, but gazed out at the water as they drove along the cliffside. To her left was the ocean, vast and deep; to her right were the gently rising foothills of deeply forested mountains. It was powerful and beautiful, exactly as she had imagined it and yet completely new and unexpected. Tears pricked her eyes, but she blinked them away. Her heart felt lighter than it had in months, years, as if she had left all her troubles on the plane.

All at once, three white puffs went up from the water about a hundred yards offshore. "Are those whales?" Bonnie cried out, twisting in her seat in time to catch a glimpse of a massive dark shape shadowing the water before disappearing.

"Yes," Claire replied, glancing in the rearview mirror before the steam dissipated entirely.

"You can drive along the highway and see whales from your car," Bonnie marveled, and Claire laughed.

Before long they reached Lahaina, Claire's adopted home-town. She happily pointed out the road to Hoʻoilo House, a bed and breakfast in the west Maui foothills run by her friends Dan and Amy; an ideal wayside for whale spotting; her favorite used bookstore; and the direction to a banyan tree at Courthouse Square, which Claire promised to show her another time.

"Where do you want to go first?" Claire asked. "The future home of Aloha Quilt Camp, the quilt shop, or my house? Eric's grilling out for us, but supper won't be ready for another hour."

Bonnie barely allowed her friend to finish before replying, "The quilt camp site, of course. You sent me only one picture of the front porch. I need to see what I have to work with."

"I like your priorities." Claire turned off the highway onto a road lined with shops and restaurants. To Bonnie's delight, Claire pulled to a stop in front of a quaint Victorian inn surrounded by palm trees, through which she glimpsed waves crashing on the sandy beach.

"You're right on the ocean?" Bonnie exclaimed. "Claire, you don't need me. Quilters will flock to this place even if all you offer is breakfast and electricity for their sewing machines."

"We both know that's not true." Claire led the way up the broad front staircase. The banisters gleamed white as if freshly painted, extending to a porch that appeared to wrap around the entire building. Balconies on the second and third floors echoed the design. "Elm Creek Quilt Camp has set the bar too high. We have to offer classes and entertainment, or why would anyone come here instead of central Pennsylvania?"

"Oh, I don't know," Bonnie teased as Claire opened the front door, upon which a wreath of hibiscus flowers hung. "Beaches? Sunshine? Abundant pineapple? We're not open during the winter, either, so we won't compete with you for half the year."

"Good. Then you can come to work for me during your off season."

Bonnie was so surprised that she laughed. "It's too soon to make me an offer like that. I've been here less than a day. Let's see how you feel after my first performance evaluation."

"I know you, Bonnie." Claire held the door open wider and gestured for Bonnie to enter. "You're creative, you're fun, you're experienced, and you're absolutely trustworthy. You're a friend. There's no one I'd prefer as my partner, and if I thought I could steal you away from the Elm Creek Quilters, I'd make you an offer right now."

"Claire . . ." Bonnie didn't know what to say. "You said you wanted to hire me as a consultant. Temporarily."

"I know." Claire was all innocence. "But let's see what happens. No pressure. After a few months, you might decide that Maui feels like home. You might decide you enjoy having half an ocean and most of the continental United States between you and Craig."

But that same distance would separate Bonnie from her children and grandchildren, as well as her dearest friends and colleagues. She no longer had a permanent home, that was true, but Elm Creek Manor had been a refuge in difficult times, and she loved working with her friends in the business they had founded and nurtured. As excited as she was to launch a new quilt camp with Claire, she couldn't imagine staying beyond the winter into spring, when her friends and students expected her back at Elm Creek Quilt Camp.

She searched her memory but couldn't recall a single conversation in which she had suggested anything to the contrary. Apparently Claire hadn't lost her habit of hearing what she wanted to hear and dismissing everything else. "I'm thrilled for the chance to help you get Aloha Quilt Camp started, but in March, I'm going home," Bonnie said firmly, ignoring the nagging voice in the back of her mind that reminded her she didn't really have a home in Pennsylvania any longer, just a place where she worked and a place to store her belongings.

But her troubled thoughts slipped away as she stepped into the foyer of the inn. Tables adorned with fragrant tropical floral arrangements flanked the entrance, directly across from a grand staircase that climbed to a second floor landing where it split into two staircases and continued up to the third floor. To the left of the staircase was a cozy sitting room decorated with bamboo furniture and historic photographs. A built-in bookcase loaded with many well-read volumes stood between a pair of windows overlooking a lush garden. Bonnie glimpsed an older couple sipping coffee at a small table outside and heard the low murmur of other unseen guests chatting. To the right of the staircase was a dining room, the table set with woven Polynesian linens and white china. On a sideboard stood two large glass pitchers—one of lemonade, Bonnie guessed, and another of iced tea—and a silver fruit bowl filled with pineapples and mangoes, with plates and glasses nearby so guests could help themselves. Gentle breezes wafted in through the open windows, stirring the sheer curtains.

It was an enticing blend of tropical and Victorian décor,

comfortable and lovely, but Bonnie was puzzled. "Where's your quilt shop?" she asked.

"In the white building across the street," Claire explained. "It's second from the end, between the sushi restaurant and the ice cream parlor. This is the Hale Kapa Kuiki, the future home of Aloha Quilt Camp, with twenty beautifully appointed guest rooms—or at least they're beautiful now. When Eric and I bought the place, it had fallen into disrepair. It's a historic building so any renovations must follow strictly enforced codes, and the former owners couldn't afford to make the necessary improvements. They were looking to retire, anyway, so Eric and I snapped it up."

"When did all this happen?"

"A year ago." Claire rolled her eyes and ran the back of her hand across her forehead as if she were still recovering. "A year of very hard work, more scrubbing and polishing and repairing than any one woman should do in a mere twelve months. The results are worth it, but my hands will never be the same."

"You never breathed a word of any of this."

"I was too busy to send out more than a generic Christmas card last year, and I didn't want to say anything in case it turned out to be a huge mistake. Anyway, you can't tell me you're not secretly glad to have avoided the real dirty work."

Bonnie shook her head, amused. "You always were good at keeping secrets, but this . . ." She turned around in place, admiring all her gaze took in. "I never imagined you as an innkeeper, but this is wonderful."

"You haven't even seen the guest rooms yet. Each has its own private lanai—that's a balcony or a patio for you mainlanders—and the furnishings are authentic 1920s Hawaiian, the same period as the inn itself. We serve breakfast each morning on the main lanai—you'd probably call it a courtyard. The garden gives our guests privacy, but they can still hear the ocean, and the beach is just a few steps away through the back gate."

"But Claire—" In the absence of specific details, Bonnie had imagined a few guest rooms over the quilt shop, with one large classroom below, certainly not an entire inn. "It's amazing, and don't take this the wrong way, but what do you know about running an inn?"

"My friends Dan and Amy let me work for them at Ho'oilo House for a few months. I know a bed and breakfast isn't the same as an inn, but it was still great training. Besides, I'm not doing it all by myself. I have Eric, you—"

"For the winter."

"And my staff." Beaming, Claire linked her arm through Bonnie's. "Come on. Let me show you to the kitchen. There's someone I want you to meet. Without her . . ." Claire shook her head to emphasize that whoever awaited them in the kitchen was indispensable.

Bonnie followed Claire across the foyer past the staircase and into a spacious kitchen where a petite woman in her late sixties was removing a batch of pineapple glazed popovers from one of the large ovens. She wore a long pink dress with an allover pattern of banana leaves in white, her black hair arranged with apparent effortless grace in a French twist. She looked to be Asian, native Hawaiian, or perhaps both.

The woman looked up at the sound of their footfalls on the gleaming wood floor, set the hot popover pan on a towel spread upon the bamboo counter, and brushed her fingertips on a tea towel. "Aloha," she greeted them, smiling as she sized up Bonnie with a single appraising glance.

"Midori, this is my best friend from college, Bonnie Markham," said Claire. "Bonnie, this is Midori Tanaka, our manager, cook, and housekeeper, all in one."

Then what was left for Claire to do? "How do you do?" Bonnie asked, shaking her hand.

"Fine, thanks." Midori's smile was both cheerful and knowing. "I've heard so much about you. You've made Claire the happiest woman on the island by agreeing to come work for her."

"For the winter," Bonnie quickly added.

Midori gave Claire an inquiring glance, which Claire seemed not to notice. "Are you hungry?" Claire asked Bonnie. "You must be starved after all that travel."

Midori took a plate from a cupboard and placed a popover upon it. "They're best when they're hot," she advised, setting it on the counter and gesturing for Bonnie to pull up a stool. "Something to drink? Jasmine tea? Lemonade?"

"Tea, please," said Bonnie, taking her seat as Claire leaned against the counter nearby. The popover was almost too warm to touch, but she tore off a piece, blew gently on it, and took a bite. It was light and flaky, with a perfect hint of sweetness from the pineapple. "Delicious," Bonnie sighed, and then laughed with delight as Midori set out a beautifully arranged dish of sliced pineapple, mango, and papaya, quickly followed by a charming tea service complete with honey and cream. "If this is how you treat all of your guests, you must be booked solid all year round."

"We're working on it," said Claire. "The inn developed a less-than-spectacular reputation under its prior owners, and once those bad reviews get on the Internet, they never disappear completely."

"We've had many good reviews since Claire took over, especially in the past four months since the restorations were finished." With a spatula, Midori deftly transferred the rest of the popovers from the pan to a wire cooling rack, except for the last, which she added to Bonnie's plate before she could demur. "In time, and God willing, I'm sure the word will spread and we'll be full to capacity every week of the year."

"You should say since *we* took over," Claire corrected, adding in an aside to Bonnie, "Honestly, I don't know what I would have done without Midori."

"You'd be lost without me," said Midori cheerfully. "Doomed to failure."

"Since we completed our renovations, we've welcomed enough guests and made enough of a profit to cover the mortgage, but little more than that," said Claire, with a helpless sigh. "I think if we can reinvent ourselves as a special destination catering to quilters, we might be able to change all that. And if we can say that our program was designed by an Elm Creek Quilter—"

"So that's why you called on me," teased Bonnie. "I have street cred."

Claire smiled. "I would have said quilt shop cred, but okay."

"I don't think you can attach the Elm Creek Quilts name to your camp," Bonnie warned. "Not without permission, and that might not come easily. You might have to guarantee each of my friends a Hawaiian vacation."

"Easily promised and easily done," Claire proclaimed. "Of course they'll want to come visit you, and we have plenty of space for the whole crew."

"They won't need to visit me," Bonnie reminded her. "They'll see me in March."

Claire hopped down from her stool. "Do you want to see what you have to work with?"

"Sure," said Bonnie, knowing Claire would never acknowledge Bonnie's intended departure date until she was on her way to the airport. "Give me the grand tour."

She had spoken partially in jest, but the tour was grand indeed. Fortunately—or rather, unfortunately, since it would have been better for the inn's financial state if they were fully booked—many of the guest rooms were unoccupied, so Bonnie was able to see several, each lovely in its own way. The Garden Rooms on the first floor opened either onto the courtyard lanai with lush gardens or offered charming views of Lahaina's Front Street. Rooms on the second and third floors boasted private balconies—lanais, Claire corrected her whenever Bonnie slipped and used the more familiar term—and some had spectacular views of the ocean. Each suite had a private bath, authentic period décor, and beautiful Hawaiian quilts on every bed.

Bonnie had seen Hawaiian quilts before, but never so many all at once, and never any so lovely. "Did you make these?" she asked, admiring two particularly exquisite quilts on twin beds in a third floor suite with dormer windows overlooking Front Street.

"I wish I could take the credit, but I can't." Claire stroked the nearest quilt, sharing in Bonnie's admiration. "Midori made these. Members of her guild made most of the rest. Midori knows everything there is to know about traditional Hawaiian quilting. If you get on her good side, she'll teach you. Trust me, it's a lesson worth learning."

Intrigued, Bonnie followed Claire down the grand staircase and outside to the courtyard lanai. Bonnie knew a little about traditional Hawaiian quilts, having seen a few in quilt shows through the years and having stocked pattern books about them in her now defunct quilt shop. She had never attempted one herself, as she preferred country colors, homespuns, and folk art designs more than the intricate, two-color appliqué patterns unique to the Hawaiian style. But quilters coming to Aloha Quilt Camp on Maui would expect at least one lesson in traditional Hawaiian quilting, so it would be essential for Bonnie to learn more, at least enough to understand what resources Claire's teacher would need, whomever that lucky woman might be. Perhaps Midori herself would take on the role, although she seemed to have enough to do already.

Claire's tour brought them to a section of the courtyard lanai that was partially enclosed, with a roof and half walls running the entire length of the wing of the inn. "This will be our classroom," Claire said. "One of Eric's friends from the service took up woodworking in his retirement. He's going to custom design sewing tables for us, and he'll get started as soon as you tell him what we need."

"Your classroom will be outdoors?" said Bonnie.

"Of course. This isn't Pennsylvania," said Claire, beaming up at the sunny skies. "Foul weather forces us inside maybe ten days out of the year. The roof will protect us from the rain, and we can light torches if we need light or heat. People don't come to Maui to stay shut up within four walls." Then Claire paused. "Also, we don't have any rooms inside large enough to accommodate a quilt class. But really, that's just as well, because we'd rather be outside."

Bonnie nodded, taking in the shaded lanai. It would be a lovely place to teach and to quilt, but it was too small to divide into separate classrooms as they did with the ballroom back at Elm Creek Manor. Aloha Quilt Camp wouldn't be able to offer multiple courses simultaneously, but perhaps that wouldn't be necessary. Since the inn had twenty guest rooms, their maximum enrollment would be forty, and not everyone came to quilt camp for structured classes. Often campers wanted nothing more than a pleasant place to work on their own projects and socialize with other quilters, far from the demands of everyday life.

Bonnie knew she would have to sit down for a long talk with Claire so she could better understand her friend's vision for Aloha Quilt Camp—but that would have to wait until she had recovered from jetlag. At the moment, her head buzzed from lack of sleep and the overwhelming impressions of so many new sights and smells and sounds.

Claire seemed to sense her fatigue. "I'll show you the quilt shop tomorrow, after you've caught up on your rest," she said. "Let's go home. Eric's expecting us."

Bonnie gratefully agreed and, after passing through the kitchen to bid Midori good-bye, they returned to Claire's convertible and were soon zipping off down the highway. Claire turned on to a rural road that wound eastward away from town as it climbed into the foothills. It took them about fifteen minutes to reach a sun-splashed bungalow tucked amidst palm trees in a small neighborhood on the hillside. The house was placed on the lot facing uphill so that the backyard surely offered the same spectacular view of the ocean and another island—Lana'i, Claire told her—that Bonnie admired from the street.

"I need a glass of wine," said Claire, pulling to a stop beside a large black SUV in the driveway.

"Make that two." Puffs of white-gray smoke drifted over the roof of the bungalow from the backyard. Bonnie's stomach rumbled when the breeze carried the aroma of charcoal and spicy meat to her, and she felt as if it had been hours since she had eaten Midori's delicious popovers.

Bonnie waited for Claire to open the trunk, but instead her friend ushered her around back, saying that Eric would bring her suitcase in later. They found him on the lanai turning fish on the grill, barefoot but clad in khaki Bermuda shorts, a white polo shirt, and dark aviator sunglasses. At the sight of Bonnie, his face lit up. He set down his tongs and hurried over to greet her with open arms.

"Aloha," he boomed, hugging her so fully her heels lifted off the ground. Eric was tall and slender, with hard, wiry muscles from years of calisthenics. "Welcome to Maui."

"It's wonderful to be here," Bonnie said, laughing as he released her.

"What did you think of the inn?" he called, striding back to the grill. His blond hair had more silvery white in it than she remembered, but his short military cut was unchanged.

"It's lovely." Bonnie seated herself on a chaise lounge while Claire went inside for drinks. As soon as the sliding glass door closed behind her friend, Bonnie asked, "What do you think of Claire's plan to turn it into a quilters' retreat?"

Eric shrugged, smiling, and lifted the fish onto a platter. "You know Claire. She doesn't get ideas, she gets obsessions. I had my doubts when I first walked through the place, but she was determined. Now that I've seen how she's transformed it, I can't remember why I ever doubted her." Eric set the platter on a shaded table and returned to the grill for some vegetables still cooking there—potatoes? Bonnie couldn't quite see. "With your help, she'll figure out how to bring in the quilters. Claire's going to make it a huge success, I'm sure of it."

"That's what he says now," teased Claire, emerging from the bungalow carrying three glasses of white wine. She closed the sliding glass door with her foot. "You should have heard him fuss and complain when I showed him the mortgage papers."

"A momentary lapse of faith," Eric protested. He had sounded so proud as he described his wife's accomplishments that Bonnie didn't doubt him for a moment. Claire apparently didn't either, for she set the drinks on the table, cupped his chin in her hand, and pulled his face close for a kiss.

Bonnie looked away, smiling, and reached for her drink. The happy couple seemed to remember her and quickly separated. "Don't stop on my account," she teased.

"Sorry." Claire took the bowl of vegetables from Eric and set them on the table. "We should be more sensitive."

"What are you talking about? Do you think that because I'm single now, or soon to be single, you two have to pretend you're not happily married?"

"Well, no," said Claire, "but we don't have to flaunt it."

"Flaunt away," Bonnie said as they seated themselves and Claire began to serve the meal. "Just because my marriage crashed and burned doesn't mean I want every other married couple to be miserable."

"If you want to talk about the divorce, we're here and ready to listen," said Eric. "Or if you'd rather we never mention his name again, we can do that, too."

"Don't be silly, Eric. I know Craig's your friend." Bonnie couldn't miss the quick glance Claire and Eric exchanged. "What?"

"We haven't liked him much for at least a dozen years," Claire confessed. "He's changed since college. Lately we've just tolerated him for your sake."

Astonished, Bonnie burst out laughing. "You can't be serious. That's a long time to tolerate someone you can't stand."

"Not if we only had to see him a couple of times a year." Eric placed a generous portion of grilled fish on her plate. "Grilled ahi with sesame glaze. Eat up. There's plenty."

"Thanks." Bonnie shook her head in amazement as she helped herself to salad. It was a shame Claire hadn't given Bonnie her honest opinion about Craig years before. Bonnie could have avoided so much pain, so much grief—but really, would it have made any difference? Several of the Elm Creek Quilters had made no secret of their poor opinion of Craig through the years, but that had not stopped Bonnie from fighting to save a marriage that was long past saving.

When Claire passed her the bowl of potatoes, Bonnie took the spoon to serve herself, but a glance into the bowl gave her pause. "These potatoes are purple."

Eric turned a laugh into a cough. "These are taro," said Claire. "They're delicious, a bit like sweet potatoes. Try some."

Dubious, Bonnie took a small serving and sampled a tiny bite. "Better than any potato," she declared, making her hosts beam. She took another bite to prove that she wasn't merely being polite. She wondered if she would be able to find taro in the grocery store back in Pennsylvania. She had never noticed them before, but she had not been looking for them.

A lot about life had escaped her notice because she had not been looking.

The fish was light and flavorful, the taro sweet and nourishing. Bonnie savored every bite while Claire and Eric entertained her with a humorous account of the purchase and refurbishing of the inn. Eventually, Bonnie found the story of her impending divorce spilling from her, how she had stumbled upon Craig's first cyber-affair a few years before, how she had thwarted the lovers' plans to meet, and how Craig's renewed commitment to their marriage had disintegrated all too soon. How he had squirreled away money in anticipation of leaving her. How Agnes had discovered his ruse. How Craig had delayed the resolution of their divorce, and how Bonnie had resorted to hiring a private detective to try to unearth something that she might use against him. How she hated having a man she once loved become her adversary.

Eric refilled their wine glasses somberly as she told them everything, everything she had been concealing from all but the Elm Creek Quilters. Eric's expression clouded over as she spoke, and sometimes he punctuated her tale with exclamations of disbelief or anger. For her part, Claire looked shocked, then horrified, and then so upset her eyes filled with tears. "Oh, Bonnie," she murmured, time and time again. She shook her head, words failing her.

Twilight had descended, and through her unshed tears her friends' compassionate gazes were difficult to make out in the dim light.

"Ancient Hawaiians believed that Hawaii was the source of all the love in the world," said Eric quietly. "Soak up that love and beauty in the months ahead, and eventually your pain will subside."

Bonnie thanked him. Her pain was already ebbing, released in the flow of words confided to her friends. Only the Elm Creek Quilters knew so much about the demise of her marriage, and for the first time Bonnie understood that she could talk about her sadness, her disappointment, her anger without feeling guilty for betraying her husband. The betrayal was his, and Bonnie was done covering for him.

Chapter Three

Bonnie slept soundly in the bedroom Claire still called "the girls' room" even though her elder had married and moved out and the younger came home only on school breaks. The two-bedroom one-bath bungalow was small but tidy, Eric's need for military order overcoming Claire's tendency to accumulate clutter. The home was charming and cozy, but even so, Bonnie was relieved when during breakfast the next morning, Claire explained that Midori had arranged a suite for her at the inn for the remainder of her stay. Bonnie knew that even the most welcome guest could become a nuisance after a while, especially in such close quarters.

After breakfast, they bade Eric farewell and drove back to Lahaina. "Eric should win Husband of the Year, every year," Bonnie told her friend as the wind whipped her short locks into a frenzy that she suspected made her resemble a brunette dandelion.

"Don't I know it," said Claire. "If I could clone him, I'd make a fortune. But if I were a billionaire I wouldn't have been motivated to open my quilt shop, and then where would I be?"

Claire's store, Plumeria Quilts, was their first stop of the morning. Bonnie felt a pang of nostalgia for her lost Grandma's Attic as Claire proudly led her inside and showed off the enticing displays of fabric bolts, notions, and pattern books, as well as an extensive collection of Hawaiian quilts and quilted décor for sale. "Many of our customers are tourists rather than quilters," Claire confided, nodding to several browsers in Crocs, sunglasses, and fanny packs, with camera bags slung over their shoulders. "They prefer to buy a finished quilt to ship home as a souvenir. Occasionally a tourist will buy a kit to make a quilted pillow in the Hawaiian style, but how many of them actually open the kits when they get home from vacation, I'll never know."

Most of their fabric off-the-bolt sales were to local residents, Claire explained as she led Bonnie past numerous bolts arranged on shelves according to color. Bonnie was tempted to shade her eyes from the bright, almost garish rainbow of hues. Her favorite country colors and homespuns were conspicuously absent, but she found batiks and tropical floral prints in abundance.

"We prefer brighter colors out here," said Claire, trying not to laugh at whatever it was she read in Bonnie's expression. "Transplanted mainlanders bring their color preferences with them, but over time, they all gradually adopt a brighter palette. The same would happen to you if you stayed long enough."

Brighter colors to reflect a brighter outlook on life? Perhaps change of that sort wouldn't hurt. Bonnie resolved to keep an open mind.

After introducing Bonnie to her employees, Sunny and Aya, who had been busy cutting fabric, assisting browsers, and ringing up sales throughout her visit, Claire suggested they get Bonnie settled in her new room at the Hale Kapa Kuiki. When Claire offered her any available room she desired, Bonnie chose a suite on the second floor with a private lanai facing the ocean. She hoped the sound of the waves would lull her to sleep at night and the glorious sunsets would work their soothing magic on her.

A turquoise-and-white Hawaiian quilt covered the queen bed, so lovely that Bonnie hesitated to sit upon it. "Go ahead," encouraged Claire, showing her how easy it was by kicking off her shoes and planting herself cross-legged in the center of the bed. Sheepishly, Bonnie followed suit, and couldn't resist running her hands over the beautiful quilt. The turquoise appliqué appeared to have been made from whole cloth, cut like a paper snowflake in shapes resembling broad leaves and small round berries on stems, symmetrical and lovely. Concentric lines of exquisitely fine quilting covered the white background, echoing the appliquéd shapes.

"Midori calls this pattern Breadfruit," said Claire. "You'll find that most if not all traditional Hawaiian quilt patterns are inspired by nature."

"It's little wonder, considering how you're surrounded by so much natural beauty here," replied Bonnie. "I admit I'm surprised that quilting has long-standing traditions in Hawaii. I wouldn't think you'd need quilts in a tropical paradise."

"You of all people should know that quilts aren't created for warmth alone."

"Of course not, but how did quilting develop here? In European cultures and colonial America, quilting evolved out of the need for warmth and the necessity to use up every precious scrap of fabric. I can understand how quilting developed in those cultures, but I wouldn't have expected quilting to develop in a place like this."

"You're right to wonder," said Claire. "Quilting isn't indigenous to the Hawaiian islands. Christian missionaries introduced the art to the native population in the eighteen hundreds. The Hawaiian people took what they learned and developed their own unique style. Midori can tell you more, if you catch her at the right time. Sometimes she'll share, other times she acts like she's guarding a treasured cultural secret to be entrusted only to the most worthy."

Claire spoke lightly, unconcerned, but her words piqued Bonnie's curiosity. Most quilters were eager to share their quilting knowledge with others. Why wouldn't Midori? Bonnie had hoped to ask Midori to teach her how to make a Hawaiian quilt, her own precious souvenir of her visit to Maui, but Claire's warning gave her pause.

Perhaps over time, if she and Midori became friends, Bonnie would feel confident enough to ask her. Perhaps if Midori learned how much Bonnie respected the rich heritage of quilting in all its diversity, Midori would consider her worthy of trust.

As Claire helped Bonnie unpack, Bonnie questioned her about her vision for Aloha Quilt Camp, how she intended to structure the week. Claire proved to be frustratingly flexible: She would confidently follow Bonnie's recommendations, whatever they turned out to be.

"You have to give me more to go on than that," protested Bonnie, hanging her last suitcase-wrinkled blouse in the closet. Ironing freshly washed yards of fabric was a pleasure, but ironing clothing was a chore to be postponed as long as possible. "You're the camp director, and you'll be running things long after I'm gone. I don't want to stick you with a program you don't like."

"If I wanted to micromanage everything, I wouldn't have hired you."

"Offering your opinion when asked isn't micromanaging,"

Bonnie said. "And we haven't even mentioned evening programs. You really ought to schedule outings around Maui in
the evenings so that everyone leaves camp feeling as if they've
enjoyed a unique, complete Hawaiian experience."

Claire nodded, amused. "Yes, *you* really ought to set up evening programs too. Just let me know what you decide. I know
you can do it."

Bonnie wished Claire had substantially less faith in her.

As Bonnie unpacked her carry-on, she came across her cell
phone and realized with a start that she hadn't turned it back
on after turning it off before her first flight more than a day
earlier. She had four messages waiting. The first was from her
daughter, Tammy, wishing her a safe trip and asking her to
call when she arrived. The second was from Darren Taylor
to confirm the hiring of a trusted private detective; Bonnie
wrote down his name and number in case she had to reach him
directly. The third was from Sarah back at Elm Creek Manor,
hoping Bonnie had arrived safely and was enjoying her first
hours in Hawaii. The fourth, left twelve hours later, was also
from Sarah, a more agitated version of her previous message
with the addition of a strained request for her to call Elm Creek
Manor to let them know she was fine, because although a plane
crashing into the Pacific would have made the national news,
any number of tragedies that might have prevented Bonnie
from calling home wouldn't have.

Bonnie blamed the pregnancy hormones for Sarah's undue
worry, but she quickly, guiltily, dialed Elm Creek Manor.
"What time is it on the East Coast?" she asked Claire as the
phone rang. "Are they six hours ahead?"

"Only five at this time of year, since we don't do Daylight
Savings Time," Claire replied. "Is something wrong?"

Bonnie shook her head as someone picked up the phone.

"So I take it you're still among the living," remarked Sylvia, who pretended to despise Caller ID but used it as scrupulously as everyone else.

"I'm so sorry I forgot to call."

"Nonsense. We knew someone would have contacted us if there had been some dire emergency. Well, some of us understood that. Others chose to worry themselves senseless."

"Will you please assure Sarah that I'm fine?"

"She knows. She's right here glaring at me. She wants her turn with you, but I want a moment to hear your first impressions of Hawaii."

There was so much to say that Bonnie couldn't put it into words. "Those who call it paradise aren't exaggerating."

"How wonderful for you. Do enjoy yourself, dear, and please fill me in later when Sarah isn't wrestling me for the phone. Here she is."

"Bonnie?" said Sarah. "Thank God you're all right. Would it have killed you to call us when your flight landed?"

Bonnie couldn't help it; she burst out laughing. "Sorry, Mom. It won't happen again."

After a moment's indignant silence, Sarah laughed too. "See that it doesn't. I guess you're forgiven." She hesitated. "I'm sorry to bring this up, but has Craig been bothering you?"

"Every day for years. Why?"

"He showed up here this morning demanding to see you."

"Why? Darren told his lawyer I would be traveling."

"Maybe he mixed up the days?"

"Or he's trying to intimidate my friends or poison my workplace."

"Impossible," said Sarah. "I haven't yet met the man who could intimidate Sylvia."

"That doesn't mean he wouldn't try."

"You don't think he's turning into a disgruntled stalker-type, do you?"

"I certainly hope not." In the background, Bonnie heard Sylvia admonish Sarah to stop frightening her. "Tell Sylvia I'm not frightened. Craig's an angry bully, but I don't think he's dangerous. I'll have Darren call Craig's lawyer and have him tell Craig not to come to Elm Creek Manor anymore. In the meantime, don't provoke him, and don't tell him where I am."

"Don't worry," said Sarah. "I'll cite a lot of employee confidentiality legalese and send him away."

"Let's hope it won't be necessary." Claire was shooting Bonnie looks of increasing alarm, so Bonnie changed the subject to a brief, cheerful description of her first day in Maui. As she hung up and dialed her daughter's number, she gave Claire a quick summary of Craig's appearance at the manor.

"It's time to get a restraining order," Claire warned, just as Tammy answered, sparing Bonnie the uncomfortable task of making excuses for him.

Tammy was considerably less frantic than Sarah had been, and she delighted in Bonnie's descriptions of the beautiful scenery and the charming inn. Tammy, in turn, entertained Bonnie with stories of her children's latest antics and promised to send her a picture the eldest had drawn in nursery school that morning. They would have chatted longer, but Bonnie noticed Claire studiously folding and putting away Bonnie's T-shirts, pretending not to eavesdrop and looking a little left out, so she wrapped up the conversation with a promise to call in a day or two with more about her Hawaiian adventures. Before hanging up, she asked her daughter for a favor.

"Sure, Mom," said Tammy. "Anything."

"Please don't tell your father where I am or how to reach me."

"Oh, Mom. I thought you wanted me to water your plants or pick up your mail or something. You know I can't take sides between you and Dad."

"This has nothing to do with taking sides and everything to do with my privacy."

"What am I supposed to do if he asks? Lie?"

"No, just tell him I asked you not to divulge that information."

"I can't say something like that to Dad."

"With any luck, he won't ask." But if he wanted to know her whereabouts badly enough to bother the Elm Creek Quilters, he wouldn't overlook asking his own daughter. "Listen, honey. He knows he's supposed to contact me only through my lawyer. Just remind him."

"How long do you think you can keep that up? Realistically, I mean. Are you and Dad never going to be in the same room together? What about when my girls graduate from college? What about when Barry gets married?"

"What? Barry's getting married?"

"Not anytime soon. Don't panic, Mom. That's just a hypothetical."

"Well, please choose a less startling hypothetical next time!" At Claire's inquiring look, Bonnie shook her head to indicate nothing was amiss. "It's a very contentious time for your father and me. After the divorce is final and the dust settles, I'm sure we'll manage to be civil, but this is the way things have to be right now. Please call your brothers and tell them the same thing, okay?"

Tammy hesitated but agreed, although Bonnie knew she wasn't happy about it.

The back-to-back calls left Bonnie disconcerted. "This is not how I expected my life to be at this point," she said, putting her cell phone into her purse and setting her purse on the nightstand. "I'm supposed to be settled. I'm supposed to be wise and secure. Happily, contentedly, maybe even boringly married. This is not what I bargained for."

Claire tucked the last of Bonnie's T-shirts into the bottom drawer of the bureau and shut it with her foot. "Bonnie, no one ever gets what they bargained for in a marriage."

"You did."

"Eric is great, without a doubt, but do you think I enjoyed packing up and moving every year or two, dragging the girls around the world behind us?"

"But you always made it sound like a grand adventure," protested Bonnie, taking her shoes from her suitcase. "So exciting and glamorous, and such a wonderful education for your daughters. You have friends in every country I've ever heard of and some I couldn't find on a map if I tried. You've seen more of the world than I ever will."

"And yet I've spent many long days wishing I had a cozy house in Pennsylvania in a neighborhood near friends I've known all my life, where I could plant bulbs in my garden in the fall and know I would be there to see the tulips come up in the spring."

Bonnie shook her head in wonder. "I had no idea. You never said anything."

"Of course not. Who complains about a saint like Eric? Faithful, dutiful, loyal to both me and our country. Overall, I've been very happy. Very. But we always long for what we can't have, don't we?"

Suddenly Claire looked so unhappy that Bonnie wanted to hug her, but her arms were full of shoes. "You're settled now. You have Eric *and* a permanent address. You can plant all the bulbs you want and enjoy every bloom."

Claire smiled wanly and carried Bonnie's toiletries bag into the bathroom. "These days I'm more into banyan trees and palms. But you're right. I can cultivate my garden with Eric by my side. That's a blessing I'll never take for granted."

It was a blessing Bonnie had wanted to give Craig, but he had rejected it. He had rejected *her*.

Bonnie knew she must have disappointed Craig in countless ways throughout the years, in big ways and small, just as he had disappointed her. It was impossible, impossible, for two people to live side by side for so many years without occasionally irritating each other, without settling into a routine, without sometimes forgetting the magic and wonder that drew them together in the first place. And yet some couples were able to forgive each other those inevitable human failings and nurture the lingering sparks of love until it burned steadily again, while others couldn't, or wouldn't.

Until Craig's betrayal, Bonnie had counted herself among the more fortunate, those whose love endured throughout the natural ebb and flow of life. When both couples were young newlyweds, there was no sign that Eric and Claire's love burned brighter than Craig and Bonnie's, that their bond was stronger, their devotion more complete. They were all young people in love, eager to build a life with the one they had chosen.

Why Eric and Claire had made it and she and Craig had not, Bonnie did not know. The explanation couldn't be as simple as concluding that Eric was a good man and Craig was bad, therefore the Markham marriage had been doomed from the start. There had to be more to it than that, for Bonnie did not believe she had married a bad man. She would not have married Craig if he had not been kind and loving to her, if she had not believed him when he promised to love her and honor her for the rest of his life. She'd had other boyfriends; she had not settled for a bad man because he was her only option. She would have lived alone before settling.

Had there been a point in their marriage, five or ten or twenty years before, when she and Craig could have changed their fate? Had they stood at a crossroads unaware? Would some other choice, some kindness offered or neglect remedied, have led them to a happier place?

And why, when the marriage was so nearly over, when she knew all too well that it was impossible to change the past, did she insist upon sifting through her memories to pinpoint exactly when and where everything had gone so terribly wrong?

⬦

While Claire went downstairs to tend to some business affairs, Bonnie finished unpacking and took in the view from her lanai. Waves crashed upon the sandy beach where couples and families relaxed and played. In the distance, she saw two other islands surrounded by aquamarine seas, forested and mysterious, one larger and one quite small. Between the distant islands and the nearby shore, sailboats danced and darted in the wind and surfers paddled out to catch the big waves. Sometimes white puffs indicated whales surfacing; tourists watched from boats that kept a respectful distance. Bonnie watched, entranced, the music of the ocean in her ears, gentle breezes bathing her in the light enticing perfume of unfamiliar flowers. Even birdsong was different here, intriguing chirps and melodies she had never heard before.

It was as if she had come to an entirely different world from the one she had left behind, a world of peace and harmony where she would never know pain.

Reluctantly she left her reverie and joined Claire in her office on the first floor to see if her friend was ready, at last, for a serious chat about quilt camp. "We've done enough work for one morning," Claire declared, brushing off Bonnie's protests that she had hardly worked at all except to unpack. "You should learn more about Maui, especially since you're going to be welcoming guests and arranging evening programs for them."

Bonnie was tempted to remind her that she would be doing the latter but not the former since their first guests wouldn't arrive until a few weeks after her return to Pennsylvania, but she let it go. "What did you have in mind? A walking tour of Lahaina?"

"Later. First you should see the big picture."

What Claire had in mind, she explained before sending Bonnie back upstairs for her sturdiest walking shoes, was a hike in the mountains to enjoy the spectacular views of the coastline and the lush valleys of Mount Kahalawai. Bonnie grabbed a hat as well as her camera, and soon they were driving north on Highway 30 past shopping centers and resort hotels. To Bonnie's surprise, Claire pulled into a parking place at a strip mall. "Are we stopping for supplies?"

"No," said Claire, smiling as she got out of the convertible. "I'm not subjecting my car to those rugged roads. We'll catch a ride from here."

Bemused, Bonnie followed her through one of several identical stucco arches leading to the various shops, passing beneath a green sign that announced in white letters, SKYLINE ECO ADVENTURES. Inside, a burly man in a dark blue shirt boasting the company logo took Claire's name and handed each of them a pen and a clipboard with a release form attached.

"A release form for a hike?" Bonnie asked, scanning the page of rather alarming warnings that she should not participate if she were pregnant, suffered from various ailments, or had been scuba diving within the past twenty-four hours. " 'Serious injury or death may occur?' We're not climbing up the side of an active volcano, are we?"

Claire breezily signed her name at the bottom of her own form, which she had apparently barely read. "Of course not. It's perfectly safe. This is a routine precaution."

Dubious, Bonnie signed the form, but her misgivings spiked when the man led her to a scale and asked her to step on it. "A weigh-in?" she protested, throwing a look to Claire rather than glancing down and viewing the grim report. She was fully dressed and had eaten a large breakfast, hardly the ideal circumstances to publicly announce her weight. "Is this Fat Camp?"

Claire's laughter pealed. "Don't be ridiculous. You don't need to lose any more weight."

"We weigh everyone," the man explained. "The harnesses have weight limits."

"And you thought I exceeded them? Wait a minute—harnesses?"

"They have minimum weight limits too," the man said, grinning. He collected their signed forms, handed each of them a sturdy water bottle with the company logo on it, and showed them to a cooler in the back corner. "After you fill your bottles, you can wait for the shuttle outside."

"Harness?" Bonnie echoed to Claire as they filled their bottles. Suddenly the word *Adventures* in the company logo seemed ominous. "What is this, mountain climbing?"

"We'll be on a mountain and we'll be climbing," Claire granted, "but it's not, strictly speaking, mountain climbing."

"Strictly speaking, what is it then?"

"It's fun and it's spectacular views and it's a great lunch half-way through. Relax, would you?"

Nothing was less likely to help Bonnie relax than Claire's

cagey assurances that she should, but she followed her friend outside where eight other men and women waited on the sidewalk. Some were older than she, some younger, some in better physical condition, and some worse. She was heartened, a little, to see that the rest of the hiking party was not comprised of twenty-something extreme athletes, so when a large van pulled up to take them to the site, she climbed aboard with everyone else. Her courage faltered a bit when she realized she was one of only four to bother with a seat belt—clearly she was among risk-takers—but she returned Claire's cheerful smile and told herself that whatever Claire was hiding couldn't be that bad.

As they drove back along the same stretch of highway she and Claire had traveled earlier, the hikers exchanged names and hometowns. One woman expressed surprise to hear that Claire was from Lahaina. "Haven't you done this dozens of times?"

"Twice," Claire said. "It never gets old."

The woman peered at Bonnie. "And you . . . this is your first time. Nervous?"

"Not really," said Bonnie, wondering what had telegraphed her novice status. "Should I be?"

A few people grinned, while others chuckled. "It's safe," a younger man reassured her. "Don't let the waiver scare you."

Before long they pulled off the highway and stopped long enough for a guide to jump down from the front passenger seat and unlock a gate. The van passed through the entrance and waited for the guide to lock the gate behind them and return to his place—and then they set off on a rough dirt road that bounced and jolted its passengers and left Bonnie fervently grateful for her seat belt. "This— must be— the reason for— the waiver," she managed to tell Claire as the van lurched up an alarmingly steep hill. Claire laughed, enjoying the ride. Claire had odd tastes sometimes.

Eventually the teeth-rattling ride ended halfway up the mountain at a small cabin with a shaded deck. The hikers disembarked and seated themselves on benches in the shade while the guide entered the cabin and returned carrying an armful of harnesses, a jumble of black straps and gleaming stainless-steel. Another guide—thin, tattooed, and multiply pierced—accompanied him carrying helmets.

"Just a precaution," Claire said before Bonnie could ask. Bonnie gnawed her lower lip and concentrated on the dark-haired guide's explanation of how to adjust the fit of the helmets. Troy bore a striking resemblance to the host of a popular reality television show that required participants to bungee jump off bridges spanning tropical gorges and eat all manner of nauseating foods considered delicacies in exotic cultures. Bonnie hoped the disconcerting similarity ended with his appearance.

Bonnie submitted to the thinner, lighter-haired guide's attention as he helped her into her harness, tightened the straps, and showed her how to attach her water bottle to the belt, cracking jokes all the while. She laughed along, a bit hysterically, but froze when a particular word caught her attention. "What's a zipline?" she asked.

The guide, Brian, laughed as if she had said something unbelievably hilarious and moved on to help the next hiker. Bonnie caught Claire's arm. "Zipline? What have you gotten me in to?"

"It's *fun*," Claire insisted. "Anyway, you can't back out now, not unless you want to sit here for the next two hours, miss lunch, and ride back down the mountain in shame while the rest of us rave about what a blast it was."

Bonnie would willingly skip lunch, but the thought of waiting around at the cabin in disgrace was more than she could
bear. Heart pounding, she followed Claire aboard another van,
this one retrofitted with tank treads instead of tires. The second
stage of the trip up the mountain was steeper and rougher
than the first, with switchbacks upon switchbacks, but the tank
treads seemed to find a surer grip, and Bonnie had new worries
to distract her from the possibility of a rollover.

All too soon and not soon enough, the van stopped near
the summit, a few yards below a large wooden platform with a
ramp that jutted out over a plunging cliff. From a complicated
rig of cables and support beams, a thick, black cable hung sus-
pended over a lush valley, ending at a similar platform on the
opposite ridge.

"Claire," Bonnie managed to say as Brian and Troy led the
group up the hiking trail toward the stairs to the platform.
"Look."

"No, you look." Claire took her by the shoulders and spun
her in the opposite direction. Bonnie drew in a breath—the
endless blue ocean, the cloud-swathed emerald of Lanaʻi, the
rainforests caressing fields of sugarcane, the resort town of
Kaanapali seeming very small and very far below. For a moment Bonnie marveled at the glorious view, which was everything Claire had promised—but then she heard Brian calling
the hikers over for a demonstration and she remembered the
cable flung into space across the chasm.

"It's only scary the first time," Claire assured her, steer-
ing her to the end of the line. Bonnie gulped and nodded.
She wanted to back out. She wanted to argue that she had
signed on for a hike, not for this, but she couldn't bear to dis-
appoint Claire or to shame herself in front of everyone else,
even though they were strangers she would never see again. If

someone else backed out, she would too, but she would not be the first, she would not be the only.

She drew closer so she wouldn't miss a word of the instructions. While Brian explained what to do, Troy hooked himself up to the zipline and demonstrated where to put her left hand to hold on to the harness, where to put her right hand to steer, where to put both hands to signal that she was out of control and needed a guide to catch her on the other side, and where not to put any hands unless she wanted them amputated in a sudden and painful manner. Then Troy strolled to the edge of the platform, stepped off into empty space, and flew across the steep valley, executing a flawless landing on the other side.

As the hikers cheered and applauded, Brian grinned and asked, "Who's first?"

A large man from Omaha volunteered, and soon he too had soared over the valley, whooping and cheering and spinning all the way. "Remember to steer," Brian reminded the others, "unless you enjoy spinning around out of control like that."

Bonnie felt sick at the thought of it, and she hung back as another man eagerly pushed forward for his turn. She checked the security of her helmet, tugged on the straps of her harness to tighten them even more, and began to question the value of her long-time friendship with anyone who would trick her into doing something so terrifying, so dangerous, so—

Bonnie rounded on Claire, barely able to keep her voice low enough for Claire's ears alone. "How could you do this to me?"

"Do what to you? Show you a beautiful bird's-eye view of Maui and Lanaʻi? Shake you out of your depression with a jolt of excitement?"

"I don't want a jolt. I don't even like roller coasters! You remember our trip to Cedar Point during sophomore year?"

"That was a long time ago. I figured you were over it." Claire tugged on her ponytail and adjusted her helmet. "Anyway, no one's ever been killed on these ziplines. I checked."

It was small consolation. "You can't make me do this."

"*I* know that. I'm glad you figured it out. No one can make you do anything." Claire turned and bounded up the stairs, harness jingling, calling to Brian, "Can I go next?"

Bonnie watched from below, silently fuming. Claire joked with Brian while he hooked her harness to the zipline, and then, without an ounce of visible fear, she darted to the end of the platform and leapt gracefully off. Swift and sure, she flew straight across the valley and alighted smoothly on the other side.

"She's done this before," Bonnie heard another woman murmur to her husband.

No one else among them had, Bonnie realized. Some of the hikers were as nervous as she, although no one seemed prepared to back out. Bonnie felt her faint courage wavering with Claire at a distance; safely remote on the other cliff, she couldn't grab Bonnie's arm if she started down the mountain on foot or chide her if she hesitated. But she also couldn't encourage her to step up and allow herself to be snapped on to that precariously thin and fragile-looking cable except in mostly inaudible shouts that were having little effect at the moment.

Bonnie knew she had to follow Claire immediately or she wouldn't go at all.

She seized the handrail and forced herself up the stairs. "I'm terrified," she confessed to Brian and he took a gadget from her belt, snapped it to the top of the zipline, clipped one part of her harness to it, and then the other.

"Terrified, huh?" he queried. All she could do was nod.

"You don't think you can do it?" She nodded again. He pointed down the ramp, grinning. "It's easy. Just walk that way until you can't anymore."

Claire shouted something unintelligible from the opposite side of the valley.

Bonnie forced the rational part of her brain to shut up, gripped the harness as tightly as she could, took one step down the ramp, and another, and another, and two more on tiptoe, and suddenly she was gliding smoothly above the rainforest, mountains rushing by on her right, sparkling ocean far below to her left. She began to turn in the harness; in a flash she remembered Brian's instructions and tried to steer, but she overcorrected and began turning too far in the other direction. With small corrections each way she managed to finish the ride facing mostly forward. All at once the platform ramp approached and she stumbled breathless up to where Troy waited to detach her from the zipline.

"Not bad," he remarked, hooking her gear onto her belt. She barely heard him over her pounding heart and Claire's cheers.

"How was it?" Claire asked when she joined her at the base of the platform to await the rest of the party. "Fun?"

"Mostly terrifying," said Bonnie, catching her breath and slowly smiling. She had done it, and lived to tell the tale. "A little fun."

When the others reached their side of the valley, Brian and Troy led them down a trail to the next platform. "See? We're hiking," Claire pointed out, as if that justified all the other more significant details she had omitted.

The next zipline, Brian announced, was slightly longer than the first and faster. Even so, Bonnie stepped up to the platform with a little less trepidation and found the ride a bit less terrifying and a lot more fun. By the third run, she was joking around with Troy as he hooked her up to the cable, and when she landed smoothly on the far distant platform, Brian declared, "You just ziplined into my heart."

Halfway down, they broke for lunch on a lookout platform high above another valley—tasty sandwiches, fruit, chips and salsa, brownies with raspberry sauce—and took in the glorious views.

"Are you still angry at me?" Claire asked after they had finished cleaning up and Bonnie took out her camera to snap photos of the spectacular views from the lookout platform.

"A little," said Bonnie, framing a shot of the beach far below. "You misled me."

"If I'd told you the truth, you wouldn't have come, and aren't you glad you did?"

"I am now," Bonnie admitted, "but that doesn't change the fact that you lied to me."

"I didn't give you every detail. That's not the same as lying."

Bonnie had to laugh. "Actually, it kind of is."

"It was the only way I knew to get you up the mountain," Claire insisted. "Disapprove on principle if you have to, but don't pretend you're sorry I did it."

And Bonnie wasn't sorry anymore, or even angry. She enjoyed every breathtaking second of each flight over the rainforest, admiring the scenery, spotting waterfalls through the foliage below and whale blow in the ocean miles away. Far too soon they came to the last zipline, which Brian announced was the guides' favorite. "Because it's the longest or the windiest?"

Brian shook his head. "Nuh-uh. Because this is the one where if people are gonna get stuck, they get stuck."

Bonnie felt a tremor of alarm. "We could get marooned halfway across?"

Troy grinned as he hooked himself to the zipline. "You probably won't, but it helps if you take a running start and cannonball across like this." He strode to the back of the platform, sprinted toward the end, and hurtled himself off the end with his knees tucked up to his chest.

One by one the other hikers waited for their turns and imitated Troy's explosive launch from the platform. No one got stuck midway, although two petite women barely made it to the edge of the platform where Troy reached out and hauled them in.

"What happens if someone gets stuck?" Bonnie asked Brian as he attached her harness to the zipline.

"It depends if we like them or not," he said. "If we like them, we go out there after them and bring 'em in."

"And if you don't like them?"

"We slide about fifty pounds of weight down the line and hope it carries them across."

Bonnie didn't dare ask which group she belonged to. Her heart pounded almost as hard as it had before the first ride. Walking down a ramp until the level cable lifted her off the ground was one thing, sprinting off a platform and leaping into space above a rainforest valley quite another. Would the harness hold? Would she make it across? If not, would she get the kindly escort the rest of the way or the grudging delivery of a burlap bag of weights?

"It's leap of faith time, Bonnie," Brian said.

She took a deep breath, backed up to the far edge of the platform, fixed her sights on the opposite ridge, ran along the wooden boards, and flung herself over the edge and into the air.

Chapter Four

Exhilarated, Bonnie and Claire chatted happily on the way back to the Hale Kapa Kuiki, reliving the most exciting moments of the zipline hike and laughing about their few minor mishaps. Clicking through the images on her digital camera, Bonnie thanked Claire for arranging the adventure, but she couldn't quite bring herself to say that Claire had been right to deceive her. There were some lines she wasn't willing to cross, no matter how well things had turned out in the end.

"We really should get some work done today," Bonnie said as they pulled into the parking lot. Claire hadn't hired her to ride ziplines and enjoy cookouts.

Claire agreed and suggested they meet in the conference room to brainstorm. "Grab a notebook and pen, put on more sunblock, change clothes if you want, and meet me on the lanai in fifteen minutes," she said. "I'll bring the drinks and snacks."

Bonnie went upstairs to freshen up and gathered her thoughts as she gathered her things. Just as she was settling down at a table on the lanai, Claire emerged from the kitchen carrying a picnic basket, a notebook stuffed with loose papers, and what appeared to be two grass mats rolled up and tucked into a beach bag. "Can you take this?" Claire asked, indicating the bag with a nod as she juggled her other burdens.

Bonnie hurried to assist, then broke into laughter as Claire led the way to a gate almost hidden in the foliage at the back of the garden. "Let me guess. Your conference room is the beach?"

"Wouldn't everyone have a beach for a conference room if they could?"

They unrolled the grass mats on the warm sand beneath an enormous beach umbrella, one of several set up for guests of the inn, and took out notebooks and pens. "I never tire of this view," said Claire dreamily, slipping off her sandals. "There are days when I almost have to pinch myself because I can't believe I'm lucky enough to live here. It's not perfect," she added quickly. "Prices are much higher than on the mainland, and we could buy a mansion in Pennsylvania for what we paid for our little bungalow. It's far from family too. We exchange visits when we can, but we can't hop in the car and drive to see the grandkids on the spur of the moment."

"Life's full of trade-offs," Bonnie agreed. "But as far as I can tell, you and Eric have it as close to perfect as anyone."

Claire smiled. "I think so, too. Tempting, isn't it? Just wait until winter, when your friends back home call you to complain about the latest blizzard. You'll never want to leave."

Bonnie laughed. "We'll see." Claire knew how to tempt her too well. She remembered how Bonnie had always hated dragging herself out of bed on cold winter mornings and bundling herself in layers for the frigid walk across campus through the snow.

They began their first official business meeting by discussing their goals for Aloha Quilt Camp. Both wanted to offer their guests a unique retreat experience with opportunities to learn new techniques, to work on individual projects, and to experience Hawaiian culture. Bonnie emphasized social activities for quilters to foster new friendships, and Claire threw around a lot of business jargon about profitability and market share that convinced Bonnie that her impulsive friend had, for once, thought ahead and planned carefully.

Then Claire quizzed Bonnie about the founding of Elm Creek Quilt Camp. Bonnie gave her the condensed version of how Sarah had devised the plan to turn Elm Creek Manor into a quilters' retreat to preserve Sylvia's family estate; how the combination of Sarah's business acumen, Sylvia's teaching experience, and Summer's Internet skills had enabled them to launch Elm Creek Quilts within a year; and how the members of their quilting bee had become the camp's first teachers.

Claire stretched out on the grass mat, tucked the empty beach bag under her head for a pillow, and frowned thoughtfully at the underside of the umbrella. "So . . . you assembled your faculty first and allowed them to teach the classes of their choice. You didn't create a program and then find the best teachers for those courses."

"We didn't really assemble our faculty," Bonnie said. "We were already friends, and several of us had already taught classes through my quilt shop. Our interests are so varied that we can cover all of the basic quilting topics and many more specialized techniques without needing to bring in outside teachers. It just worked out that way."

"Unfortunately, I don't have a ready-made team of teachers hanging around," said Claire, sighing. "I'll have to find them and recruit them."

"Surely your quilt shop helps you keep in touch with all of the local quilting teachers."

"Yes, but whether they'd want to leave their current gigs to help me is another question."

"They wouldn't be doing it as a favor. You *are* planning to pay them, right?" In response, Claire swatted her lightly with the nearest suitable object, a piece of fallen palm leaf. "Working at a quilters' retreat benefits your teachers, too, and not just because of a paycheck. It's great experience and wonderful exposure if they enjoy traveling to teach workshops at quilt guilds or if they sell their own pattern lines."

"You've convinced me," said Claire. "Now convince them."

"First we have to decide whether you'll need one teacher and an assistant or two, or several teachers with different areas of expertise. And that depends upon how you want to set up your program."

"I just figured we'd duplicate what you do at Elm Creek Quilt Camp."

"You can't, not really. You only have one classroom." Bonnie traced patterns in the sand with the palm leaf. "Maybe Aloha Quilt Camp could offer classes in a different quilting technique each morning, so that campers could sign up for those that appeal to them and skip the others. Or you could offer instruction on a single, advanced project, such as a traditional Hawaiian quilt from start to finish, with new steps presented each day in a morning seminar."

"Why can't we do both? Why couldn't we have one week focused on a single project followed by a week offering a variety of classes?"

"That'll make hiring teachers more difficult," Bonnie pointed out. "A steady job is more appealing than working only every other week."

"But it would be steady work. One week each instructor could offer a workshop on her favorite quilting technique, one each morning. The next week they could team-teach the week-long project."

"That's asking a lot of our teachers."

"I know they can manage with you to lead them."

Bonnie groaned. "Again, I won't be here and you know it. Sometimes you drive me crazy."

"And sometimes you drive me crazy, so we're even." Claire tucked her hands beneath her head and closed her eyes. "If it helps, I've already started a list of potential local quilting instructors who might be willing to teach for us. We can also ask Midori to inquire at her quilt guild. I don't know if any of them have taught before, but there are some fantastic quilters in that group and it wouldn't hurt to ask. I bet Midori would have some great suggestions for evening programs, too."

"I'll take that list, thanks, and I'll definitely talk to Midori." Following Claire's example, Bonnie set her notebook and pen aside and stretched out on her grass mat. She wondered if Skyline Eco Adventures offered evening hikes and how many of their campers might surprise themselves by daring more than they had ever thought possible. She wondered if like her they would feel the surge of pride and the renewal of confidence born of confronting risk and fear and taking a leap of faith above a rainforest canopy.

❖

Over the next few days, Bonnie described the founding of Elm Creek Quilt Camp in greater detail, occasionally phoning or emailing her friends back home to refresh her memory or to seek advice. Together she and Claire developed a master schedule with a tentative grand opening for the first week of April. Claire suggested that they hold a "soft opening" in late February or early March, a test run of the quilt camp with trusted friends invited to be their first campers. With any luck, they could work through any unforeseen problems that appeared during their dress rehearsal before Bonnie left for home.

Every night Bonnie watched the sunset from her lanai, the play of color and light filling her with awe and wonder. Every morning she woke refreshed and ready to continue her work, energized by the act of creation. She took her morning walks through Lahaina, along the ocean and around Courthouse Square, where an enormous banyan tree rose about sixty feet into the air and shaded nearly two-thirds of an acre, with a dozen aerial roots as thick as trunks stretching down to plunge back into the earth. In those early morning hours just after dawn, she passed other walkers and joggers admiring the scenery as they exercised, wetsuit-clad surfers carrying boards to the beach, and men and women on their way to work clad in uniforms bearing logos of shops and restaurants. Not a resident, not quite a tourist, Bonnie felt as if she tread a narrow path between those two groups, belonging to one and catching hidden glimpses of the other.

No matter how early she rose or how quickly she completed her route, by the time she showered, dressed, and came down to the kitchen, Midori was always there working busily, baking popovers or muffins, cutting pineapple and mango for beautifully arranged tropical fruit plates, or pressing halved oranges in the juicer. Bonnie always offered to help, and by her third morning as a guest of the inn, she had begun to think of certain tasks as her responsibility—filling small pitchers with cream and tucking napkins into rings without asking Midori for an assignment.

Sometimes Midori was too busy for small talk, but other times she greeted Bonnie with a relaxed friendliness that invited questions. Bonnie learned that Midori was born on Oahu but had moved to Maui more than forty years before. Her late husband, a musician, had played ukulele with several different bands throughout his career, performing everywhere from small bars only locals knew about to exclusive resorts frequented by tourists from around the world. When their youngest child started school, Midori began working as a housekeeper at a hotel in Kaanapali, eventually working her way up the ladder and learning all aspects of hotel management along the way. "This is my retirement job," she told Bonnie, smiling as she deftly sliced off the top of a pineapple. "I do this for fun, so I don't slow down and grow old. It's also the only way I can live rent-free on the ocean." She smiled to herself and added, "Claire thinks I chose my suite because it's more private, off on its own, but I chose it for the view."

"I chose my room for the view and for the quilt on the bed," said Bonnie, folding napkins into a graceful fan as Midori had shown her. "Claire called it the Breadfruit pattern."

"Oh, yes. You're in the room with the turquoise-and-white one, isn't that right?" When Bonnie nodded, Midori added, "That's one of several Breadfruit variations I made for the inn. I think it's my favorite."

"Variations?" echoed Bonnie. "You didn't use the same pattern each time?"

"Of course not." Midori's knife sliced through the pineapple core and struck the wooden cutting board with a sharp thwack. "No two quilts you create should be exactly alike, just as no two children you bear are perfectly alike. Even twins. Even identical twins," she emphasized, as if she expected a challenge. "Everything in God's creation is unique, though there may be superficial similarities. So too should our quilts also be unique. This is the Hawaiian way. Everything is special and created with love. No mass-produced, factory assembled quilts for me and my loved ones, thank you very much, although that might be the way of things on the mainland."

Bonnie nodded in reply and continued working, worried that she had offended the older woman. "I think I saw a few of the other Breadfruit variations when Claire gave me the grand tour," she said, when the silence, for her at least, had become uncomfortable. "I recall a green one on the second floor, and a fuchsia one down the hall from my room. I thought they were the same at first, but now that you mention it, there were differences. The green one had a different border than the one in my room, and both of the others had narrower leaves."

Midori nodded her approval. "That's right. You have a good memory. There's an orange variation in a first-floor suite, too. The room's occupied or I'd show it to you."

"They were all beautiful, but the turquoise one seemed so cool and soothing that I knew I'd have good dreams beneath it." Bonnie laughed a little to conceal how badly she needed to take every measure possible to secure good dreams. "It was so lovely that I was afraid to sit upon it."

"I'm glad you didn't," declared Midori. "Most mainlanders aren't aware of what a great insult that is to Hawaiian quilters. They toss their suitcases on the quilts, lie on top of them with shoes full of beach sand, all without a thought for the quilter who put so much of her heart and soul into every stitch. Even Claire, a quilter herself, doesn't seem to know any better. I caught her sitting on the quilt I made her and Eric for their anniversary, although she jumped right off when she saw me in the doorway and swore it was the first and only time."

Bonnie hid her dismay as best she could, imagining Midori's reaction if she had seen Claire and Bonnie sitting cross-legged on the turquoise-and-white Breadfruit quilt. "I hope you forgave her."

"Of course I did, both for sitting on my quilt and for trying to cover up her bad habit with a lie." Midori smiled, sighed, and tucked a loose strand of black hair back into her French twist. "That's Claire for you. She can't help herself, as I'm sure you know."

"She could help herself, she just doesn't," said Bonnie, remembering how they had often exasperated each other as roommates back at college. Still, it had always been impossible to stay angry with her impulsive, irrepressible friend, as younger women because they had been kindred spirits despite their differences, and in later years because their friendship had become all the more precious for its long duration. Apparently Midori had also fallen under the spell of Claire's charm. "How did you and Claire meet?" Bonnie asked.

"Eric's a close friend of my nephew," said Midori. "They were stationed on Oahu together."

"So you've known Claire a long time."

"Oh, yes. Years."

"And in all that time, you never taught her how to make a Hawaiian quilt?"

Midori set down her knife and gave her a curious, appraising look. "She never asked me to. I didn't think she cared to learn."

"I don't know that she does," Bonnie hastened to explain. "I just thought—well, every bed in the inn has a Hawaiian quilt spread upon it, but Claire made none of them. Since she obviously loves the style, I assumed that she would have made one of her own if she knew how."

"I would teach Claire if she asked me to," Midori said, arranging the pineapple spears on the platter. "But you've taken a tour of her shop and you know her temperament. Claire prefers Mariner's Compasses and stars arranged in traditional blocks and rows. She has a dozen projects going on all at once and she zooms from start to finish so she can display them in her shop to sell patterns and fabric. Her favorite tool is her rotary cutter, and her second favorite is her sewing machine with a computer built in. I think one reason Claire admires Hawaiian quilts so much is that she knows she doesn't have the time or inclination to create one herself." Midori shrugged and shook her head. "It's not a criticism. I say this with love."

Every word rang true, even the last, which from any other person might have sounded ironic. "Maybe she'll never make a Hawaiian quilt herself, but only because she doesn't think she'll do it justice. She never attempts anything unless she's confident of success."

"And that is why she succeeds at everything she tries," said Midori with a cryptic smile.

Perhaps it was Bonnie's sudden discomfort at gossiping about a dear friend that made her change the subject to something she otherwise would not have mentioned until she and Midori were better acquainted. "I'd like to learn how to make a Hawaiian quilt," she heard herself say. "I'm not saying that I'm any more skilled or persevering than Claire, but I'd love to learn."

"Is that so?"

"I've been quilting since college, so your lessons wouldn't have to begin at square one. I could show you some photos of my work, if you like, if you're concerned that I might not be able to do the handwork."

"That's not necessary. Claire's told me all about your quilting, how you used to sew those blocks for your grandmother when she fell ill. And you're an Elm Creek Quilter, which says a lot." Midori fell silent, thinking. "My quilt guild, the Laulima Quilters, meets tonight. You can come and sit in with us and see how it's done. After that, if you still want to learn, I'll teach you."

"Thank you," said Bonnie. "After I see your friends working on their Hawaiian quilts, I know I'll want to make my own even more."

"We'll see," said Midori. "But there's something you should understand. You won't be making a Hawaiian quilt. You will only be able to make a quilt in the Hawaiian style."

"That's fine," said Bonnie, puzzled by the emphasis Midori had placed on the last two words. What was the difference? "Either way, I promise to never sit on it."

She knew from Midori's smile that she had responded perfectly.

⬦

That evening, Bonnie packed a small sewing kit and met Midori in the front hall, eager and more nervous than she thought she ought to be considering she was on her way to meet other quilters. They walked about ten minutes through downtown Lahaina to the church meeting room where the Laulima Quilters gathered every two weeks to work on their own projects and assist friends with tasks that were more easily completed by many hands working together. Eleven other women, most of them Asian, Hawaiian, or an apparent mix like Midori, were gathered around several lunch tables covered in bright fabric, bundles of soft cotton batting, spools of thread, and sewing notions. Most of the women held quilts in various stages of completion on their laps; some were sewing complex, radial symmetric appliqués of turquoise, scarlet, or emerald to white backgrounds, while others held quilt hoops and were stitching top, batting, and backing fabric together with tiny stitches in fine lines of echo quilting. Nearby, three women had layered

backing, batting, and a brilliant butter yellow quilt top with
a design reminiscent of a grove of banyan trees over a table
and were basting the three layers together with large, zigzag
stitches. Lingering near the doorway as Midori continued inside, Bonnie watched as one of the women set aside her quilt
hoop, took a large piece of folded butcher paper from a tote
bag, and took it to one of the quilters helping to baste the butter yellow quilt top. Bonnie couldn't hear what the first woman
said, but the second accepted the folded paper with a cry of
delight and embraced the giver.

"Maya gave Danielle a quilt pattern," Midori explained as
she and Bonnie watched the two women carefully unfold the
paper on a table while their friends gathered around to admire
it. "All true Hawaiian quilt patterns are unique, made especially
for a particular person, purpose, or occasion. An original quilt
pattern is a precious gift and a sign of great friendship because
of the prayers and good wishes—part of the very spirit of the
designer—that go into its creation."

Danielle, the woman who had received the gift, had clasped
her hands to her heart, and her eyes shone as Maya gestured
to several graceful curves and elegant arcs, explaining their
symbolism, or so Bonnie imagined. "Will the other members
of your bee share the pattern after Danielle makes hers?"

"Not likely, but you shouldn't interpret that as selfishness,"
Midori said. "You mainlanders share patterns readily, whether
you made them up yourself, learned them from your grandmother, copied them from a friend, or downloaded them from
the Internet. That's your way and that's fine for you, but that's
not our way."

"Well . . ." Bonnie noticed that a few of the quilters were
watching her and Midori with friendly curiosity. "What's
wrong with sharing?"

"Nothing's wrong with it, but in our tradition, patterns were a carefully guarded secret," Midori repeated. "Whenever a quilter created a design, it was a unique, original work. If one quilter copied another's design, it was considered stealing, taking not only the design but also part of the spirit of the designer. Such theft brought great shame upon the person who copied another's design, even if she changed it here or there to alter it and try to make it her own."

"But I've seen books of published Hawaiian quilt patterns," said Bonnie, bewildered. "Kits, too, in Claire's shop and elsewhere."

"If a pattern is freely given or sold, of course it isn't considered theft," said Midori. "But most traditionalists will consider a quilter who uses another's patterns or a kit to be less of an artist than a quilter who creates her own original design or uses an original design created especially for her."

Midori nodded to indicate the lucky woman who had received the gift of the pattern. Danielle was carefully, lovingly folding the paper, with a faraway look in her eye that told Bonnie she was imagining herself choosing the perfect fabric, tracing the pattern, cutting out her appliqué, and taking the first tiny stitches of thousands. Her quilt, when complete, would become a cherished heirloom, rich with the memories of the woman who had designed it for her. Though Bonnie had always freely shared patterns before, she understood how this pattern represented a deep and abiding friendship and how dismayed both designer and quiltmaker would be if another quilter copied it. The unique artistry of their quilt would be diminished by the existence of a copy that carried with it none of the good wishes, prayers, and symbolism of their friendship.

But what of the novice quilter? Bonnie had created original quilts, but only from traditional blocks created by unknown quilters of generations long past. Her color palette, fabric choices, border designs, and arrangement of those traditional blocks were what made her quilts original works. Despite her experience as a quilter and teacher, she had never considered herself innovative enough to create her own original blocks, and she marveled at her friends who could do so. If she lacked confidence in her ability to create a simple block in a style she was very familiar with, how could she ever hope to create her own unique Hawaiian-style quilt? After what she had witnessed, she could not bear to be seen as a lesser artist who copied another's design. But how else was she to learn?

"Let me introduce you to everyone," said Midori, beckoning her into the room. Bonnie concealed her newfound worries behind a friendly smile as Midori made introductions. Everyone welcomed her kindly, and when she explained that she hoped to learn how to make a quilt in the Hawaiian style, they responded with cheerful encouragement, as she would have expected from any gathering of quilters on the mainland. Perhaps Midori was the strictest traditionalist of them all, and the others would be more patient and tolerant of her ignorance and her mistakes.

"Before you can make a quilt in the Hawaiian style, you need to know Hawaiian quilts," Midori told her after introductions were finished and the quilters returned to their work. "You'll see some lovely examples tonight, and I'll show you more at the inn tomorrow if you're willing to help me change the linens."

"Of course," Bonnie agreed. "Anything."

Midori led her to a corner table where they could sit and talk without disturbing the others. "First, a bit of history. Perhaps you've heard that quilting wasn't practiced among our native peoples, but was introduced by Europeans."

Bonnie nodded. "Claire said missionaries taught native Hawaiians to quilt."

Midori nodded as if she had expected Bonnie's response. "That's what most people believe, but that's not the whole truth. For centuries before any Europeans so much as glimpsed the islands, the Hawaiian people had made a cloth called *kapa* from the bark of paper mulberry trees. They made bed coverings called *kappa moe* by sewing together several layers of *kapa* with large running stitches and decorating the top with traditional patterns made from natural dyes."

"So native Hawaiians had a wholecloth quilting tradition," mused Bonnie. "I assume, then, that the missionaries introduced them to patchwork?"

"That's right," said Midori. "But even before the missionaries came, European whalers and traders had already brought fine needles, scissors, and threads to the islands, making sewing much easier than with our traditional tools and bone needles."

"I can imagine," said Bonnie.

"When the Christian missionaries arrived, they taught young Hawaiian girls how to do patchwork as a part of their domestic training. But sadly, as our young people were learning Western skills and Western values, many of the old traditions fell away. Our people's religions, languages, and customs were gradually fading, and often what replaced them had little meaning for us. Patchwork, for example, was meaningful to the missionary women who taught it, but it had no cultural significance for their students."

Bonnie nodded, thinking of all the evocative quilt block names that called to mind historic events, geographic locations, beloved or notorious people—but only for those familiar with mainland culture. "But quilting did catch on here,"

Bonnie said, realizing even as she spoke, "but not patchwork. Appliqué is what flourished."

Midori nodded, and Bonnie hoped it wasn't her imagination that Midori seemed pleased. "That's right, for the most part. You'll find many examples of nineteenth-century patchwork quilts in our history, as well as Crazy Quilts and other designs with strong Western influences. But the two-color, large scale appliqué quilts that Hawaii is best known for is a style uniquely our own."

Midori gestured to indicate her friends, smiling and chatting as they worked, their conversation occasionally punctuated by bursts of laughter. "You see the many variations in our quilts, as well as the striking similarities. They reflect our values as a people. When so much of our culture was being lost, our quilts became a way to preserve those things we held most dear. Our designs reflected our love for the natural beauty of our island home, our respect for our ancestors, and our longing for what had been lost. That's why you'll find images of native plants and animals in our appliquéd patterns, as well as traditional artifacts and family crests." She pushed back her chair and rose. "Come. I'll show you."

Midori led Bonnie to the three women basting together the butter yellow quilt top, batting, and backing, making large, exaggerated stitches to keep the three layers from shifting until the fine quilting could be added.

"The three main parts of a Hawaiian quilt top are the center, the branches, and the *lei,* or border," Midori said. "Tia's quilt, as you see, has a solid center or *piko*. A *piko* can be solid or open, but it must be balanced so that love and energy can flow freely."

"Tia's quilt is all about love," remarked the oldest of the three women, smiling over the rims of her glasses at the youngest, who blushed and continued basting.

"A solid center represents family," said Danielle. "Whole and intact, the strong core of a person's life."

"A solid center can also represent Mother Earth, or the quilter's own center," said Tia.

"That's true, but not in this case," declared the eldest. "We know you chose a solid *piko* for David."

"Her fiancé," Midori added for Bonnie's benefit. "This will be their wedding quilt. I don't think Tia minds if I divulge that, do you, Tia?"

"Of course not," said Tia lightly, but her blush deepened with her smile.

Bonnie drew closer to study the pattern. "This reminds me of the banyan tree in Courthouse Square."

"I told you so," the eldest quilter declared to Tia, triumphant. "And you said no one would recognize it."

"David proposed to her beneath that banyan tree," said Danielle, nudging Tia, who smiled and kept on basting. "Tia, tell the rest."

Tia set down her needle, pressed a hand to her lower back, and arched her spine as if she felt stiff from hours bent over the quilt. "Our marriage should be like the banyan tree," she said, gesturing to the four thick trunks branching off from the solid center. "Strong and solid, deeply rooted, able to withstand the winds of change. These aerial roots—" She indicated narrower branches falling from the trunks, intersecting, fusing, weaving, and fanning outward. "They're our friends and family, supporting us, strengthening us, nourishing us so that we may grow in love together."

"It's lovely," said Bonnie.

Tia thanked her, and Midori touched her lightly on the arm. "Tia rightly chose a solid *piko* for a quilt representing the creation of a new family. An open *piko* represents the gateway between the physical world and the spiritual. Our people believed they could travel into the spiritual world to consult with their gods and ancestors and return to the physical world unharmed and enlightened. If Tia had chosen an open *piko* for her quilt, it would have changed the pattern's symbolic meaning considerably."

"Tia isn't marrying David for his handsome spirit," Danielle teased, "although I'm sure she's hoping he'll take her to heaven!"

All the women laughed, except for Tia, who grinned, took up her needle, and ordered everyone back to work. With some good-natured complaining, they complied.

Midori gestured to the appliquéd trunks and aerial roots as the three quilters basted around them, large stitches that would be removed later after the finer quilting stitches were added. "Branches from the center of the quilt are another important feature of the Hawaiian quilt," she said. "As they reach from the center to the borders, they represent personal, spiritual, and family growth, and the quilter's love reaching out and blessing everyone she knows."

"Also very appropriate for a wedding quilt," remarked the eldest, taking two more basting stitches and tying off the end of her thread.

"Let's bother some of my other friends for a while," said Midori, smiling as she led Bonnie to four women who had arranged their chairs in a circle, quilt hoops in their laps. "The last part of a Hawaiian quilt is the *lei*, or border."

"When you say *lei*, do you mean the sort of *lei* you wear around your neck?" asked Bonnie. "Or maybe I misunderstood and it's not the same word."

"No, it's the same word," said Midori. "*Leis* are recognized around the world as a symbol of Hawaii and the aloha spirit.

Leis are made with love and given in love, so it was only natural for quilters to bring them into their designs. The *lei* of a quilt can symbolize the lands beyond Hawaii, with the center of the quilt representing Hawaii itself. Since the *leis* are unbroken, they also represent the circle of life, and life continuing into eternity, even after death."

"Midori's going philosophical on us again," remarked one of the seated ladies.

"Oh, hush, and show us your quilt," retorted Midori cheerfully. As the woman obliged, holding up the hoop and spreading open the folds of fabric and batting, Midori lifted the edge so Bonnie could see it better. "*Leis* can take several forms. This one is called a border *lei*. It's part of the edge of the quilt, so that the inner edge echoes the center design but the outer edges are solid. June's quilt—could you show us, June?" Another woman in the circle rose and held her quilt wide, her arms outspread. "June's *lei* is what we call a full *lei*, because it stands apart, separate from the center as well as the outer edges of the quilt."

"There's a third kind," said June, sitting back down and readjusting her hoop on her lap. "The attached *lei*. It's a border *lei* with branches connecting it to the center design." She raised her voice so that it carried throughout the room. "Does anyone have an attached *lei* she could show our guest?"

A woman at another table called them over to see the appliqué she had finished cutting out only moments before. At first, Bonnie couldn't quite picture how it differed from a border *lei*, but then the woman spread her white background fabric upon a table and asked Midori and Bonnie to help her place the intricately cut appliqué upon it. The contrast between scarlet appliqué and yellow background helped Bonnie see how the border, *lei,* and center were all of a single piece.

"A bit overwhelming, is it?" Midori asked as Bonnie stepped

back to take in one beautiful quilt after another, all in different stages of completion, each rich with symbolism and meaning she never would have imagined.

"Overwhelming but wonderful," said Bonnie.

Midori allowed the faintest of smiles. "Then I suppose I haven't discouraged you from attempting one of your own?"

"Was that your intention?"

"No, not really, though I did want to see if you were serious."

"I am." Bonnie was a bit nervous, a bit uncertain about her design skills, but very serious, and more determined than ever to make the attempt. If she tried and failed, so be it. All the same, she would treasure her quilt as a learning experience and a souvenir of her stay in Maui.

Midori joined one of the clusters of women and left Bonnie to wander the room, observing the Laulima Quilters, admiring their patterns and fine needlework, and occasionally helping with basting or adjusting a quilt in a hoop. They offered her so much good advice that she despaired of remembering everything, but her heart lifted when one of the quilters sensed her distress and assured her that she should feel free to ask any of them for advice any time.

She had not thought she would have the opportunity, but if Midori didn't consider it an intrusion, she would be delighted to return to the circle of quilters the next time they met—and every time thereafter for the duration of her visit.

At the end of the evening, she and Midori walked back to the hotel, chatting about the beautiful quilts they had seen, which ones Bonnie particularly admired, and what she had learned. "I can't pick just any old pattern and dive in," said Bonnie, noting the most important of all the evening's lessons. "It must be meaningful as well as beautiful."

"You don't have to decide right now," said Midori as they

climbed the front steps of the Hale Kapa Kuiki. "Perhaps inspiration will come to you in your dreams."

They parted after agreeing that Bonnie would help Midori change linens as she made up the guest rooms after checkout the next day. Bonnie would still have plenty of time for her own work, and if she helped Midori finish her tasks early, perhaps they could squeeze in a quilt lesson.

Bonnie hurried upstairs, hoping to catch the last of the sunset from her lanai. When she entered her room, she discovered a surprise set out for her on the nightstand: a plate of two chocolate chip cookies, a small bottle of milk on ice, and a note.

"A little treat to help bring sweet dreams," Claire had written. "I know the months ahead will be challenging, but you won't have to face them alone. Whatever happens, whatever you discover, I'm here for you."

After brooding over the divorce for months, Bonnie had, for a few blissful hours among Midori's friends, forgotten it entirely. Now, somehow, the reminder did not bring her pain, but rather a sad acceptance. Whatever happened would happen. She would retain her solid center and stretch forth her branches in love for friends like Claire who would support her in the times to come.

She watched the fading light over the Pacific, dunking the crisp cookies in cold milk, savoring the sweetness, her thoughts a gently shifting kaleidoscope of pattern and color.

Chapter Five

When Bonnie came down for breakfast the next morning after her walk and shower, she found Claire seated at the center island sipping coffee and sorting paperwork while Midori sliced bananas. Bonnie helped Midori serve breakfast to their guests—only ten that week, which couldn't be good for the inn's bottom line—and spent the rest of the morning conferring with Claire in her office. After checkout time, Bonnie met Midori in the laundry room and together they carried baskets of fresh linens to the vacated rooms. Claire intended to hire a housekeeper as soon as they regularly filled enough rooms to justify the expense, but until then, she and Midori, and now Bonnie, would clean everything themselves.

Each room boasted at least one beautiful Hawaiian quilt, each with evocative images reflecting the islands' natural beauties—Plumeria, Lehua, Ocean Palm—or Hawaiian history. Within the grandest guest suite was a stunning quilt Midori called Crowns and Kahili, impressive not only for its vivid color scheme, yellow appliqué on red, but also for the bold power of its design. Radial symmetric, four leafy fans lay on the horizontal and vertical axes, while four tall, faceted crowns reached out on the diagonals. "The crowns honor our Hawaiian kings and queens," said Midori. "The *kahili* are feather standards displayed in throne rooms and carried in royal processions."

There was a note of pride in her voice that Bonnie had not heard before, even when Midori had spoken of other lovely quilts she had made. "This quilt is one of yours, isn't it?" she asked.

"I made the quilt," Midori explained. "My nephew designed the pattern."

Bonnie searched her memory. "The nephew who was in the service with Eric?"

"One and the same."

Bonnie studied the quilt. "He's quite an artist."

"He is, and I'm excessively proud of him. He's earned a reputation as one of Maui's leaders in preserving Hawaiian language, arts, and culture." Midori turned a speculative gaze upon Bonnie. "You know, I'm not sure what you had in mind for your evening programs. Maybe you were thinking of strolls on the beach and mai tais, with a ten-minute hula lesson thrown in to give things a Hawaiian gloss. If, on the other hand, you want to give your quilt campers a true sense of the real Hawaii, you should speak with my nephew. If you want your guests to take home more than a superficial understanding of Hawaii, he could help you."

"I'd always choose the real over the superficial," said Bonnie.

"I'll call him," said Midori. "I'll tell him to expect your visit."

One o'clock found them with several rooms left to clean, but they decided to break for lunch before finishing. Claire met them in the kitchen and announced that she was taking them out, and afterward, she would show Bonnie around Lahaina. After a tasty lunch of Japanese noodles at a small shop on Laukini Street, Midori begged off the tour and returned to the inn, leaving Claire and Bonnie on their own. They passed a couple hours window-shopping and walking along the beach, reminiscing about their college days and enjoying the beautiful sunshine and clear skies. But it was impossible to think about the old times without wondering what Craig was up to and what the detective might be observing at that very moment, so eventually Bonnie reminded Claire that they too had business awaiting them back at the inn.

Later, Bonnie was on the lanai working on a job announcement that Claire intended to post in her shop, run in the Maui Quilt Guild's newsletter, and mail to a select group of potential teachers throughout Hawaii when Midori approached. "Are you ready for a break?" she inquired.

Bonnie set down her pen and pushed the papers away. "Not just ready. Grateful." She had been stuck on the same few sentences for twenty minutes, unable to describe Claire's unusual proposed schedule clearly and attractively. Although Elm Creek Quilts had recently hired two new teachers, Sarah and Summer had written all of their ads and Bonnie felt out of practice.

"I have a few minutes free and I thought you might like a lesson in pattern designing," said Midori.

"Absolutely," said Bonnie, surprised. She had expected Midori to take longer to mull over her suitability as a student. Either Bonnie had made a better impression at the quilting bee than she had thought, or Claire had told Midori all about the impending divorce and she had been moved by pity.

While Bonnie slipped her haphazard rough drafts into a folder and set them aside, Midori went back inside and reappeared a few minutes later carrying a roll of white paper, a few pencils, and a pair of scissors. "You should begin with a small project, a wall-hanging," she told Bonnie, spreading out her supplies on the table. "Something to whet your appetite for a larger masterpiece later."

With practiced deftness, Midori unrolled the paper, cut a length, and neatly trimmed it to a square about three feet wide. "You've made paper snowflakes before?" she asked. When Bonnie nodded, Midori continued, "Hawaiian quilt patterns follow the same principle of design. Experienced quilters sometimes skip this step and draw on the appliqué fabric instead of making a paper pattern, but this way works best for beginners since you can correct any problems with your design before you cut your fabric."

Midori folded the paper in half once to make a rectangle, and again to make a square, and then one last fold along the diagonal to make a triangle. "You can use half-fold or quarter-folded paper, but the one-eighth fold is the most popular method," she said, taking up a pencil. "Now you draw your design. Be sure to leave some space around the outer edges. An inch or two should do for a quilt this size. I prefer to place some of my design on the folds, but remember that you will be creating mirror images."

"This is the part that concerns me most," said Bonnie. "How do you know what to draw?"

Midori smiled as she sketched half of a leaf along the fold. "Take your inspiration from nature, history, or your family. Whatever subject you want to honor."

"But how do you know what to draw on this folded paper so that it looks right when you unfold it?"

"Ah. That's the challenge." A twining vine appeared beneath the tip of Midori's pencil. "You must envision the finished whole from this small segment before you. Isn't that how we all try to understand the glory of God? We glimpse only the material world, one small facet of His creation, and from this alone we attempt to comprehend the eternal world of the spirit."

Bonnie watched as Midori's design took shape. She had never considered herself much of an artist and couldn't draw anything more complex than stick figures. Her shortcomings had never bothered her until now, for they had not prevented her from creating beautiful quilts. Now it mattered. Would her wish to create a Hawaiian quilt uniquely her own be thwarted before she ever threaded a needle?

Midori set down her pencil, glanced up from her work, and read the misery in Bonnie's expression. "It takes practice, that's all," she said. "It's only paper. Try and try again until you create a pattern that pleases you. If you're worried, before you cut, hold the folded edge of the paper up to a mirror to see what the finished design will look like."

"I'll try that," said Bonnie, relieved. She could imagine herself cutting one ill-conceived pattern after another until she used up the entire roll of paper.

Taking up the scissors, Midori cut along the drawn line, snipping points and concave angles carefully. Then she unfolded the paper, smoothed out the creases, and laid it upon the table. Bonnie shook her head in amazement at the lovely design that appeared, eight elegant clusters of segmented leaves on long, graceful stems.

"Monstera leaves," said Midori, inspecting her work with a critical eye. "You don't have to make anything quite this complicated for your first quilt. Try to avoid sharp turns in your design, and make nothing narrower than an inch or you'll regret it when it comes time to sew."

"I think I'll use a mirror," said Bonnie. "And a pencil with a large eraser."

"Draw something fun," Midori advised. "Something that makes you happy. Even a small quilt will require many, many days, so it should be something that you enjoy and want to keep forever."

"I can't think of anything at the moment."

"The more you know of Hawaii, the more inspiration you will find. My nephew, Hinano Paoa, might be able to offer you some guidance. He's expecting you."

"Today?"

"This afternoon. He'll be in his shop, and he said you should feel free to stop by whenever you have time."

❖

Bonnie helped Midori clean up from the pattern designing lesson, left a note on Claire's desk explaining that she was going on a research trip, and set off with a notebook tucked into her purse and her cell phone set to vibrate. Midori's directions took her through Lahaina beyond the route she and Claire had taken earlier that day to a part of town she had not visited before. Once Bonnie was sure she had taken a wrong turn, but a young woman working behind the counter at a surf shop assured her she was only a few blocks away.

She heard faint melodic strumming before she saw the sign above the door: NĀ MELE HAWAIʻI MUSIC SHOP. At the sight, she gasped and froze in place, staring: gold letters on a red background, the same size, same typeface as the sign that had once hung above the door to Grandma's Attic. Then she blinked and shook herself. It was not exactly the same, only similar. This sign was a bit smaller than hers, and the rustic quality to the letters had a Polynesian look whereas hers had been quaintly country.

She missed her quilt shop, so naturally, painfully, she caught glimpses of it everywhere, just as she sometimes thought she recognized the faces of absent loved ones in a crowd of strangers. Sights, smells, sounds—any of her senses could be triggered, reminding her of the shop she had built from the ground up and lost. Even in Maui, completely new and unfamiliar, she risked the pull of memory.

Instinctively she dug into her purse and checked her cell phone—no voicemails, battery fully charged as she had known it would be. Chiding herself, she took a deep breath and entered the store just as a young man about the age of her younger son was leaving, a ukulele tucked under his arm.

She entered and discovered that the shop was unexpectedly small, a little wider than the front door and storefront window, with shelves of books and sheet music near the front, where a few curious tourists mingled among serious shoppers. Behind the long counter at the back of the room hung ukuleles of various sizes and wood grains, dark and light, graceful, gleaming, and beautiful. A white-haired man with skin the color of caramel sat on a tall stool near the cash register, strumming a dark ukulele while three customers listened, enthralled. The poignant melody tickled Bonnie's memory, and after a few measures she recognized not a traditional Hawaiian tune, but one of her favorite songs, the Beatles' "Here, There, and Everywhere."

She smiled.

As the last notes faded, everyone in the store burst into applause. The man good-naturedly waved off the praise, carefully placed the ukulele into a case lying open on the counter, and rang up the purchase. As the customer left with his two companions, carrying the ukulele case as if it cradled something rare and precious, Bonnie approached the counter. She tried to catch the man's eye, but he had already turned to take down another instrument from a shelf beside a closed door.

"Excuse me," she said. "Are you Hinano Paoa?"

"The one and only." When he turned around to set the ukulele on the counter, Bonnie realized the thick white hair was misleading. He looked to be no older than she, with only a few lines around kind, intelligent eyes that quickly sized her up. "You Bonnie?"

"Yes," she replied, surprised to be recognized.

"Eh, howzit, Bonnie? My aunt told me to expect you." He smiled quizzically, folding muscular arms over a broad chest. "So, you want me to give your quilting friends ukulele lessons?"

"Well, no," she said, flustered. How exactly had Midori explained the reason for her visit?

His brow furrowed. "So you don't want them to learn to play?"

"Maybe, I suppose. I mean, I haven't ruled it out." Wishing she could start the conversation over, Bonnie shook her head slightly to clear it and briefly explained the purpose of evening programs at quilt camp—to offer entertainment, relaxation, and socializing for their guests after a busy day of quilting. For Aloha Quilt Camp, she told him, she wanted to provide guests with a unique Hawaiian experience, something they would find only in Maui, something no other quilt camp could duplicate. "We—Claire and I—want our guests to experience Hawaii beyond the usual tourist spots," she said. "Your aunt recommended you. She said you're very knowledgeable about Hawaiian culture and could advise me about excursions, lectures, or other events for our quilters."

To her astonishment, Hinano laughed, a deep, rich laugh tinged with irony. "Auntie Midori recommended me?" he asked, shaking his head. "She hasn't always appreciated my opinions about the state of Hawaiian culture, especially when it comes to serving it up for tourists."

A blond man bending over to peer through the glass counter straightened indignantly, but when Hinano gave him a disarming shrug, he smiled uncertainly and resumed browsing.

"Our campers aren't tourists in the usual sense," Bonnie explained. "They're coming to Maui to learn, not to loll around on beaches working on their tans. Not that there's anything wrong with that."

"Your quilting friends aren't interested in the real Hawaii," said Hinano. "What you need are the brochures you can pick up at one of those visitor information kiosks outside the big hotels. Your quilters could do a little snorkeling, go to a luau, maybe take a boat ride out to Molokai. That's enough for most kine folks."

His tone was so charming and patronizing all at once that Bonnie bristled. "How do you know that my quilting friends aren't interested in the real Hawaii?" she demanded. "You don't even know them. Quilters are passionate about art, about history, about community and family— How can you just dismiss them as superficial tourists? Sorry," she added automatically to the blond man at the counter, who scowled and left the store.

Hinano sighed. "You just cost me a customer."

Bonnie dismissed his complaint with a wave of her hand. "He wasn't going to buy anything. I've run a store myself. I know the signs. Anyway, you're the one who lost him, with your condescending remarks about tourists."

The door behind the counter opened while Bonnie spoke, and a young man entered, grinning as he caught her last words. "That's part of my dad's charm," he said, reading from a receipt as he punched keys on the cash register. "You know. Sweet native guy full of the aloha spirit. He used to drape *leis* over every customer who came in, but we made him stop. All our profits went to buy flowers."

Bonnie expected Hinano to rebuke his son, but instead Hinano snorted as if trying not to laugh. "Don't go making up stories about me, Kai," he said. "The truth is bad enough."

Bonnie was inclined to agree with him for a change, and she wondered why on earth Midori had recommended her nephew. Was it another test of Bonnie's commitment to discovering the real Hawaii, whether quilts or music or culture? If so, Bonnie had failed. She'd find another, less patronizing advisor. Somehow. "This was obviously a bad idea," she said, turning to go. "I've wasted enough of your time. Excuse me."

At that moment, her cell phone rang.

She fumbled around in her purse as the ringtone grew persistently louder. She could have sworn she had set the phone to vibrate. She saw Hinano and Kai exchange a look—tourists and their ubiquitous cell phones, it said—but any embarrassment she might have felt swiftly vanished with one glance at the caller ID.

It was Darren Taylor.

Bonnie felt as if the breath had been squeezed from her body, but she took the call. "Hello?" she said, turning her back on father and son and taking a few steps away. "Darren?"

"Hello, Bonnie. How are you?"

"Oh, fine, I suppose." Her heart was pounding. "It must be late there. Do you have news?"

"Yes. Last Friday the detective followed Craig to Penn State. He stayed at the Hotel State College all weekend."

"Oh." Was that all? That was nothing. "Craig's a huge Nittany Lions fan. He'd make that trip every home game of the season if he could."

"A woman met him for dinner at the Allen Street Grill Friday evening at seven o'clock."

"Oh," repeated Bonnie in a small voice.

"The detective took pictures of them holding hands, kissing across the table, feeding each other, the works. Bonnie, I know this must be painful to hear. Should I stop?"

"No, no, go on," said Bonnie, desperately wanting him to say no more.

"Afterward, the detective tailed them to a club where they drank and danced. From there, they returned to the hotel, where the detective snapped a great shot of them kissing while Craig fumbled to unlock the door." In the background was the light tapping of computer keys. "They didn't come out until morning. They ate breakfast at the Corner Room, strolled around campus, stopped by an alumni association tailgater, attended the football game, and shared the same hotel room that night as well."

"I see." Slowly the facts of the tryst sank in. Bonnie had agreed to let Craig keep their season tickets in exchange for their family photo albums. Some strange woman had sat in Bonnie's seat in Beaver Stadium, beside *her* husband, cheering on *her* favorite team, enjoying a meal in *her* favorite restaurant, and spending two nights in *her* favorite hotel. It was as if Craig had designed the weekend to inflict as much insult and injury upon Bonnie as possible. Imagining the lovers' weekend, picturing them in all those familiar places, Bonnie knew she could never enjoy any of those favorite things again.

"The good news is that we already have enough to make a strong case for divorce on the grounds of adultery."

"You're right. This is good news."

"Do you want me to email you the photos?"

"No," said Bonnie vehemently. "I don't need to see the pictures. Just—just do what you have to do to get me out of this marriage as soon as possible."

"Understood. I'll wait for the detective's final report and I'll contact Craig's lawyer on Monday."

Bonnie thanked him and hung up. Ducking her head, she flung her phone into her purse and angrily flicked away the two tears that had betrayed her and were slipping down her cheeks. Her gaze fell upon Hinano and Kai, who had heard her every word and were watching her in astonished sympathy.

"You said 'This is good news,'" said Kai uneasily, "but you sure don't look it."

"Kai," said Hinano, a quiet warning.

"That was my lawyer," said Bonnie as more tears threatened, shrugging, smiling as if it were no big deal. "Really, it's nothing. My husband met some strange other woman for a big romantic date, you know, but it's okay because the detective got pictures and so now I'll be able to get my divorce, which really is for the best, and it's what I want—" Bonnie forced herself to stop babbling. "I have to go."

Hinano studied her. "Are you sure you're okay?"

"Perfect! Great. Never better." She dug around in her purse for Midori's directions. "I just have to find my way back to the inn and I'll be fine."

"Hold on." Hinano came around from behind the counter. "You want to get a cup of coffee or something first?"

"I—I don't think so."

"One cup of coffee." He gave her a disarming smile not unlike the one he had given the disgruntled tourist. "My favorite coffee shop's down the block."

"Well—" It would give her time to clear her thoughts so she would be less likely to get lost on the way back to the inn and stumble into the ocean or an active volcano. And she needed the information Midori had assured her Hinano could provide. It would be a shame to go away empty-handed. "Okay," she said, taking a deep breath. "Sure. Why not?"

"Maui coffee," Hinano remarked as he brought their steaming cups over to the table Bonnie had selected near the front corner. The café was long and narrow, with large windows facing Courthouse Square and original art by Maui residents on the walls, or so the discreet price tags announced. By her count, at least four people had greeted Hinano as an old friend while he waited in line. "Pure Hawaiian and better even than Kona."

"Lesson one for my campers will be to drink only Hawaiian coffee."

"Not just any Hawaiian coffee, Maui coffee. Our soil gives the beans a special flavor— What are you doing?"

Bonnie had retrieved her notebook from her purse and uncapped her pen. "Taking notes, of course. Drink only Maui coffee." She had to smile when Hinano's eyebrows rose in surprise. "I'm kidding. I'm not going to micromanage their visits to that extent. Besides, your aunt Midori is in charge of selecting the coffee."

"No, no, you misunderstand. I'm surprised because I didn't expect you to take my advice."

"That *is* why your aunt sent me to see you," Bonnie reminded him, and she tried again to explain what she had in mind for the evening programs. Either he wasn't as condescending as his first impression had suggested or he was behaving himself out of sympathy, for he listened without making any more insulting comments about "her quilters."

"I think I can help you," he said when she had finished. "I know some good places to visit and things to do that are off the beaten track but still accessible. But first you could start with the Old Lahaina Lu'au. Most people think it's the best and the most authentic luau in Maui, and even guests who want an alternative Hawaiian experience are going to expect a luau."

Hinano continued to describe several other places and events he thought might interest guests of Aloha Quilt Camp, everything from ecologically sensitive hikes through pristine rainforest on private land to a visit to a remote village where ancient Hawaiian customs were still practiced. Fascinated, Bonnie jotted notes as Hinano spoke, her coffee cooling and barely tasted.

When he finished, Hinano said, "You should check out these places yourself first to make sure they're what you had in mind. Don't take my word for it."

Bonnie wouldn't dream of scheduling an event for her campers sight unseen, but to be polite, she said, "I will, though I'm sure it's not necessary. You came very highly recommended."

"By my aunt," he pointed out. "Hardly an objective source."

She sipped her coffee, now barely lukewarm, pretending to consider the point. "That's certainly true."

"And I made a very bad first impression."

"That, you did." With her pen she tapped her notebook, which now held several pages of useful notes. "But you've made up for it since."

"Glad to hear it. Aunt Midori would tan my hide if she heard I wasn't nice to you. And Eric might not be too happy, either."

Bonnie had to laugh at the thought of petite Midori intimidating her much larger nephew. "Yes, your aunt mentioned that you and Eric served together."

"That's right." He regarded her over the rim of his coffee cup before continuing. "We were stationed on Oahu together for a couple of years. We stayed in touch after."

"Did you retire, too, as Eric did?"

He frowned slightly, looked past her shoulder, and exchanged a quick greeting with another customer who was walking toward the exit. "I guess you could say that. I got wounded in the Persian Gulf War—the first one—got an honorable discharge, came home to Maui, and opened the shop."

She sensed that he didn't want to discuss his military service. "It seems like a successful store, despite your tendency to insult your customers," she said. "Do you and your son run it together?"

"Kai helps out on school breaks." A note of pride rang in Hinano's voice. "He's a senior at the University of Hawaii on Oahu, majoring in Oceanography. He's only home for the weekend."

"It must be nice to have him so close."

"He's my only kid, so I hope he stays close after graduation. He's thinking about graduate school." Hinano raised his hand in greeting to a man and woman who had just joined the queue at the coffee bar. Did he know everyone in Lahaina? "Kai's a half decent ukulele player, too. You have any kids?"

"Three. Two sons and a daughter, all back home in Pennsylvania." Bonnie glanced at Hinano's left hand and saw that he wasn't wearing a wedding ring. Perhaps he was divorced, and that was why he had sympathized with her. She wished that Darren had waited five minutes to call her or that she hadn't lost her composure in the music shop. She would enjoy the coffee and conversation much more if genuine interest in her project rather than pity had inspired Hinano's invitation.

"Since you brought it up . . ." Bonnie glanced through her notes. "I'm surprised you haven't mentioned anything about the ukulele. You missed a great opportunity to work a visit to your store into our campers' itinerary."

"I thought that would be crass marketing."

"Whatever it takes to get people through the door." If she had heeded Summer's pleas to improve her marketing strategies, Grandma's Attic might still be in business. To Hinano's questioning look, she replied, "For many years I ran a quilt shop. I had to close it down last spring."

"That's too bad." He leaned forward and rested his arms on the table. "What happened?"

"It's complicated. Competition from a chain store, slow-down in the economy, financial ruin brought on by teenage vandals— You know. The usual."

"Right," he said, nodding slowly. "The usual."

"It's a long story."

"I'd like to hear it."

Bonnie hesitated. "I'm afraid it would bore you. And it doesn't have a happy ending."

"Some of the most interesting stories I've ever heard don't have happy endings."

So Bonnie told him everything—how she had opened Grandma's Attic after receiving an inheritance from her grandmother, after whom she named the shop; how she had enjoyed a long, rewarding run in business and had made many wonderful friends; how the opening of a Fabric Warehouse on the outskirts of town had lured away all but her most loyal customers; and how a thoughtless act of cruelty and destruction had pushed her shop over the edge into bankruptcy. Then, thanks to one of the Elm Creek Quilters, the vandals who had broken into and trashed her shop had been caught, and the long-delayed insurance settlement had come through. Reopening her old store was out of the question since the building had been sold for redevelopment, but Sylvia had invited her to open a shop within Elm Creek Manor, or she could probably find a vacancy downtown, a few blocks away from her old location.

"But I don't know if that's what I want," Bonnie concluded, resting her chin on her hand. "Running a quilt shop was my dream, but that dream ended when I took down the sign above the door. I think maybe I need to accept that this part of my life is over, and that I need to move on."

"Move on to what?" asked Hinano.

"That's the real question, isn't it? I still have Elm Creek Quilt Camp, of course, but beyond that . . ." She shook her head. "I don't know. That's one of the reasons I accepted Claire's invitation to come to Maui for the winter, to give myself time to think."

"So you're a snowbird, but you're a snowbird with a mission." Hinano sat back in his chair, regarding her with a faint smile. "Your story won't be finished until you decide. You may get a happy ending after all."

"I'm working on it," said Bonnie wryly, and Hinano laughed sympathetically.

As they left the coffee shop, he asked if she was sure she knew how to find her way back to the Hale Kapa Kuiki or if she wanted him to see her there. Bonnie felt guilty enough for taking up so much of his time and leaving his son to run the music shop alone, so she assured him she would be fine on her own.

"I do want to learn more about your music," she told him as they stood outside the café, tourists passing by on either side. "I think the quilt campers would, too."

"Come by the store sometime," he said. "I'll give you a brief history of the ukulele and a concert, and you can decide if it's worth sharing with your quilter friends."

Bonnie was sure it would be, and she told him she would come by soon.

She had almost reached the end of the block when she heard Hinano call, "Be sure to tell Aunt Midori and Eric that I was nice to you!"

She smiled, and for the first time since Darren Taylor's call, her heart ached a little less.

⬦

Bonnie told Claire about Darren's call as soon as she returned to the inn, but waited until morning to email her friends back at Elm Creek Manor about the detective's discoveries. Mere moments after she logged off, her cell phone rang—Sarah, appalled and angry, and sounding as if she were ready to jump in her truck and race off to confront Craig herself. Bonnie had sent the email because she had hoped to avoid rehashing all the details over the phone, but after Sarah's anger subsided and Bonnie took her own turn to vent, she felt much better.

Her calm somewhat restored, Bonnie retrieved her folder from Claire's office, settled herself on the lanai, and tackled the job announcement with new determination to get it right. After reading over what she had written the previous day, she drew a large X through all but the paragraph containing contact information and started fresh. This time the words came easily, and after an hour of intense writing and revising, Bonnie thought she had captured the fun and camaraderie of quilt camp in her description of the new teachers' proposed duties. She hoped that every qualified quilting instructor who read it would be intrigued enough to send in a résumé.

Bonnie stood up and stretched, pleased with a job well done. As she gathered up her papers to take inside to show Claire, her gaze fell upon a strikingly familiar shape nestled within the low green garden foliage. She drew closer, and at first glance she thought someone had dropped a whole pineapple into the planting beds. Then she spotted another pineapple, and another, and several more, each sitting firmly upright in the middle of a whorl of long, narrow, green leaves.

She must have cried out in astonishment, for a moment later, Midori appeared at the kitchen window. "Bonnie? Are you all right?"

"There are pineapples," she exclaimed. "Growing here! In your garden!"

She heard the screen door slide open and shut, and soon Midori was at her side. "Well, what do you know," said Midori, barely concealing her amusement as she studied the pineapple patch and nodded to show she agreed with Bonnie's assessment. "Of course, Hawaii is rather well known for pineapple, so we probably shouldn't be surprised."

"But they're growing here, on the ground. Real pineapples."

"Of course they're real. I've tried growing the fake kind and it doesn't thrive."

"Stop teasing me," protested Bonnie, laughing at herself. "It just threw me for a minute. I know pineapple grows in Hawaii, but I wasn't expecting to see it here."

"Where did you expect it to grow?"

"I don't know. On tall trees, in pineapple orchards."

Midori folded her arms and regarded her. "You need to get out more."

"I do get out. I don't just work all day. I see a lot on my morning walks."

"There's more to Hawaii than the streets of Lahaina."

"I know, and your nephew gave me some great suggestions for what to see first."

"Did he, now?" Midori's eyebrows rose. "I hope he was a gentleman."

"Oh, absolutely," said Bonnie, perhaps a bit too emphatically, for Midori made a scoffing sound. "He was very helpful. I have pages of notes and lots of great ideas."

"Did he give you his usual political lecture?"

"No," said Bonnie, puzzled. "He didn't say a word about politics."

"He's probably saving that for when he knows you better." Midori bent over the pineapple plants and grasped hold of one large fruit. "Here's a good one. Do you want to pick it?"

"Me?"

"I'll do all the work if you insist, but I thought since you've probably never picked a *real* pineapple before, you might like to try it yourself."

"Of course." Bonnie managed to refrain from asking if the pineapple was edible, sparing herself additional teasing. "How do I do it?"

"Just reach down and pluck it."

Tentatively Bonnie obeyed, the firm skin of the pineapple rough against her palms. "A real pineapple," she said, brushing off bits of broken leaves, not caring if her wonder and delight were amusing.

But to her surprise, Midori said, "It's a pleasure to see someone enjoying a simple task, a simple gift, one that is far too easy for those of us accustomed to it to take for granted." She took the pineapple from Bonnie and indicated the kitchen door with a tilt of her head. "Come inside. Let's have a taste."

Quickly Bonnie gathered up her papers and followed Midori to the kitchen. Deftly Midori sliced off the leafy, plumed top with a sharp knife, then the bottom, and set the rest on her favorite koa wood cutting board. She pared off the rough skin and cut the fruit into spears, setting the core aside. When Midori beckoned, Bonnie helped herself to the sweet, juicy pineapple, without a doubt the freshest, most delicious she had ever tasted.

"Thank you," she told Midori after they had eaten their fill. "This was a rare treat."

Midori looked up from cleaning the cutting board to smile at her. "Thank *you*."

❖

Later, after the day's work was finished, Bonnie borrowed paper, pencil, and scissors from Midori and returned to the courtyard lanai, greeting guests in passing, answering questions, offering suggestions for their dinner plans. Then, left to her own devices, she set herself to work.

Inspiration had come to her as she and Claire collaborated in Claire's cozy office earlier that day, making a few minor changes to the job description and discussing how best to distribute it. As she considered the response the ad might generate, Bonnie reflected upon how welcome she had felt at the Hale Kapa Kuiki since the moment she arrived. Soon, if the job description succeeded, it would be up to her to pass along that same aloha spirit of welcome to the applicants for their teaching staff, just as she and the Elm Creek Quilters had done the previous summer at the manor.

For her first quilt in the Hawaiian style, Bonnie decided to draw upon the natural beauties of the islands as well as a traditional symbol of welcome: the pineapple. The foundation paper pieced Pineapple block was one of her favorites, making this new interpretation of the theme even more appropriate and meaningful.

She cut a piece of paper one yard square, and then folded it into eighths as Midori had shown her. Studying the pineapples growing in the lanai garden, sketching, erasing, trying again,

Bonnie drew a plump, ripe pineapple crowned with short, spiky leaves, set snugly within a flourish of long, slender, tapering fronds. She tried to imagine how her pattern would look after she cut it out and unfolded it, and when she thought she had it just about right, she carried her supplies upstairs to her suite and held the edge of the folded paper up to her bathroom mirror. The reflected image gave her a better idea of what the whole pattern would look like when complete, and she was inspired to make a few changes—an erasure here, a smoother curve there—until at last she was pleased with what she saw.

It was time to commit herself, to put scissors to paper and see if what she had created matched what she had envisioned.

On the privacy of her lanai overlooking the sandy beach where vacationers relaxed and played, Bonnie carefully trimmed the folded paper along the drawn lines. Leaves and fruit took shape with every snip, until at last she trimmed away the final excess piece, set aside the scissors, and carefully unfolded the paper.

She held it up to the sunlight and, against a background of green palms, sandy beach, and surging ocean, she beheld four pineapples nestled within a sunburst of tapered leaves, an ordered, symmetrical rendition of the garden's beauty. The pattern looked almost as she had thought it would as she had worked upon the eighth-fold paper, using her imagination and aided by mirrors, but new curves appeared in unexpected places, extra leaves where she had not thought she had drawn any. But rather than detracting from the design she had imagined, the new and unanticipated changes to her pattern delighted her.

She had created more beauty than she had been able to imagine by glimpsing the fragment and envisioning the whole.

Chapter Six

O n Tuesday morning, Darren Taylor phoned. He had received the detective's final report about Craig's weekend tryst, including the woman's name.

"There must be some mistake," said Bonnie. "Terri— that was the woman from his first cyber-affair. He intended to meet her at the Penn State Blue and White game but I tagged along and spoiled things. You must have mixed up your notes."

Gently, Darren said, "There's no mix-up, Bonnie."

"But she met me," said Bonnie numbly. "She liked me. Now all this time later, they went through with it after all?" Another thought triggered a flood of doubt and revulsion. "How long have they been meeting?"

Darren didn't know, but the detective had collected pages of detailed notes about Craig and Terri's rendezvous, including more incriminating photos—all of which he could forward to Bonnie via email, if she wished. She didn't.

The next step, Darren reminded her, was to present the new evidence to Craig's lawyer. With it in hand, any judge would grant Bonnie a divorce on grounds of adultery. Craig could still delay the process by contesting the division of property, but he couldn't hold out forever, and if their pressure tactics worked, he would agree to the original settlement rather than expose the affair, and possibly ruin Terri.

Time would tell whether Craig cared more about money or his lover.

"Do what you have to do," she told Darren, wishing she were clever enough to think of another way to free herself from her failed marriage. Then her heart hardened. She owed Terri nothing. Terri was divorced—or at least she had been the first time around—but she had children who depended upon her. Terri should have thought of them before she got involved with a married man.

Darren's call left Bonnie snappish and angry for the rest of the day. When a call came from Elm Creek Manor, she didn't answer. When Claire invited her for lunch on the beach, she said she wasn't hungry. When Midori offered her another quilting lesson, she hesitated before explaining that her heart wasn't in it.

"If your heart isn't in your quilting," Midori asked, "where is it?"

Shattered into a thousand pieces and rattling around the bottom of her ribcage was what it felt like, but Bonnie thought it melodramatic to say so. "I didn't sleep well," she said by way of excuse. "I'll feel better after a good night's rest."

And she did, a little. The next morning she extended her walk and even broke into a jog part of the way, reminding herself to appreciate the beauty of the whitecaps dancing along the edge of the waves as they swept the beach, the fragrance of the abundant flowers, the unfailing sunshine, and the majesty of the West Maui mountains, green and lush, their tops often swathed in white clouds. She could not fail to appreciate the beauty all around her because of the disappointments of the past or worries about the future. She could not miss a moment of her once-in-a-lifetime visit to a land so rich in beauty.

She barred Craig from her thoughts and focused on work, a welcome diversion. Every day she helped Midori prepare breakfast and tend guest rooms. Claire had sent the job announcement out into the quilting world and they eagerly awaited the first responses. She went through Hinano's notes and made plans to investigate each location, each event. At the bottom of the list she added a second visit to the Nä Mele Hawai'i Music Shop. Why not? Hinano had invited her, and she didn't have to follow the list in any particular order.

Later that week, Bonnie attended a second meeting of Midori's quilting bee and found herself welcomed back warmly. When she showed the circle of quilters her Pineapple pattern, several praised her design and everyone was curious about her color and fabric preferences.

Bonnie soon learned that apparently Hawaiian quilters were not unanimous in their opinions on the subject of fabric selection. Some referred to their ancestors' belief that it was bad luck to have more than two colors in a quilt, and they urged her to choose a traditional scheme of two solid fabrics, one dark and one light. Others remarked that in recent years, some Hawaiian quilters had begun using multicolored batiks for their quilts with stunningly beautiful results, and some had departed from the single-cut pattern by layering appliqués of different colored fabrics in a style reminiscent of the appliqué one saw in mainland quilts. With few exceptions, the divide fell along generational lines, with most of the older women advocating tradition and the younger ones encouraging her to explore new alternatives.

When they teased her to choose a side, Bonnie laughingly responded that she would consider everything she had heard, but she was sure to have difficulty deciding. In truth, she favored a traditional, two-color scheme. That was what she had envisioned when she had first asked Midori to teach her, and that was what she imagined hanging on her wall when it was complete.

She couldn't envision which wall or what dwelling it belonged to, but at least she could see the quilt.

⟡

A few days before Halloween, guests began filling the Hale Kapa Kuiki in such numbers that for the first time since Bonnie's arrival, the inn had no vacancies. Work on Aloha Quilt Camp was abandoned in the sudden dramatic increase in activity. Claire, who always worked best under pressure, seemed to be in constant motion—greeting guests, offering sightseeing advice, resolving computer glitches, managing a shortage of beach towels—all with a smile and seemingly inexhaustible good cheer. Even Eric pitched in as porter, mechanic, and jack-of-all-trades. Bonnie was glad to see more of him, even if they could only exchange a few words in passing as they rushed from one task to another.

Although Bonnie found the unexpected increase in her workload overwhelming at times, she was happy for her friend's windfall of success. "Claire's marketing strategies are really paying off," she remarked to Midori one morning as she quickly squeezed oranges to fill a second pitcher.

"It's not the marketing," said Midori. "It's the holiday. Halloween is a big deal in Lahaina. So many tourists come for the party that even places averaging only two stars out of five on the Internet fill up fast."

"We won't be stuck at two stars for long," said Claire, sailing into the kitchen with a laundry basket of napkins fresh from the dryer. "Maybe our current guests settled for us because they couldn't get rooms elsewhere, but this is our chance to impress them. Next time, they'll forget about the big chain resorts and make us their first choice."

"Then let's impress them already," Midori called after Claire as she dashed from the kitchen, already intent on another errand. With a wry smile, she added to Bonnie, "We'll start with these guests, and later we'll get around to the rest of the thirty thousand."

"Thirty thousand?" Bonnie exclaimed. It didn't seem possible that Lahaina could accommodate so many. "Just for Halloween?"

"We like a good party," said Midori. "It started out among some mainland transplants when Lahaina was still a small town. Since everybody knew everybody, dressing up for Halloween gave us some anonymity for a change. It probably startled visitors at first to see half the town in costume, but they must have gotten into the spirit of it because year after year, more tourists have joined in. Eventually the crowds grew and grew until one year the town had to take it over and turn it into an official event just to manage the chaos."

"We could use a little help with chaos management ourselves," remarked Bonnie, hurrying outside to the lanai with the refreshed pitcher of orange juice.

Later Bonnie learned from Eric and Claire that Halloween in Lahaina was not quite the uncontrolled revelry Midori had implied, at least, not until after nightfall. The festivities began in a family friendly way at five o'clock with a children's costume parade and a Halloween Arts Festival in Courthouse Square, with food booths, music, crafts, and entertainment for all ages. Restaurants and bars throughout town sponsored costume contests where local residents and visitors alike vied for cash prizes while entertaining sightseers with their imaginative, humorous, and daring disguises. Sensible parents whisked their children home after the sun went down, away from the raucous celebration that commenced later in the evening.

"We'll be safe inside by then," Claire assured Bonnie, explaining that she planned to throw a private Halloween party for their guests on the lanai, complete with delicious treats from Midori's kitchen and beautiful music courtesy of her nephew's band.

"Hinano will play for us here?" asked Bonnie.

"We didn't ask him because he's Midori's nephew," Claire hastened to add. "He's exceptionally good."

"Oh, I know," Bonnie said. "I've heard him. A little. I've been looking forward to hearing more."

But of course, she wouldn't have the opportunity to sit down and enjoy his performance. She would be busy working, helping Claire and Midori run the party. She would probably spend most of the evening in the kitchen. It was hardly worth finding herself a costume.

Claire apparently thought otherwise, for after tidying the kitchen from breakfast on Halloween morning, she invited Bonnie to the office and surprised her with a garment bag. "What's this?" asked Bonnie warily.

Claire was almost dancing with excitement. "It's your costume, of course. You can't host a Halloween party without a costume, and I know you didn't bring one from home."

Bonnie unzipped the garment bag and discovered a flowing dress made from a white, silky fabric that shimmered like snow in sunlight. Attached to the hanger was a girdle trimmed in gold cord and a golden bangle to wear around her upper arm.

"I have a pair of gold sandals you can borrow," said Claire, beaming eagerly.

"So . . . what am I supposed to be?" asked Bonnie, dubious. "Some sort of Greek goddess?"

"Not just any Greek goddess." From behind her back, Claire produced a small plush owl with large eyes and a surprised expression that was probably meant to convey intelligence. "Pin this to your shoulder and you become Athena, the goddess of wisdom. It's perfect for you. You're the wisest woman I know, and you'll look gorgeous in this dress."

Bonnie didn't feel particularly wise as she smothered a laugh and accepted the owl. "Don't you think I should be Hera? Wasn't she the protector of marriage, even though Zeus cheated on her all the time? Or maybe *because* he cheated on her all the time."

Claire dismissed that with a wave. "Athena was also the goddess of military victory and the goddess of crafts. She invented all kinds of important tools and musical instruments, and she was also in charge of women's arts like weaving, cooking, and spinning."

"And quilting?"

"If they had quilting in ancient Greece, I'm sure it fell under her jurisdiction."

"All right, then, I'll be Athena." Bonnie tucked the toy owl into the garment bag and zipped it shut. "Who are you going to be? Aphrodite?"

"No, I thought that would be too obvious. I'm going to be a Penn State cheerleader. Eric's going as a basketball player, and you know I'm his most devoted fan."

From late morning through the afternoon, Midori, Claire, and Bonnie worked in the kitchen and on the lanai, preparing for the party. Once Bonnie had to run out to the grocery store, and to her surprise, the town looked almost as it did on any other day, with little sign of the festivities to come except for a few city workers setting up booths around Courthouse Square. She had prepared herself for long lines of cars pulling into parking lots, early risers staking out prime spots on the parade route, and tourists racing from store to store searching for essential costume accessories they had forgotten to pack. Apparently the storm of activity would strike all at once later that day, just as Midori had forecast.

Bonnie was so busy that she barely had time to call her kids and grandkids to wish them a happy Halloween, much less try on her costume. She hoped it would fit well, and if it did, that people would have a chance to admire it before she spilled something on herself, the inevitable consequence of wearing a white dress in a kitchen.

When she finally reached her younger son on his cell phone, Barry was hurrying to get ready to meet his friends at a Halloween party, where he had been assured there would be a keg and lots of "hot girls" in skimpy costumes.

"Halloween is awesome," he enthused, almost dropping the phone in his rush out the door. "Girls love having an excuse to dress sexy in public without being considered—well, you know."

Bonnie wasn't sure she knew and wasn't sure she wanted to. "Maybe you should stay home and pass out candy to trick-or-treaters instead."

Barry laughed, though Bonnie had been at least half serious. "Oh, I forgot," he said. "Dad asked me to give you a message."

Bonnie's heart thumped. "When did he call?"

"I don't remember. Maybe a week ago?"

Before his trip to Penn State to meet Terri, then. "What did he want?"

"He asked you to please stop refusing to divide stuff equally. What's up with that, Mom? You were always telling us kids to share things fairly and now you won't do it."

"Are you kidding me?" Bonnie exclaimed. "I'm the one who wanted a fifty-fifty split. It's your father who insists upon—" She forced herself to stop. "I shouldn't discuss this with you. Your father and I will resolve this through our lawyers."

"Why don't you just talk to him, Mom? I know he misses you."

Barry could be so oblivious sometimes. "Honey, he doesn't, and that isn't the point. You're just going to have to trust me on this. And remember—"

"I know, I know. Don't tell him how to reach you."

"No matter how hard he begs or threatens or whatever."

"I know." Barry sighed heavily and said he had to go. Reluctantly, Bonnie left it at that and wished him a happy Halloween, unable to resist adding a reminder to be careful. Barry had always seemed to need the reminder more than his brother and sister.

Bonnie, Claire, and Midori finished all but the last-minute preparations with time to spare, so Claire suggested they put on their costumes and join the celebration outside. Midori had seen enough Halloweens in Lahaina that she preferred to remain behind, but Claire insisted Bonnie accompany her. Bonnie hurried upstairs to change, eager to take in the spectacle. She slipped the silky dress over her head, fastened the girdle snug around her waist, put on the arm bangle, pinned the stuffed owl to her shoulder, and slid her feet into the borrowed sandals. As she went to the bathroom to brush her hair, she stopped short at the sight of herself in the mirror. The cut of the dress complemented her curves, nipping in her waist and emphasizing her generous bosom. Maybe too generous, and maybe too much emphasis. She tugged the bodice into a slightly more modest arrangement, but as soon as she reached for the hairbrush, everything fell back into place. It would have to do, Bonnie told herself after a few more useless adjustments. Besides, with all of the scantily clad twenty-somethings out there, no one would be looking at her.

She ran the brush through her short, dark locks, touched up her makeup, and peered at her face in the mirror. The color of the fabric made her skin positively glow in a way it hadn't in years, or maybe it was a trick of the twilight. The wide-eyed plush owl on her shoulder looked as surprised as she felt. She shook her head, set down the brush, and hurried downstairs to meet Claire. She should have made an appointment with her ophthalmologist before leaving home. Her vision was obviously going south. Next stop, bifocals.

"You look radiant," gushed Claire, watching from the foyer as Bonnie descended the stairs.

"Me? Look at you," Bonnie exclaimed, taking in her friend's bouncy light brown ponytail and blue-and-white cheerleader's uniform complete with pom-poms. "You should be on the sidelines of Beaver Stadium. With those legs, you could pass for an undergrad. Can you still do a back handspring?"

"My handspringing days are long gone," said Claire, taking something from the bamboo credenza. "As for you, your costume needs only one last touch." Smiling, she placed a light wreath of greenery on Bonnie's head.

"Laurel?" asked Bonnie, touching the leaves carefully. It

was wonderfully fragrant, reminiscent of vanilla and fresh woodland air, sweet and spicy and woodsy all at once.

"It's called *maile*." Claire's eyes danced with merriment as she slipped her arm through Bonnie's and led her from the inn and down Front Street. "I've missed dressing you up for a night out."

"I've missed your fashion sense," Bonnie admitted. "Speaking of fashion, I love what that bride across the street is wearing. I never thought to accessorize a wedding gown with a machete through the chest and a gallon of fake blood, but on her it works."

The gory bride was only the first and not even the most noteworthy of the quirky costumes they saw during their stroll down Front Street and around Courthouse Square. Amidst the plethora of superheroes, monsters, Elizabethan royalty, and pirates, they spotted a giant piece of candy corn, a Rubik's Cube, a sparkling disco ball, and a great white shark with a mannequin's legs dangling from the mouth. Bonnie's favorites were the group costumes, especially the four men dressed as Mount Rushmore in white face paint, white wigs, and an elaborate, papier-mâché mountain.

Impossible to ignore were the legion of couples in costume—Romeo and Juliet, Fred and Wilma Flintstone, Marc Antony and Cleopatra, Adam and Eve wearing little more than leis and fig leaves, and a fly swatter and fly. Bonnie and Craig had never coordinated their costumes for Halloween, not even for fraternity parties when all their friends and their dates did. On one painful, memorable trip to Penn State, Craig had even complained about wearing the matching Nittany Lions sweatshirts Bonnie had bought them for the last home game of the season. He wore it because she hadn't packed him an alternative, but he groused all through breakfast at the College Avenue Diner, spoiling her appetite. While he paid the check, Bonnie had hurried back to their hotel room to change, trying not to mind that Craig apparently didn't want anyone to realize they were a couple.

But that was long ago and far away. In Lahaina, music filled the air, delicious smells wafted from the food booths, and thousands of people laughed, shouted, people-watched, and enjoyed every moment. Caught up in the celebration, Bonnie and Claire lost track of time. Half-past eight found them sprinting back to the Hale Kapa Kuiki a mere half-hour before their own private party was to begin.

"Back so soon?" Midori inquired dryly when they burst into the kitchen babbling apologies. She had already filled the punch bowl and had begun setting out platters of food, but there was much more to do and she quickly ordered Claire and Bonnie to it.

Bonnie snatched up a fruit tray and carried it out to the lanai, past the hired bartender to a long buffet table where a few costumed early arrivals lingered hopefully. Midori had wisely decided to keep plates and utensils covered until the last moment so that no one dove in too early. "It won't be much longer," Bonnie assured the guests as she found a place for her tray, but suddenly her attention was captured by a melodious strum.

At the other end of the lanai, Hinano, Kai, and two other musicians were setting up and tuning their instruments—ukulele, slack key guitar, bass, and drums. Kai tested the microphones and joked with his father, who grinned as he plucked a few notes, sweet and pure.

Instinctively Bonnie smoothed her goddess gown over her hips and adjusted her leafy crown. She caught herself, chided herself, and got herself back into the kitchen. "The band's here," she announced brightly.

"The band's *been* here," said Midori.

"I should go welcome them," said Claire, wiping up a spill on the counter and draping the towel over the sink. Glancing through the window from time to time as she arranged short-bread cookies shaped like pineapples on a tiered tray, Bonnie glimpsed her friend crossing the lanai and greeting the musicians like old friends. A few moments later, Eric joined them clad in what looked to be an official Penn State basketball uniform. When he put his arm around Claire's shoulders with an unconscious, comfortable familiarity, Claire instinctively drew closer to him. Bonnie smiled, but she suddenly became so wistful that she had to turn away. She missed knowing that tenderness, that closeness shared with a trusted, lifelong companion.

She missed it, but really, had she ever truly known it?

❖

Before long, the party was underway. Bathed in torchlight and sheltered from the wilder celebration on the streets outside, guests mingled, admired one another's costumes, savored delicious hors d'oeuvres and sweets, and listened to beautiful traditional Hawaiian music. Playing hostess and assistant cook for a full house, Bonnie had no time to sit down with a glass of wine and enjoy the performance but only caught a few bars here and there in passing.

Two hours later, when the momentum of the party carried it along, Midori shooed her out to the lanai with orders to feed herself and put her feet up. The borrowed sandals were comfortable, but Bonnie had been racing around on them all evening. She accepted Midori's offer gratefully with promises that she would come running back if summoned.

Bonnie filled a small plate from the buffet, collected a glass of white wine from the bar, and found a seat at a table on the discreet fringes of the party with a good view of both the band as well as the kitchen in case Midori beckoned. The band was in the middle of a song that for Bonnie evoked images of moonlit beaches and palm trees swaying in a gentle, misty breeze. Though she did not understand the lyrics except for "aloha," repeated in the refrain, Hinano's baritone conveyed gentle longing with every unfamiliar word.

The song ended and Bonnie joined in the applause. Hinano said something over his shoulder to the rest of his band, then turned back to the microphone and gave his ukulele two, quick strums. "I know what you're thinking," he said to the crowd, tightening a tuning peg, "but no, my guitar didn't shrink."

A smattering of laughter rose from the audience.

"This is a ukulele," he continued, giving the word the same unusual lilt Bonnie had heard from him before. "Most people think of it as a Hawaiian instrument, and it's true we've adopted it as our own, but it actually was brought to the islands by Portuguese immigrants who came in the late nineteen hundreds to work in the sugar cane fields."

He strummed another chord and adjusted the microphone. "When the Hawaiian people saw the newcomers playing, they loved the music and were impressed by the speed of the musicians' fingers as they raced up and down the fingerboard. The Hawaiians gave the instrument the name ukulele, which translates to 'jumping flea.' " Hinano played a few quick scales up and down, his fingers jumping and dancing on the fingerboard. "You can see how that image came to mind."

The audience responded with murmurs and nods.

"But that's only one version of the story." Suddenly Hinano's glance fell on Bonnie, and she froze with her wine glass halfway to her lips until he looked away. "According to our

Queen Liliʻuokalani, ukulele came from two Hawaiian words, *uku*, a gift or reward, and *lele*, to come. So the ukulele is 'the gift that came here.' " He played a few soft, wistful chords. "I've heard a half-dozen other origin stories, but these are my two favorite, so those are the only two you'll get out of me tonight."

His listeners laughed.

"Enough talk." Hinano turned again to nod to his companions. "Let's play."

They launched into a quick, cheerful melody and the party's liveliness quickly resumed. Bonnie listened for a little while longer before returning to work. Guests had been filtering in from the street festival all evening, requiring an ongoing replenishment of the buffet table. As Bonnie watched their supply of prepared treats dwindling, she worried that they might run out of food. "No need to panic just yet," Claire assured her as they crossed paths on the lanai. "I did a head count. Most of our guests have already eaten. As long as people restrain themselves to only third helpings, we should be able to hold out until the party wraps up."

Bonnie hoped she was right. "But if they clear the entire buffet?"

"We'll send out for pizza. Next time we'll know, and we'll plan for this."

Bonnie knew Claire couldn't possibly feel as nonchalant as she sounded. The party had to be a huge, resounding success if they wanted their guests to go away completely satisfied and reward them with glowing reviews on every site in cyberspace.

A little before one o'clock in the morning, the band went on a break just as Bonnie was refilling the trays, bowls, and platters for what was sure to be the last time, since they had not a single appetizer or cookie left in reserve. She had just finished rearranging the buffet to disguise the dwindling quantities when

114   Jennifer Chiaverini

the musicians came over to help themselves. "Go easy," Hinano urged his friends in an undertone.

But the band had entertained their guests all evening, and Bonnie couldn't bear to let them go hungry. "There's plenty," she assured them, smiling. "Go ahead. We know you've worked up an appetite. If we polish off the buffet, we'll just skip ahead a few hours and start serving breakfast."

The musicians laughed, but it occurred to Bonnie that she might have hit upon the solution. She was about to hurry off and suggest it to Midori as a last resort, but Hinano caught her by the elbow. "You mean you're not going to join us?"

"I—" Bonnie shrugged, helpless. Why not? She couldn't replenish the buffet even if she wanted to, and she couldn't clean up until the party ended. "Sure. I think your aunt could spare me for a few minutes."

She joined the band at the last unoccupied table, and after Hinano made introductions, Kai and the other members of the band began discussing the next set. Hinano made a few suggestions but then quickly turned his attention to Bonnie. "There's more to the history of the ukulele in Hawaii than that brief intro I just gave you."

"I figured there probably was," said Bonnie, determined not to make too much of his choice to say *you* instead of *your guests*.

"Some of the Portuguese immigrants who introduced the ukulele here were also skilled woodworkers, and they began making new instruments for others as the music of the ukulele caught on. It quickly became our most popular instrument both among the common people and the royalty."

"You mentioned a queen," Bonnie recalled, "and her thoughts on the origin of the name."

Hinano nodded. "Queen Lili'uokalani, our last queen. She

played the ukulele, as did King Kalakaua, Prince Leleiohoku, and Princess Likelike."

"I don't know anything about Hawaiian royalty," said Bonnie apologetically. "What happened? Did the monarchy get phased out after Hawaii joined the United States?"

Hinano's eyebrows rose and he regarded her for a moment as if not sure whether she was joking. Eventually he must have decided that she honestly didn't know, for he said, "It wasn't quite like that. Hawaii was a sovereign nation and recognized by international heads of state as such. In 1893, Queen Lili'uokalani was deposed in a coup organized by Stanford Dole—"

"The pineapple guy's cousin," Kai broke in. "But that was after he forced that constitution on us. Tell her about that, Dad."

"Kai's right. If you go further back, you find more injustice." Hinano hesitated, flexing his hands as if to keep them limber for more music soon. "In 1887, Dole helped organize local politicians, businessmen, and sugar planters to create a constitution for the Kingdom of Hawaii that stripped Asians and all but the most elite native Hawaiians of their voting rights. It also shifted power from the monarch to the Privy Council, the royal cabinet. All of this gave the elite native Hawaiians, Europeans, and Americans greater control and influence at the expense of the common people."

"Same kine story the world over," said the drummer. "Rich and powerful end up running everything."

"Many of the same people involved in the 1887 constitution participated in the 1893 coup," Hinano said. "The Kingdom of Hawaii was taken over by the United States with the full threat of the use of their vastly superior military force. When the U.S. Marines landed in Honolulu, Queen Lili'uokalani stepped aside under protest to prevent the loss of life. She fully intended to regain her rightful place eventually, believing that the international community would denounce America's illegal actions."

"Hinano," the bass player broke in cautiously, "this is a friendly party."

"Wait. Hawaii was invaded by the United States Marines?" asked Bonnie. "You didn't want to become a state?"

"Not that way," said Kai, and with a glance at his father, added, "and some people would say not any way."

"Some people believe that Hawaii isn't a state at all, but a sovereign nation under prolonged occupation," said Hinano. "Some believe that the Hawaiian people ought to have the same rights to self-governance that many Native American tribes on the mainland possess."

Bonnie studied him. "Some people, meaning you. But you were in the military."

Hinano shrugged, but that small, ostensibly dismissive motion suggested fathomless depths of conflict. "I've fought for my country. I took a bullet for my country. I'm a proud American the same as you. But America doesn't exactly have a great track record when it comes to dealing with indigenous peoples, and the law was broken. It's never too late to correct an injustice."

"Easy, Hinano," said the bass player. "Queen Lili'uokalani reconciled herself to it. Maybe you should too."

"What choice did she have?" Hinano countered. "After imprisonment, after President Cleveland broke his promise to support her? What was she supposed to do?"

The bass player held up his palms and shook his head, exchanging a long look with the drummer that implied they had been through this same debate before.

"But the coup was so long ago," Bonnie said. "And from

what you said, there was no blood shed over it. Surely you don't think Hawaii would be better off if it weren't a part of the United States?"

She knew at once that it was the worst thing she could have said.

"You're posing a hypothetical that avoids the real issues," Hinano said quietly. "Ask Native Americans on the mainland if they would be better off today if Europeans had never come to the New World. Ask African-Americans if they would be better off today if their ancestors had never been brought to the Colonies as slaves. If you want good answers, you have to ask the right questions." He pushed back his chair and stood. "And blood *has* been shed over this issue. It's not all in the past. Look beyond the resorts and the beaches and you'll see a host of social ills that are the direct result of our native lands being colonized. Our people can't find affordable homes. We work two or three jobs just to keep up with the cost of living, and many of us have to leave our beloved *aina* when we can't support our families here any longer. We suffer from a serious brain drain. Kai isn't the only Hawaiian college kid who'll probably have to take a job on the mainland instead of his own island home if he ever wants to get ahead. Rich *haole* from the mainland want to turn our islands into their own private playground of vacation homes in gated communities."

"I'm sorry," Bonnie said as the other musicians rose, averting their gazes as if to spare her further embarrassment. "There's obviously a lot I don't know. I didn't mean to offend you."

"No problem." Hinano smiled, but it did not touch his eyes. "You should just know that we're not all happy natives draping leis and dancing the hula for tourists."

Mortified, Bonnie nodded in reply, but Hinano had already turned away and didn't see it. Biting her lips together, she busied herself with clearing their table and had returned to the kitchen with the dirty dishes by the time the band struck up another song.

Midori took one look at her and frowned. "What did he say?"

"Nothing. What do you mean?" Bonnie rinsed off plates and stacked them on the counter above the dishwasher, which was already running its third load of the night.

"I saw you sitting with my nephew and from the look on your face I know he said something wrong. And after he was going on and on to Eric and Claire about how lovely you looked." She shook her head. "Always he does this."

"I was the one who said something wrong." Then Midori's last words registered—Hinano thought she looked lovely? Well, it didn't matter now. "I offended him. I said something stupid about Hawaiian sovereignty, and I didn't even know there was a controversy."

"Naturally. Why should there be a controversy? Who wouldn't want to be ruled by the United States?" Midori's tone was so ambiguous that Bonnie couldn't tell if she was mocking her nephew, Bonnie, both, or neither. "Don't mind him. That's a sensitive issue for my nephew."

"As I discovered the hard way."

"Unless you denounced Queen Liliʻuokalani and proposed a toast to Stanford B. Dole, he'll get over it. And it won't take him long. Before he leaves tonight, I'm sure he'll come to you and apologize for being such a big baby."

Bonnie didn't give him the opportunity. When the party ended at two o'clock, Hinano lingered after the other musicians departed, but Bonnie had so much work to do that she managed to avoid him. It wasn't that difficult. As far as she could tell, he made little effort to speak to her. Despite what

Midori thought, he couldn't have wanted to apologize too badly or he would have done so.

Besides, she didn't really think he owed her an apology, except for that snide remark about leis, hulas, and tourists. What she had said was worse, but she had spoken out of ignorance and had meant no harm. Hinano, on the other hand . . .

She didn't notice when he left, only that he was gone. Her heart felt strangely heavy as she, Claire, Midori, and Eric restored order to the lanai, but she told herself it was merely fatigue. At last Claire decided that they had done enough to make the kitchen and lanai suitable for breakfast the next morning. Wearily, Bonnie was about to drag herself upstairs and collapse into bed when Claire called her into the office.

There, Bonnie saw that Claire had turned on her computer and opened the web browser. "The party was the treat," she said, beckoning Bonnie closer. "Now it's time for a Halloween trick."

Blinking from exhaustion, Bonnie scanned the web page. "The Revenge Guy?" she read aloud.

"There's also the Revenge Gal, but I don't think they're related. Look." Claire clicked back to a Google search results page. "There are more than eighty-one million sites about revenge. We can find the perfect way to get back at Craig and Terri."

"Only eighty-one million?" Bonnie pulled up a chair and studied the computer. "Are you sure this is legal?"

"Some of it's a bit borderline, but we're just browsing. Look. This company will send Craig a fake letter from the IRS telling him he's going to be audited in a week. They'll mangle and stamp the envelope so it looks like it was delayed in the mail. Or—here. You can disguise your phone number so it won't show up on caller ID, then leave a message at Terri's workplace pretending to be her doctor calling with the results of her AIDS test."

"Claire, this is so ugly," Bonnie exclaimed.

Claire laughed. "Maybe, but it's not even in the same league of ugly as what they've done to you."

"Ordinarily I'd rather take the high road." Bonnie reached for the mouse. "However, in honor of Halloween, I might just indulge in a trick for them as a treat for me."

"Now, now, Bonnie." Claire playfully slapped the back of Bonnie's hand and scooted the mouse away. "We're just having fun. We aren't actually going to do any of these things."

"Not tonight," Bonnie acknowledged. "It's late and we're both tired. I'll bookmark some of these sites and we can look them over tomorrow."

"No, Bonnie. You shouldn't seek revenge tomorrow or the next day or the next. Just let it go, okay? I'm sorry I brought it up. I only wanted to make you laugh at the end of a long day."

"Maybe you meant it as a joke, but you're right. I deserve payback."

"You deserve peace of mind," said Claire. "Revenge won't bring you that."

"Maybe not, but it might be worth it."

"Come on, Bonnie. You don't really mean that. You don't want to become like them, do you? You're better than that. You'd never take pleasure in hurting people. That's not you. Just let it go."

"How can I let it go when I can't stop thinking about it?" demanded Bonnie, suddenly tearful. "And I do think about it! Day and night. Sleeping and waking. I need to *stop* thinking about it. You want to help me? Help me forget this whole terrible nightmare ever happened! Help me forget that women like Terri even exist."

"I'm so sorry," said Claire, stricken. "I should have known better than to joke about something like this."

"No, it's all right. It's okay to imagine what I might like to do to Craig, but I know I'd feel terrible if I followed through." Bonnie took a deep, shaky breath and tried to smile. "The party was a huge success. We're successful and happy and I'm perfectly fine without him. That's the best revenge of all."

She wasn't perfectly fine, not yet.

Chapter Seven

Claire must have seen Hinano's list of must-see Maui events in Bonnie's notebook, for the following week, Claire and Eric surprised Bonnie with a night out at the Old Lahaina Luʻau. They were greeted with beautiful, fragrant flower *leis* and enjoyed a delicious feast of kalua puaʻa—pork roasted in a beachside underground oven called an *imu*—as well as fish, poi, chicken, vegetables, fruit, and salads. After the feast, the guests were spellbound by a wonderful performance of traditional Hawaiian music, dances, and chants performed against the stunning backdrop of the sunset over the ocean. Once Bonnie recalled Hinano's scathing remark about *leis* and hulas, and she wondered if he would find the luau authentic enough to meet his high standards or if he would dismiss it as just another commercial display for the tourists. He must have believed it represented the real Hawaii, she decided, or he wouldn't have recommended it. Either way, she knew the quilt campers would have as wonderful a time there as she was having, so she resolved to include an evening at the Old Lahaina Luʻau during each week of camp, either early in the week to introduce the campers to Hawaii, or perhaps at the end, as a farewell banquet.

Another week passed, and as Bonnie and Claire awaited the response to the job announcement they had posted in the quilt shop, on their website, and in the newsletter of every quilting guild in Hawaii, Bonnie resumed work on her Pineapple Patch quilt. First she created a border *lei* to complement the center, then browsed through the aisles of Plumeria Quilts admiring the rainbow of bolts, selecting a few of the prettiest and setting them aside on the cutting table to unroll, inspect, and compare. After considering several possible combinations of focus fabrics and backgrounds, she selected a vibrant emerald green tone-on-tone print for the appliqué. She had originally intended to choose a solid fabric in keeping with tradition, but the subtle print offered the slightest hint of texture when compared to a solid fabric, which she thought might appear too flat. For the background she chose a creamy ivory fabric, after ruling out white as too easily dirtied and too bright for the emerald green. Contrast was good and necessary in a quilt, but the ivory fabric glowed when placed next to the green, whereas the bright white seemed to glare.

Claire assured her she had chosen the two prettiest fabrics in the store and that her quilt was destined to be a masterpiece. She also refused to let Bonnie pay for her purchases, but folded the yardage, wrapped the bundles in tissue paper, and tucked them into a shopping bag while ignoring the cash Bonnie set on the counter. Bonnie tried to leave it there, but Claire slipped it back into her purse while one of her employees distracted her. It was so silly and obvious that Bonnie had to laugh, but she felt a twinge of guilt as she left the store. Even though she had selected only enough fabric and thread for a wallhanging, she wouldn't have chosen an expensive batik if she had known Claire intended to give it to her. She had been a shopkeeper long enough to know that every penny counted.

Back at the Hale Kapa Kuiki, she tracked down Midori in the laundry room and tentatively showed her the two fabrics, expecting a rebuke for not choosing solids. Instead, Midori nodded her approval, remarked that the ivory brought out subtle hints of gold in the emerald appliqué fabric, and suggested Bonnie wash the fabric yardage separately just in case the emerald bled.

"You're okay with this?" asked Bonnie before loading the emerald green print into the washer. She had expected a sigh of disappointment at best, a refusal to continue their lessons at worst.

"What does it matter what I think?" inquired Midori, balancing a laundry basket full of freshly washed and folded towels on her hip. "You're the one who's going to have to work with it and look at it every day when it's done."

"I guess I hoped you'd approve."

Midori set down the laundry basket and scrutinized the two fabrics more carefully. "It's a pretty combination. The tone-on-tone gives it a nice texture, but not too much. It's not strictly traditional, but you could have done worse."

Somehow that honest, restrained approval meant as much as all the lavish praise Claire had heaped upon her at the store.

Later, after the fabrics were washed and dried, Midori instructed Bonnie to iron the emerald green appliqué fabric, fold it in eighths with right sides facing, and iron the creases of the folds. Then she urged Bonnie to either pin or baste all around the edges of the thick fabric triangle. "That will keep the layers from shifting while you trace your pattern and cut out the appliqué," she explained. "It's a little extra work now that will save you big headaches later."

Bonnie decided to baste, thinking that she could always secure loose places with pins if she snipped through the basting threads while cutting out her design. Then Midori told her to cut her paper pattern on its folds so that only the eighth-fold section she had drawn remained. Bonnie hesitated, reluctant to ruin her pattern.

"You aren't ruining it," Midori told her. "You need only the one-eighth section. A more advanced Hawaiian quilter wouldn't have cut out the entire paper pattern at this stage anyway. I had you do it so that you could unfold the paper and see what your whole design looked like. You seemed to need that reassurance."

Bonnie couldn't dispute that, and so she placed her trust in her mentor and trimmed her Pineapple pattern so that only the one-eighth section she had drawn remained. Making sure the grain lines and biases were aligned, she placed the one-eighth pattern on the fabric triangle so that the edges of the paper met the folds of the fabric.

"Some quilters prefer to pin or baste their pattern in place," Midori said. "Others trust the steadiness of their hands and don't bother."

Midori's tone suggested she didn't think much of quilters who skipped that step, so Bonnie threaded her needle again and basted the pattern in place with large stitches just within the pattern line. After she tied the knot and snipped the dangling length of thread, Midori again offered her two options of how to proceed: She could trace around her pattern so that the outline was marked on the fabric itself, or she could cut around the pattern without tracing.

If Bonnie had pinned the paper pattern to the fabric, she might have chosen to trace around the pattern and remove the paper before cutting, but since she had already gone to the trouble of basting the pattern in place, she decided to take the second option.

Making careful snips with Midori's sharpest scissors, she cut the emerald green fabric one-eighth of an inch outside the edges of the pattern. "The extra eighth inch is your fabric allowance," Midori told her, confirming Bonnie's guess. "You'll tuck the raw edge under your appliqué as you sew it to the background fabric."

Midori left her on her own to finish, admonishing her to take her time. Bonnie would have done so in any case, knowing that a simple slip of the scissors could ruin all her efforts up to that point. She felt no need to rush, but allowed the shapes she had drawn to gradually emerge from the fabric—plump pineapples, short tufted tops, and long, graceful leaves.

With one last snip, she finished. She cut the basting stitches, brushed away loose threads, and piled the scraps on the far side of the table, clearing the space in front of her. Then, handling the bias edges carefully rather than risk stretching them even slightly and distorting her appliqué, she unfolded it on the table and stood up to inspect it.

She was pleased to see that her design appealed to her even more in fabric than on paper, and she prepared the *lei* with greater confidence.

Midori returned while Bonnie was cleaning up the table and asked if she was ready to move ahead to the next step. "It will take you more time than anything you've done so far, except, perhaps, designing your pattern," she warned.

"What's the next step?" asked Bonnie, sweeping snipped threads and fabric scraps off the table and into a trash bag.

"Preparing the background fabric and basting the appliqué in place," said Midori. "When I make my quilts, I like to get my appliqué basted down right away to secure those bias edges."

"If you have time to teach, I have time to learn," Bonnie replied.

Since she had already washed the ivory background fabric, her next step was to iron it as she had done with the emerald fabric earlier. After Bonnie pressed the folds into crisp creases, Midori instructed her to unfold the background fabric right side up on one of the large tables in the covered part of the lanai. "Lay your appliqués upon the background," Midori said, showing her how to ease the emerald green pieces into place without stretching them, matching the pressed creases of the appliqués to those in the background fabric. When the creases were aligned, the pineapples and leaves were perfectly centered on the ivory background.

Midori helped her pin the appliqué in place, first the *lei* and then the center, taking care to keep the creases aligned.

"Next we baste." Then Midori eyed her appraisingly. "Yes, more preparation. Eventually you will begin to appliqué, if you don't give up in frustration first."

"I haven't complained," Bonnie reminded her mildly, reaching across the table for needle and thread. Then she hesitated, watching Midori curiously. "Tell me, Midori. Are you accustomed to having your apprentices question your every lesson?"

"No," said Midori, brow furrowing. "Quite the contrary. Why do you ask?"

"Because from the beginning, you've been telling me what to do and then emphasizing why I must do it exactly so or I'll regret it, almost as if you expect me to dispute the point. I'm here to learn, not to argue. I'm not second-guessing you."

Midori frowned slightly and her gaze turned inward, as if she were replaying their lessons in her mind's eye. "Sometimes experienced quilters make the most stubborn students. They think they already know the best way so they aren't open to new ideas."

"I'm well aware that I don't know everything and I welcome genuine efforts to help me learn. Just give me a chance."

Midori's eyebrows rose. "You think I don't genuinely want to teach you? If I didn't, I could just give you a book and let you figure it out on your own."

"Of course I know you want to help me," said Bonnie, flustered. "You've been very generous with your time and advice, and you introduced me to your guild. Just forget it. I'm being too sensitive. I don't know what I'm talking about."

But she did know, and from Midori's expression, she thought Midori knew, too.

"Sometimes the people who are the quickest to anger are quickest to forgive, once they realize no offense was intended," said Midori kindly. "Those sorts of people can become the most loyal friends of all, once you get past that bristly exterior." She studied the emerald green appliqué and bent over to smooth a wrinkle in a long, tapering leaf. "Sometimes people have good reasons for their defenses, reasons you would never suspect. But never mind that now. We have work to do."

With a length of white thread to contrast with the emerald green, Bonnie basted the appliqué to the background fabric with large running stitches, first across the diagonals and then on the horizontal and vertical axes. Then, following Midori's directions, she carefully basted every curve and point, every leaf and fruit, one quarter of an inch within the edges of the entire emerald piece. "A precise quarter inch is essential," Midori said. "You'll see why when it comes time to appliqué."

An experienced quilter, Bonnie had already figured it out, but she merely nodded and thanked Midori for the tip rather than appear to be one of those stubborn experienced quilters who assumed they knew everything.

Once satisfied that Bonnie would not rush through the

task or grow careless with the spacing of her basting stitches, Midori left Bonnie to finish on her own. Basting every curve and point was painstaking work that left her with pinpricked fingertips and an aching neck, so she took occasional breaks to stretch and to rest her eyes by looking around the garden or the shaded lanai, their future classroom. As the hours passed, her thoughts drifted from the repetitive motions of needle and thread to Aloha Quilt Camp. In a few months, the very lanai where she now worked would be filled with beginning quilters taking their first stitches or experienced quilters mastering new techniques. Or so they would if Bonnie planned well, if she accomplished the tasks Claire had assigned her, not the least of which was finding qualified instructors.

Their recruiting had stalled after an initial bustle of responses from local quilters, most of whom were fine quilters but lacked teaching experience. Bonnie had inquired with the Laulima Quilters too, but most of them had other full-time careers, cared for small children or grandchildren at home, or were enjoying retirement too much to consider returning to work. Bonnie also knew that there was a world of difference between helping friends at a quilt guild meeting and designing and leading a structured course in a classroom setting, so even those few who had offered to teach for them might not have the sort of experience that Aloha Quilt Camp needed. Despite all this, Claire insisted that advertising in local quilt guild newsletters and distributing flyers would eventually pay off. Bonnie lacked her certainty, and believed they shouldn't rely upon that alone.

With every stitch, Bonnie became more convinced that they needed to advertise in a national quilting magazine. It was an expensive but necessary investment in the future of Aloha Quilt Camp. Advertising had worked for Elm Creek

Quilts and it would work for them. Claire juggled numbers as adeptly as Sarah McClure, so surely she could trim expenses here or there until she came up with enough to cover the costs if she wanted to.

The question was, *did* Claire want to?

It was early evening when Bonnie put the last basting stitch into her quilt top, tied a knot, and snipped the trailing thread. She packed her supplies and rolled up her quilt top rather than folding it to avoid creasing the fabric. After putting everything in her room for safekeeping, she returned downstairs and found Claire in the office.

Claire looked up at Bonnie's approach and quickly shut down her web browser, and although she smiled a welcome, she looked so tired that Bonnie considered merely wishing her a good night and leaving her alone. But just as she was about to say good night, Claire said, "Midori really had you working hard today."

"Oh, no. It was my choice. I took breaks every once in a while."

"That's good." Claire glanced back at the computer screen, now showing only her desktop, and gave an involuntary sigh before turning back to Bonnie with some of her usual brightness restored. "Do you want to have dinner with me and Eric tonight? You must be tired of cooking for one."

She wasn't, actually. For most of her adult life, Bonnie had planned what and when to eat based upon Craig and the children's schedules and preferences. Eating what she wanted when she wanted was a refreshing novelty. But she didn't always dine alone. Often she and Midori prepared a simple meal for two together and chatted about quilting, Hawaii, or the challenges facing the Hale Kapa Kuiki, sometimes lingering at the table long after they finished eating to continue their conversation. In many ways, Bonnie had learned more about the inn and Lahaina from Midori than from Claire.

"I don't mind cooking for myself," Bonnie assured her, "but I'd love to join you and Eric. Why don't we bring along a copy of the budget? Maybe if the three of us go over it together, we'll find a way to pay for an ad." Suddenly inspired, she added, "Maybe we could borrow from the advertising budget for the camp itself."

Claire pursed her lips and shook her head. "If we did, when it comes time to announce our launch, we won't be able to reach potential customers as well. Enrollment will suffer."

"It won't matter if we have an inn full of campers if we have no one to teach them."

"We'll find teachers." Claire gestured to the wire basket on her desk. "Two résumés came in today's mail and I'm sure more will follow."

Bonnie wondered why Claire had not mentioned the good news earlier. "If I were a suspicious person," she teased, "I might think you were deliberately putting less than your best effort into the search for teachers so that I'll agree to stay rather than leave you understaffed."

Claire frowned, rose, and pushed in her chair. "I don't have any ulterior motives. I would never want you to stay here if your heart wasn't in it."

"Oh, come on, Claire. Don't be angry. I was only teasing."

"I haven't made any secret of the fact that I'd like you to stay. I don't need to resort to underhanded tricks when there are a hundred obvious reasons for you to choose Aloha Quilt Camp over anything else."

Bonnie had to admit that this made a certain kind of sense, but she still disagreed with Claire's decision. "You have an advertising budget for Aloha Quilt Camp. Let's take some of those funds and pay for a help-wanted ad in a prominent magazine with a high circulation to get the most for our money. If we don't have teachers, we won't need to advertise the quilt camp because there won't *be* a quilt camp. Even if I stayed, I couldn't teach every class."

"We couldn't do that even if we wanted to," Claire said. "It's not like putting an ad in the newspaper. Magazines like *Quilter's Newsletter* need a few months' lead time. We're too late."

"Then let's buy ad space on their website," said Bonnie, remembering one of Sarah's more recent marketing campaigns for Elm Creek Quilt Camp. "They don't need much lead time for that. For the same price as a single print ad, we could probably buy banner ads on the websites of several different quilting magazines."

Claire studied her for a long moment, then sighed, clasped a hand to her brow, and ran her fingers through her long, light brown hair. "I suppose those ads could be considered an early announcement of our grand opening," she said at last. "They might generate some buzz. We'll include a link to Aloha Quilt Camp website and create a mailing list for when we're set up and ready to accept registrations."

"It's never too soon to start spreading the word to potential future campers."

Claire retrieved a manila folder from a filing cabinet. "I'll bring the budget," she said. "It'll be a working dinner. But dessert will be strictly social."

Bonnie smiled, relieved that the conflict had been resolved as quickly as it had arisen. "Agreed."

❖

Over mahimahi, taro, and pineapple salsa, Claire, Eric, and Bonnie went over the budget line by line. It was late by the time

Eric drove Bonnie back to the inn. "Thanks for pursuading Claire to buy advertising," he told her as he walked her to the door in a completely unnecessary but charming show of chivalry. "I've believed all along that it's the only way you're going to drum up enough candidates for the job, but Claire insisted it wasn't necessary, and I hate to argue."

"You hate to argue with Claire," Bonnie corrected, for with anyone else, Eric never avoided confrontation when he knew he was in the right. "You hate it when she's displeased with you."

He spread his hands helplessly. "What can I say? I'm in love with her."

"That's why Claire could always get away with anything, even when we were in school," teased Bonnie. "I wish Craig—"

Eric winced. "Let's not spoil a nice evening by bringing him up."

Bonnie nodded, wished Eric a good night, and went upstairs to bed. She had been about to say that she wished Craig had learned a few things from Eric's example all those years ago back in college—how to treat the woman he loved, for one. How to be a good, decent, and honorable man. But even back then, Craig had not been inclined to follow Eric's example in much of anything. They had been friends, but privately, Craig had criticized Eric for tolerating too much from Claire. "I would never put up with that," Craig had told Bonnie after, in his opinion, Claire had flirted with other guys at a frat party. "If I were Eric, I'd dump her and let her find another ride home."

Though Bonnie had been displeased by Craig's criticism of her friend, she had nodded and murmured lukewarm agreement before changing the subject. She had always gone along to get along, had pretended to agree when she didn't really, merely to keep the peace. No wonder Craig had ended up treating her like a doormat so many years later—no, worse than a doormat. Like the dirt beneath his feet.

If she had stood up for herself long ago, if she had been a little bit more like Claire and a little less willing to tolerate everything for the sake of harmony, she might not be on the wrong side of fifty and facing divorce.

She had always considered tolerance and cooperativeness virtues, but perhaps in certain circumstances they weren't. She hadn't permitted disrespectful behavior from her children and they had all grown up to be responsible adults. She hadn't allowed Craig to get away with meeting Terri that first time, and that had given her a second chance to save her marriage. She hadn't let Midori discourage her from learning to make a quilt in the Hawaiian style, and as a result, she was making a beautiful quilt top and possibly even a friend. She had challenged Claire about her reluctance to advertise the teaching positions, and Claire had relented. Whenever Bonnie remembered she had a backbone and that "being nice" wasn't always the highest priority, good things followed.

The next day, Bonnie pondered this new insight as she went for her morning walk and with every step her resolve strengthened. What did she have to lose if she started speaking her mind? Would she anger people? Perhaps, but they would get over it as Claire had done. Would she lose friends? If honesty scared them away, they were never her friends in the first place. Would she astonish people who had grown accustomed to the nice, pleasant, acquiescent Bonnie? Almost certainly, but it might do them good to have their expectations challenged. It had done Bonnie good already, and she was just getting started.

Resolved, she walked faster and faster, pumping her fists, working up a good sweat. She found her steps leading her off her usual route, away from the beach toward central Lahaina. When she passed the coffee shop where she had interviewed Hinano, she realized what her destination must be.

The lights were off in Nä Mele Hawai'i Music Shop when she arrived, the sign hanging in the front window turned to CLOSED. She peered inside, hoping to see Hinano working behind the counter and preparing to open the store for the day, but there was no sign of anyone moving in the darkened store. She knocked on the door anyway, determined to speak to him before she lost her nerve. She waited, knocked again, and had reluctantly decided to come back later when suddenly the door behind the counter opened and Hinano appeared. He stopped short at the sight of her, but he quickly masked his astonishment and made his way from the back of the store.

He gave her one quick, appraising glance as he unlocked the door and pushed it open. "Howzit, Bonnie?" He glanced up at the morning sky. "If you're here to buy a ukulele, we don't open for another hour."

She wasn't sure whether he was teasing her. "I'm here to talk, if that's okay."

He shrugged and opened the door wider. "Come on in." When she stepped inside, he locked the door behind her and headed for the back of the store. "You want some coffee?"

"Sure, thanks."

She followed him around the corner and through the door to the back. She had expected an office but was surprised to discover three long tables covered in pieces of wood of various colors and grains, woodworking tools, strings, tuning pegs, and ukuleles in various stages of completion. Long, thin strips of wood soaked in a deep utility sink filled with water near the entrance. On a nearby table, a piece of wood of similar size and shape had been molded around the sides of an unfinished ukulele, held in place with small clamps and giving off the faint odor of glue. Bulletin boards, posters of surfers and musicians, and metal shelves stocked with boxes lined the walls. Two small windows flanked an outside door and a stairwell. The smell of sawdust tickled Bonnie's nostrils and she pressed the back of her hand to her nose to keep from sneezing.

"Did you make these yourself?" she asked, admiring a beautiful ukulele made of koa wood and ivory on a nearby table, finished except for the strings.

"Some of them," he said, nodding to the one she had admired as well as a few other finished instruments on a table near the entrance to the shop. "Some are my students' work."

Bonnie was impressed in spite of herself. "You teach people how to make ukuleles as well as how to play them?"

"Of course. Knowledge is meant to be passed on, not hoarded. When musicians make their own ukuleles, they treasure them more than any other instrument." Hinano picked up a fingerboard, blew off a bit of sawdust, and held it close to his eye to examine the frets. "The instrument becomes a part of them."

"Does it also help them to play better if they use an instrument they've made themselves?"

"Sometimes. Most of my students are experienced ukulele players who want something unique they can't buy in a store. Others are serious musicians who decide to learn to make a ukulele so that they can better understand how the sound is produced." Hinano smiled ruefully and returned the fingerboard to the table. "I do get the occasional woodworker who can't play a note on the first day of class but expects to be ready to play at their neighbor's luau when their ukulele is finished. I hate to see them so disappointed, but what do they expect? You don't learn to become a master chef by eating at five-star restaurants. You have to train and you have to practice."

Bonnie smiled knowingly. "But I'm sure you offer to help these disappointed students by enrolling them in your music lessons."

Hinano laughed. "Hey, you've been checking up on me."

"No, I just figure you're a shrewd businessman."

Hinano mulled over the compliment as if not sure whether it was one. "Shrewd. I guess that's better than some of the other things you could have called me."

"About Halloween—"

He held up a hand. "You don't have to say a word. My auntie already let me have it."

"She did?"

"Oh, yeah. Told me she was ashamed of me and that if I can't speak nicely to her friends I'm not allowed to speak to them at all. She also banned me from the family Thanksgiving dinner but Kai convinced her to give me another chance."

"I had no idea," Bonnie said. "I didn't ask her to intervene."

"I figured that. But in any case . . . I'm sorry."

Bonnie was so pleased to learn that Midori had referred to her as a friend that she was almost willing to let it go.

Almost.

"Apology accepted," Bonnie said. "However, there's something more I'm sure your aunt didn't mention."

Hinano winced and folded his arms across his chest. "Okay. Let me have it."

"I had freely admitted that I knew nothing about Hawaiian royalty," Bonnie said. "Obviously I said the wrong thing, and I'm sorry that my ignorance offended you, but it was unfair of you to make that snide remark and stalk away from the table. I wouldn't have done that in your place if you had unknowingly said something offensive about—about Pennsylvania history or quilting."

Hinano frowned, considering her words. "Actually, I know more about quilting than you might think."

Bonnie remembered that he had designed beautiful quilt patterns for his aunt, but his attempt to distract her sparked her temper. "Fine. The point is, by being a jerk, you missed an opportunity to teach me about something that's clearly important to you. It's not fair for you to be indignant about mainlanders' ignorance about Hawaiian issues, and yet also be unwilling to enlighten us. Knowledge is meant to be passed on, not hoarded, remember? Or does that apply only to music? Maybe it's easier to dismiss mainlanders as hopelessly prejudiced instead of having to make a genuine effort to explain your point of view. Maybe you'd rather just stay angry."

"I have good reason to be angry. I'm sure Aunt Midori's told you everything."

"She's told me nothing except that you're an expert on Hawaiian culture and you have a temper," said Bonnie, exasperated. "I've seen enough to know that she's right on both counts. But she also hinted that you're worth getting to know despite your irritating, off-putting manner, and I have yet to see much evidence of that."

His eyebrows rose. "She called me irritating and off-putting?"

Bonnie tried to recall the exact phrase. "Maybe not in so many words, but that was the general idea."

"Man." Hinano shook his head. "I thought I was her favorite nephew."

"Maybe you are," Bonnie shot back. "Maybe your cousins are ten times worse, in which case I hope I never meet them."

Hinano stared at her for a long moment before bursting into laughter. "Don't worry," he said. "I'm by far the worst."

Bonnie folded her arms. "This isn't funny."

"You're right." Hinano struggled to keep a straight face. "It's not funny at all. You know, you have a strange way of accepting apologies. Usually when I admit I was wrong, I don't get yelled at for it."

"I find it hard to believe you admit you're wrong often enough to be able to make that judgment," said Bonnie, deliberately lowering her voice. "Maybe on those rare occasions, people don't yell at you because they're speechless from shock."

Hinano's shoulders shook from suppressed laughter. "Stop it, snowbird, or I'm gonna bust a gut."

Bonnie scowled at him while he struggled to compose himself, feeling more foolish with every passing second. She had not intended to scold him. She had not even intended to come to see him. How ridiculous he must think her, in her running shoes and sweaty workout clothes, flushed with anger and exercise, prissily upbraiding him like an old schoolmarm.

"I should go," she said, deflated.

But when she turned around, Hinano caught her by the arm. "Wait," he said. "I didn't mean to laugh at you any more than you meant to go off on me. Want some coffee? Offer's still good."

Bonnie glanced around but saw only woodworking tools, shelves of supplies, and a small desk with an old computer, printer, and reams of paper. No coffeepot was in sight, nor did she smell any brewing. "Is this another joke?"

"Coffee's upstairs," he said. "Have a seat, relax, and I'll bring some down. I can't let you go back to the Hale Kapa Kuiki this upset or Aunt Midori will banish me from Thanksgiving *and* Christmas for the next decade."

He steered her to a stool and all but pushed her onto it. He ordered her not to move, promised to be back shortly, and disappeared up the stairs in the back. She heard faint footsteps fading, then silence except for a delivery truck passing outside.

She waited and considered sneaking away, but regretfully dismissed that idea when she realized she would then have to apologize to him the next time they met. Someone had to break the cycle of apologies. She sighed, rose, and wandered around the workshop, admiring the instruments in progress and trying to picture Hinano at the front of a classroom. Surely he didn't belittle his students or storm from the room if one of them made an innocent, foolish remark or he would have gone out of business long ago. The Hinano that Midori claimed lay beneath the prickly exterior, the Hinano she had glimpsed on that awful day when Darren Taylor phoned with the detective's report—that must be the Hinano who made such beautiful instruments and music and who taught others to do the same.

She turned around quickly when Hinano suddenly reappeared with two mugs of coffee in one hand and a pint carton of 2 percent milk and two red plastic stirrers in the other. "Maui coffee," he said, handing her a mug. He dug a few paper sugar packets from his pocket and tossed them on the closest table. "Best coffee in the world."

Though tempted to goad him about his obvious bias, she thanked him for the coffee, stirred in a packet of sugar, and took a self-conscious sip. His hands had brushed hers as he handed her the mug, and his palms and fingertips were callused from ukulele strings and woodworking, or so she guessed. She had calluses of her own from years of needle scrapes and pinpricks. Even those things she loved best in the world had left her with scars.

"So," Bonnie said, floundering for something benign to talk about, "I guess you have a staff lounge upstairs?"

"No," he replied, amused. "We're not that big of an operation. That's my apartment."

"Oh." She thought of Grandma's Attic, and how once upon a time her morning commute had consisted of descending a back staircase from her family's third floor condo to her beloved quilt shop. "I used to live above my store, too."

"Yeah, you mentioned that. Until your husband locked you out, and you stayed with a friend, and you finally had to agree to sell the place . . ."

As Hinano's voice trailed away, she realized that he knew much more about her than she knew about him. Somehow this seemed to give him an advantage. "What about you?" she asked.

He took a slow drink of coffee. "What *about* me?"

She gestured, glancing up at the ceiling to indicate the apartment above. "Do you live alone?"

"When Kai's not home from school, yeah."

She could see he was determined to be as reticent as possible. "Divorced?"

"Widowed. Or is it widowered?" He frowned and shook his head. "My wife passed away almost ten years ago."

Her irritation vanished. "Oh, Hinano. I'm sorry."

He studied her quizzically. "My aunt didn't mention any of this?"

Bonnie shook her head at him in feigned bewilderment. "You seem to be under the impression that we sit around chatting about you all day. I'm sorry to bruise your ego but that's simply not the case."

Hinano laughed and slapped his palm to his chest. "Ouch! The truth hurts."

"Sorry."

"You don't sound sorry."

She was, if not in the way he meant. "I am."

He shrugged and looked away, managing a hard smile. "They say life goes on."

"What do 'they' know?" she scoffed. "'They' always have opinions and sometimes I think 'they' ought to just shut up."

"I couldn't agree more." Hinano raised his coffee mug in salute, and after a moment's hesitation, she clinked her mug against his. "If one more person tells me that Nani is in a better place now, I might punch them."

"If one more person tells me how much better off I am without my soon-to-be ex-husband, I'll scream."

"At last. Common ground," said Hinano dryly.

"You might find we have more than that in common if you forget for ten minutes that I'm an ignorant mainlander and treat me like a human being."

"All right." Hinano drained the last of his coffee, set the mug on the table, and folded his arms over his chest. "That's fair enough. Does this mean you want another lesson in Hawaiian history?"

"Yes. I'd like that." She set her mug, still half-full, beside his. "But not now. I have to get back to the inn."

He glanced at the clock on the wall above the computer desk. "And I should probably open the store sooner or later."

She smiled and thanked him for the coffee. He accompanied her back into the store, flipping on the lights as they went and unlocking the front door. "We'll talk," he said as she left. "We'll set up a date for history class soon."

Bonnie agreed and hurried off, quickening her pace at the thought of Midori preparing and serving breakfast on her own.

Later, after the guests had eaten and Bonnie had helped

Midori tidy up, she mentioned that she had seen Hinano that morning on her walk. "Is that why you were so late?" inquired Midori, stacking plates in the cupboard. "My nephew talked your ear off and you couldn't sneak away?"

"Quite the opposite," said Bonnie, rinsing a dishcloth in the sink and wringing it out. "He says very little about himself, at least to me. He seems to think that you've told me all about him, though."

Midori snorted. "Because we have nothing better to discuss. Men. Honestly."

"He told me that he lost his wife ten years ago."

Midori paused before shutting the cupboard. "Yes." She brushed crumbs from a plate into the trash and opened the dishwasher. "It was sad. Very sad. Hinano lost the love of his life and Kai lost his mother. He was only eleven years old."

"What happened?" Quickly Bonnie added, "I know it's not really any of my business."

For a moment, Midori seemed engrossed in loading the dishwasher. "That's Hinano's story to tell."

"Maybe he hopes you'll tell me so he doesn't have to." When Midori shot her a skeptical look, Bonnie added, "He always seems surprised that you haven't told me everything about him."

Midori frowned and shook her head. "So much of their sorrow was exposed to the public, it's no wonder he assumes everyone knows."

"What happened?" asked Bonnie again, curiosity giving way to concern.

"Some say it was an accident, some say it was murder."

"What?"

"Nani was very active in the Hawaiian independence movement," Midori explained. "Back then, Hinano was more ambivalent about sovereignty than he is today. He always cared about preserving Hawaiian culture, of course, but thoughts of Hawaii seceding from the union or reinstating the monarchy were simply inconceivable to him." She fell silent, reflecting. "It's really the only thing I can recall them arguing about."

"Hinano's wife—Nani—she believed Hawaii should leave the United States?"

Midori shook her head. "Nani didn't believe that was a practical goal. She wanted reparations for stolen lands, government support to the preservation of native culture, and a formal apology from the United States government—and as a botanist, she also wanted a strong federal commitment to protect the islands' native ecology."

"None of that sounds unreasonable," said Bonnie, although she wasn't sure it was realistic. As far as she knew, the United States didn't customarily go out of its way to make reparations to indigenous peoples, even when it did issue an official apology.

"Nani also didn't want reparations limited to native Hawaiians alone, but to the descendants of all people of all ethnicities who had pledged their loyalty to the Kingdom of Hawaii before the overthrow—Hawaiian, Asian, and European alike," Midori continued. "This put her at odds with others who believed only native Hawaiians deserved compensation. You have to understand, the Hawaiian sovereignty movement was and still is fractured. Different people with different ideas of what is right and what should be done, sometimes so busy arguing among themselves that little good is accomplished."

"I gather that Nani made enemies."

"It would have been impossible not to make a few, even for someone less outspoken than Nani. But even so, she was well regarded by all sides. She was educated and passionate, and she knew how to speak so that even people who disagreed with her would listen." She smiled faintly. "She was as diplomatic as Hinano is abrasive."

"He's not that bad," said Bonnie.

"Nani knew that unless the different factions could unite, or at least cooperate, they would never make any real progress." Midori closed the dishwasher and took a seat on one of the stools at the center island. "She met with leaders of various groups to help them find common ground, certain principles that they could all stand behind. She hoped that if they could achieve even one small goal by working together, they would see the wisdom in putting aside their differences and forming a lasting alliance."

Bonnie leaned back against the counter. "Did she have any success?"

"She did." Midori nudged the koa wood cutting board out of the way and rested her elbows on the island's marble surface. "She organized a May Day parade on Oahu. Representatives from community, social, and political groups marched from a park in downtown Honolulu to the 'Iolani Palace, where their leaders made speeches about Hawaiian unity. Though they marched under different banners and shouted different slogans along the way, the mood was positive, and for a while it seemed as if Nani had achieved her goal of unifying a very divided movement."

"For a while?"

"For a few hours." Midori sighed and shook her head, reluctant to continue. "The march itself was peaceful and the first few speeches went off without a hitch. But then a radical group got it into their heads that they should overtake the palace and declare one of the descendants of the last elected monarch king."

"Oh, no."

"I was watching Kai on a school playground nearby when the chaos broke out." Midori inhaled deeply, her gaze far away. "I couldn't see Nani and Hinano—they were going to meet us at the playground afterward. I saw the police come in riot gear, people screaming and running— I didn't know what else to do. I grabbed Kai's hand and ran, ran away until we left the screams and sirens behind."

Bonnie pressed a hand to her mouth, horrified. "What happened to Nani and Hinano?"

"Hours passed with no word. I managed to get us a ride back to their house—they lived near the university then. We waited and waited, afraid to call anyone in case Hinano and Nani called us. It was different in those days. Now everyone has a cell phone, but back then you had to wait by the phone, and hope and pray."

Bonnie sank onto a stool. "Did they finally make it home?"

Midori shook her head. "Hinano finally called from the hospital. It was evening and Kai was already asleep in bed." She took a deep, shaky breath. "Hinano and Nani had been separated in the riot. Hinano searched frantically for her, trying to figure out where she might have gone when the crowd tore her from his side. Then he spotted a single island of stillness in the flood of rushing people and he knew she must be at the center of it. He hoped that she was restoring calm, but his heart was full of dread."

"Was she there?" Bonnie asked, afraid of what Midori might say next. "Had he found her?"

Midori nodded. "Those few people weren't moving because they had gathered around Nani where she had fallen to protect her from the riot. Hinano heard them shouting for an ambulance as he struggled to reach them. Finally he made his

way through the crowd and found her, unconscious and bleed-
ing on the grass."

"Oh, my God."

"It took more than an hour to get her to the hospital because
of the upheaval. Nani had been struck over the head—with a
sign or something, we never found out what. A blunt instrument, the police said. She never regained consciousness."

The horrifying scene was all too vivid. Bonnie closed her
eyes and shook her head, but she could still see the nightmare
playing out.

She blinked away tears, heart aching for the young family,
divided so cruelly.

Brooding, Midori traced a pattern of dark threads in the
marble countertop. "My nephew will never forgive himself for
those ten minutes they were separated."

"What could he have done?" asked Bonnie. "In all that confusion, even if he had been right beside her, how could he have
prevented such a terrible accident?"

"Terrible, yes. Accident . . ." Midori pursed her lips, thinking. "That's the question that haunts us. Hinano especially."

"You don't think it was a deliberate attack?"

"I think I'll never know for certain."

Bonnie shook her head, imagining the violence swirling
around Hinano and his wife on that terrible day, a day of such
hope and promise turned tragically wrong. "Anything could
have happened in all that mayhem. It's a wonder more people
weren't hurt."

She had meant that in all likelihood Nani's death was indeed a tragic accident, but Midori pounced. "Exactly. Anything could have happened. The riot was a perfect cover for a
deliberate killing. An assassination. And yes, it's quite remarkable that except for minor bumps and bruises, no one else was

injured that day. No one was injured or killed except for the woman who had brought all those feuding groups together and could have eventually united them as one. Together they would have been powerful, *too* powerful to suit those who benefited from the ongoing strife in the sovereignty movement."

Bonnie studied her, uncertain. "Then you and Hinano believe Nani was murdered to keep the Hawaiian independence movement fractured?"

"We have no proof." Midori lifted her hands and let them fall to her lap, a gesture that suggested years of fruitless searching. "The police never found a weapon or had any description of it other than 'blunt instrument,' and no suspects were ever named or questioned except for the leaders of the different groups invited to participate in the unity celebration."

Perplexed, Bonnie asked, "No one investigated opponents of Hawaiian sovereignty? Those would have been Nani's real political enemies, wouldn't they?"

Midori jabbed a finger in the air. "Ah, but they weren't anywhere near the 'Iolani Palace grounds that day, were they? They had no reason to attend that march and hear those speeches. Therefore it must have been a tragic accident, the outcome of a mob out of control, or a terrible crime committed by a rival faction."

"But it doesn't sound like Nani led a faction. She worked on behalf of all."

"Unless you count the biology department at the University of Hawaii, you're right, Nani had no faction of her own." Midori laughed, short and bitter. "You know how dangerous those botanists can be when they want to protect native plants from invasive species."

"How can a woman be killed under such questionable circumstances and no one investigates her political enemies?"

Bonnie asked. "Where's the public outcry? Doesn't anyone care?"

"Her friends fought as hard as they could," said Midori. "Hinano kept on long after everyone else had given up. But when a death takes place within a crowd of thousands and no one sees anything, there's little any single man can do."

"His wife brutally killed, no justice, no resolution—how could he bear it?"

"He had a son to live for," Midori said. "What choice did he have? He could keep fighting and fighting and getting no-where, or he could devote himself to raising his son and try to move on."

Bonnie might have made the same choice in Hinano's place. Kai seemed like a fine young man—bright, confident, cheerful. She never would have guessed he had grown up in the shadow of such grief. "Hinano's done well by his son. It couldn't have been easy to raise Kai on his own."

"Kai is a wonderful boy," said Midori proudly. "But Hinano hasn't raised him alone. Our *ohana*, our family, has always been there to help him. Kai lost his mother and there is no making up for that, but he still grew up surrounded by love."

"He should have had his mother, too."

"Hinano would be the first to agree with you."

They fell silent. Bonnie pondered Midori's tale, imagining a grief-stricken father raising his son after his beloved wife was so cruelly taken from them. It was little wonder he had become angry and defensive, mistrustful of outsiders. The real wonder was that he was not more so.

"As you've learned, Hinano adopted Nani's cause as his own," Midori said, breaking the silence. "How could he not, after she had died for it? He won't give up on the hope of ob-taining some measure of sovereignty for his nation and justice for his people, the justice that was denied his wife." Midori sighed, rose, and carried the koa wood cutting board to the sink, where slowly, methodically, she washed it. "I doubt he will ever trust the government to do right by the people. It's sad. He served his country proudly for many years, but when the time came that he needed them, they let him down. He knows the name of everyone who played even the smallest part in preventing a full investigation into Nani's death. I doubt he will ever forget those names, nor will he ever forgive."

Bonnie thought of the burden of anger and grief Hinano had carried for so many years, and her heart went out to him.

Chapter Eight

———— ⚜ ————

Once persuaded to advertise their teaching positions, Claire worked quickly to design an attractive, appealing banner ad that would soon appear on the home pages of several quilting magazine websites as well as other popular quilting sites. A few other applications had arrived by mail thanks to Sylvia's referrals, and two or three of them seemed quite promising. This hopeful turn of fortune gave Bonnie much to be thankful for during the fourth week of November, which made the thought of spending Thanksgiving without her children or grandchildren a little easier to bear.

The Hale Kapa Kuiki was not quite filled to capacity for the Thanksgiving holiday weekend, but it was nearly so, with more guests than they had hosted since Halloween. After helping Midori serve their guests a special Thanksgiving breakfast that included pumpkin muffins, pineapple pecan bread, and savory turkey omelets, Bonnie returned to her room to call her family and wish them a happy Thanksgiving. Because of the time difference their celebrations would already be under way, so after calling her mother at her retirement community in Erie, Bonnie planned to call her mother-in-law in Scranton, where her children and grandchildren were attending the traditional family gathering.

She had always liked her mother-in-law, but she felt a flutter of trepidation as she wrapped up her first call and prepared herself for the second. She had not spoken with Linda since the divorce proceedings had begun. As the contentious rift between Craig and Bonnie had widened, Bonnie had felt increasingly anxious and uncertain as she pondered the inevitable changes to her relationships with her soon-to-be-former in-laws. Would Linda now hate her as much as she had once loved her? Was it inappropriate to call until the divorce was resolved or until she received Craig's permission? Her stomach churned at the thought of calling him to humbly ask if she could speak to people she had considered family for nearly thirty years. And what if he forbade it?

She could wait until later that night after her children returned to their own homes, or she could call their cell phones. But she knew Tammy's cell phone would be tucked into a pocket of the diaper bag, the ring muffled and inaudible in the din. Barry never had service in the Scranton area, and C.J. was so often harassed with after-hours calls from work that he refused to switch on his cell phone on holidays. Bonnie's only reasonable options were to call the Markham home or not speak to her children and grandchildren on Thanksgiving, and she couldn't bear to do that. After much hesitation, she dialed her mother-in-law's number.

Her sister-in-law picked up, and they spent a few moments engaged in awkward small talk before Linda finished setting out pies for dessert and came to the phone. "Bonnie, dear," she greeted her. "How are you? What time is it where you are?"

The unbridled warmth in her voice brought tears to Bonnie's eyes. "It's only ten in the morning here," she said. "The sun's shining, the sky is blue, just another beautiful day in paradise."

Linda insisted Bonnie tell her all about it, and so Bonnie gave her the highlights of her adventures in Hawaii without revealing too many details that Linda might inadvertently pass on to Craig, enabling him to figure out her exact location. Linda sounded genuinely happy for her, which Bonnie had not expected, and a little wistful, which she had.

"I don't suppose you want to talk to Craig?" Linda said when Bonnie finished her travelogue.

"I'm sorry, but I think it's best if I don't."

"I understand." Linda hesitated. "Well, Bonnie, it was sure nice talking to you. Please don't be a stranger. I've thought of you as a daughter all these many years and I can't just switch that off. You might have divorced Craig, but you didn't divorce me."

Throat constricting, Bonnie promised to remember that, and she asked to speak to C.J.

"Oh, here's Tammy," Linda said brightly, and handed off the phone.

"Hi, Mom," said Tammy. "Happy Thanksgiving."

"Happy Thanksgiving to you too." It was so wonderful to hear her daughter's voice. "How's the baby?"

They chatted happily on that subject for a good fifteen minutes, the voices and clamor of the family in the background sometimes drowning out Tammy's words. Bonnie was telling Tammy about her plans to celebrate Thanksgiving at a luau at the home of Midori's eldest daughter when the baby began to fuss. "You have your hands full," said Bonnie, laughing. "Why don't you put C.J. on?"

"Didn't Grandma tell you?"

"Tell me what?"

"C.J. isn't here. They're spending Thanksgiving with Julie's family."

"But I thought this was the Markhams' year for Thanksgiving." C.J. and his wife alternated their holiday plans: One year they spent Thanksgiving with the Markhams and Christmas with Julie's family, and the next year they switched. "Did something come up? Will they spend Christmas in Scranton instead? That would make Grandma Markham happy. You know how much she enjoys seeing everyone around the tree on Christmas morning."

Tammy hesitated. "Well, no, C.J. said he was thinking of spending Christmas in Hawaii with you."

"I'd love that, but I still don't understand why he changed his Thanksgiving plans. Is it because I'm not there?" Despite Linda's friendliness, it would have been awkward for Bonnie to show up for Thanksgiving dinner with the divorce in such a contentious state. It was impossible to believe that her relationship with Craig would ever again be cordial enough for Bonnie to consider celebrating holidays with the Markham family. Claire's invitation to spend the winter in Hawaii had spared Bonnie the difficult and painful task of asking the children to decide between spending the holidays with their mother or their father. Next year she would not be able to avoid it.

The background voices faded, as if Tammy had carried the cordless phone into a secluded room. "C.J. didn't stay away because you *aren't* here," she said, "but because Dad *is* here."

"You mean they still haven't made up?"

"Mom, you have no idea. For the past month, things have been getting worse and worse between them. A few days ago C.J. told Grandma that he was very sorry to miss seeing her on Thanksgiving, but he can't be under the same roof as his father."

"He shouldn't have told Grandma that," said Bonnie, dismayed. "He could have come up with some other excuse without stretching the truth too much."

"I know. Nice of him to drag Grandma into the middle of the conflict." Tammy sighed. "He's your staunchest defender, Mom, and he's determined to make everyone in the family see Dad as the villain."

"Well," said Bonnie carefully, "he is the villain, sweetie. He had an affair. He emptied our joint bank account and opened another in his own name. He hid assets from me. He changed the locks when I was away from home."

"I know, Mom, I know. If Jason ever did to me what Dad did to you, I don't think I could stay with him either. But deep down, I know Dad isn't a bad person. He's just going through a midlife crisis or something."

Bonnie had read the books and advice columns and knew it was harmful for divorcing parents to criticize the estranged spouse in front of the children. Even so, she could not bear for her daughter to think that she and Craig were equally complicit in the failure of their marriage. "The simple truth is that your father has done some very bad things. I know you love him and you don't want anyone to speak ill of him, but please don't ignore the facts out of loyalty. That's not fair."

"I won't." Tammy's voice was subdued. "I know you never wanted things to turn out this way. But neither did he."

Bonnie was past caring what Craig wanted. "Then he should have made different choices along the way, wouldn't you agree?"

"He messed up. I won't deny it." The noise of conversation and laughter resumed, as if Tammy had rejoined the party.

"Last time I saw Barry, he was in the backyard playing football with the cousins. I'll find him and put him on."

"Thanks, sweetie. Happy Thanksgiving. Aloha!"

Tammy laughed. "Aloha to you too, Mom."

Bonnie stayed on the line while Tammy sought out her younger brother, the sounds of the gathering rising and falling in the background. Then Bonnie heard a low voice rise above the other voices, and Tammy's reply, and then a jumble of rustling and scraping as someone grabbed the phone.

"What the hell kind of stunt was that?" Craig barked in her ear. "You're sending spies after me now?"

As the sounds of the party swiftly faded, Bonnie imagined Craig striding down the long hallway toward the rear of the house, phone clenched in his fist. "Craig, give the phone back to Tammy."

"Isn't it bad enough that you ruined my life, but you have to ruin Terri's too? Her ex-husband could use this to screw up her custody of their kids."

"I didn't ruin your life or hers," Bonnie snapped, voice shaking. "You and Terri brought this upon yourselves."

"If you think you can blackmail me into giving up what's rightfully mine, you've got a lot to learn. I earned that money. It's mine. And who the hell do you think you are, calling my mother's house on Thanksgiving?"

"I only wanted to speak to the kids. Please just give the phone to Barry."

"Why should I? Why should I let you speak to him when you won't let C.J. speak to me?"

"I have nothing to do with that. I never told C.J.—"

"You forget who you're talking to. I know you better than you know yourself, Bonnie. You think you can keep my first-born son away from me, you think you can force me and Terri apart, but you're wrong, and if you don't stop it, you're going to be very sorry. I can play hardball too—"

Quickly Bonnie hung up the phone, heart pounding. Such venom in his voice, such outrage. She never should have called his mother's home. It had been so refreshing to chat with Linda, to clear the air—but the cost was too high. Her heart was racing, her head spinning, her breath catching in her throat. She had not realized how safe and secure she felt having no direct contact with Craig until she heard his voice.

It was the way it had to be. No contact, except through their lawyers. Craig had upset her too much, had sent her emotions spinning in a kaleidoscope of confusion and pain with a single conversation. She could not give him such control over her. Until she knew she could face him with complete indifference, she must avoid all places and situations where she might encounter him, whether in person or over the phone.

She would not make that mistake again.

❖

Soberly Bonnie dressed for the luau and tried to put the upsetting conflict out of her mind. Never before had she been so thankful for the continent and ocean separating her from Craig. After the holiday weekend, she would have to contact Darren Taylor and tell him about the incident. She wasn't afraid of Craig, not exactly, if only because he had never laid a hand on her. He had hurled insults at her before, words as caustic as acid, but this time there was a different note in his voice. He sounded like a man who had lost nearly everything and was determined to hold on to the little he had left.

She said nothing of Craig's outburst as Eric drove her, Claire, and Midori to the home of Midori's eldest daughter,

Keilana, in the town of Kuau on Maui's north shore. The house Keilana shared with her husband and three children was a single story, but raised up on stilts to a second-floor height with room to park cars beneath. A shaded lanai wrapped around the house, and upon it adults and children alike talked, laughed, and enjoyed what was surely a wonderful view of the ocean, just across the busy highway behind a row of beachfront houses on long, narrow lots. Cars lined both sides of the street, so Eric parked on the ocean side some distance away. Even from there Bonnie heard music coming from the backyard—ukulele and guitar, and a woman singing. Carrying the pineapple upside-down cake Midori had baked, she followed her friends up the gravel driveway, breaking into a smile at the sight of the festivities already under way in the yard—clusters of adults chatting and laughing, children darting about engrossed in play, men and women arranging picnic tables into a long row and covering them with tablecloths, a few musicians taking instruments from cases on the lanai. She thought she might find Hinano among them—Midori had told her that he and Kai would attend the party—but he was not yet there.

She soon discovered that Midori's *ohana* included friends and neighbors as well as actual relatives, for the party quickly grew until it was nearly as large as the group that had celebrated Halloween at the Hale Kapa Kuiki. Bonnie had never been among such a friendly, cheerful gathering of such extraordinary diversity—different races, every age from infant to elderly, different accents, shapes, and sizes—everyone mixing and mingling and getting along better than most real families did.

It was almost time for the main feast to begin when she finally bumped into Hinano. "Hey, snowbird," he greeted her, raising his beer bottle to her in salute. "What do you think of your first Hawaiian Thanksgiving?"

"It's wonderful." Everyone had welcomed her so warmly, as if she were a long-lost member of the extended *ohana*. "I'm surprised you're not up there with the band."

"Eh, we take turns. It's nothing formal. When Denis gets tired, I'll probably take over for him."

A sudden stir in a back corner of the yard caught their attention. "You don't want to miss this," Hinano said, taking her by the elbow and guiding her through the crowd. "They're opening the *imu* and bringing out the pig and the turkeys."

From her visit to the Old Lahaina Lu'au Bonnie knew that an *imu* was an underground oven, but she was still surprised. "You mean they cook the turkeys in there, too? Can you do that?"

"Of course," he said, amused. "It's a hole in the ground. The technology's not that specialized. You can *kalua* just about anything, and it taste so good it break da mout."

As she puzzled out his last words, Hinano grinned at her bewilderment and brought her closer to the *imu*, where three large Hawaiian men were shoveling aside a thick layer of loose sand to reveal what appeared to be a thick covering of kapa cloth, woven mats, and burlap bags. The men carefully lifted the covering without spilling any sand into the pit below, releasing a gust of steam and the most delicious, mouth-watering aroma Bonnie had ever savored.

Others came forward then to help lift the cooked meats wrapped in blackened *ti* and banana leaves from the pit and carry them off to the serving tables. "The meat'll fall off the bone," Hinano promised. "Just wait till you taste it. This will be the best meal you've ever had. Make sure you take a bit of everything."

Eyeing the impressive spread, Bonnie didn't think it would be possible to take even a single spoonful of everything. As she passed through the buffet line, she gave in to other guests' urging to pile her plate high. "You have to start eating like a Hawaiian," one man told her, "and at a luau, we don't just eat until we're full or stuffed, but until we can barely move!"

Balancing her plate, a glass of wine, and utensils wrapped in a napkin, Bonnie spotted Claire and Eric sitting on a blanket spread on the grass on the other side of the yard. When Claire waved frantically for her to join them, she made her way to them, realizing only after she sat down that Hinano had not followed her. She extinguished a flash of disappointment and quickly launched into a reminiscence of a long-ago Thanksgiving at Penn State, when she and Claire had tried to cook a Thanksgiving feast in the dorm for all of their friends who had remained on campus for the holiday rather than miss the football game against Notre Dame. They lost the game and burned the frozen pumpkin pie so badly that smoke billowed throughout the entire floor, setting their Resident Assistant into a panic and prompting an official, campus-wide investigation into the failure of the smoke detectors. Some people might have considered that a holiday disaster, but it had become one of Bonnie and Claire's favorite memories of Penn State.

Bonnie savored every delicious morsel of pork and turkey, cornbread and sausage stuffing, taro and poi, and a surprising number of side dishes made with Spam, macaroni, or both. "I don't think I could eat like a Hawaiian every day," Bonnie told Claire and Eric, groaning, when she had finally eaten her fill. She lay back on the blanket the couple had spread out, propped herself up on her elbows, and considered defying social conventions and unbuttoning her slacks for greater comfort.

"Not even Hawaiians eat like Hawaiians every day," remarked Eric, taking another bite of succulent pork and licking his fingertips.

Bonnie smiled and let her gaze wander, taking in the festive scene, so unlike any other Thanksgiving she had ever celebrated. She spotted Hinano at a table on the lanai, still eating and engaged in animated conversation with Kai and a few other men. He seemed completely engrossed in the moment and the pleasure of his friends' company, and when he threw back his head and laughed, Bonnie also saw no trace of the grief Midori had described. But looking around, Bonnie understood what Midori had meant when she had said Hinano had not been forced to raise Kai alone. Surrounded by their family and the many friends considered *ohana*, he had not been truly alone. And yet it was not the same, not complete. It never could have been.

When Bonnie offered to clear away their dishes, Eric and Claire, who were as full as she was, made only token protests as they handed her their plates and stretched out on the blanket. Hinano and Kai had joined the band, filling the yard with such lovely music that Bonnie's heart ached to listen. On her way back to her friends, she passed a few of the women from the Laulima quilt guild. They seemed delighted to see her and invited her to sit down, so she did, and happily joined in their lively debate about the best needles to use for appliqué. Bonnie had tried nearly every manufacturer's best varieties at every Quilt Market trade show for more than a decade, so she had much to share. She hardly noticed the passing of time as the discussion turned to preferred threads and favorite fabric designers, until one of her new friends put on a sweater and she noticed Midori's son-in-law making his way around the lanai and the yard lighting tiki torches.

The air had grown much cooler with the approach of

evening, so Bonnie excused herself and went to retrieve her sweater, which she had left in the car. Carrying Eric's keys, she made her way down the street alone, humming along to the music and contemplating dessert.

She was on her way back when she spied Hinano walking down the gravel driveway. "Hey, snowbird," he said. "Flying off early?"

Bonnie had to laugh. It was almost twilight, hardly early; they had been eating and celebrating for hours. "I went to the car for my sweater," she said. "I don't think anyone's ready to leave just yet."

Hinano nodded and fell in step beside her as she walked back to the house. "Can't leave without dessert. You'll insult all those aunties and grandmas who've been cooking for days."

"How did you know I haven't had dessert yet?"

Hinano barely hesitated. "No crumbs on your shirt."

Amused, she realized he had been watching her. "I think I know how to eat a piece of pie without making a mess of myself. I'm not four years old."

"Lucky guess, then." He jerked his head toward the buffet tables, where the empty platters from the luau feast had been replaced with cake plates and pie pans with tempting treats of every variety. "Come on. I know who baked what and I can advise you."

She pretended to consider it. "All right, but I must insist upon Maui coffee with my dessert—only Maui coffee."

Hinano grinned and waved an arm gallantly to allow her to precede him. She followed the example of others ahead of her in line and took tiny pieces of three different treats—a narrow slice of pineapple pecan pie, a piece of something that looked like white custard that Hinano said would taste like coconut pudding, and of course, a thin slice of Midori's pineapple upside-down cake.

After they found seats on the lanai, Hinano disappeared for a few moments and returned with two cups of coffee. One sip told Bonnie he had fixed hers exactly the way she liked it—black with two sugars—although she had not told him her preferences. He must have been paying attention when they'd had coffee together.

"How are you doing with that list I gave you?" Hinano asked as he sat down beside her.

"I'm about a third of the way through it," Bonnie replied. "So far I've only seen the sites and events in Lahaina, places I can walk to from the Hale Kapa Kuiki. It's harder to get farther afield."

"I hadn't thought of that." He took a bite of chocolate brownie. "I can drive you if you want."

She hadn't meant to hint that he should offer her a ride. "That's not the problem. Claire would let me borrow her car. It's just difficult to get away because we're so busy at the inn and trying to get Aloha Quilt Camp off the ground."

"I see." He sipped his coffee. "Well, the offer stands if you change your mind. I'll try to think of a few other places you should add to that list too."

Bonnie thanked him and they fell silent, listening to the music. Kai was leading some of his young cousins in a rousing, rather aggressive tune that sounded vaguely familiar, although Bonnie was sure she had never heard it played on ukulele and slack-key guitar before.

"Metallica," said Hinano, noting her scrutiny. "Kai likes to push the boundaries of the traditional ukulele repertoire."

"I wonder where he gets that from," teased Bonnie.

"His mother," said Hinano absently, his eyes on his son.

"I was going to say from you," said Bonnie, surprised. "The first time I came to your music store, you were playing a Beatles song on your ukulele."

He looked away from Kai to smile at her, eyebrows raised. "You remember that?"

"Well, yes." Bonnie felt strangely embarrassed. "It's not every day you hear the Beatles on the ukulele."

His brow furrowed. "Yeah it is."

"Maybe for you," said Bonnie. "Not for normal people."

His laugh, rich and booming, earned them glances of amused curiosity from the *ohana* sitting nearby. "Snowbird, around here, I'm the normal one. You're the—"

"I know. I'm the *haole*."

He winced. "You know that's not a compliment, right?"

"I know."

"I never called you *haole*."

"I know that, too." He had referred to rich *haole* on Halloween, but he had not meant her. A teenager had shouted the word at her a few days after her arrival, when she had carelessly stepped into the path of his bicycle while crossing the street. She had heard it a few times since, only occasionally directed at her. "I think it's a bit racist, actually."

"If you knew the history, you might not think so. Are you trying to start another fight?"

"Not really." They did seem to debate more than converse. Then again, she sometimes disagreed with the Elm Creek Quilters and their friendship was an unbreakable bond. In contrast, she had rarely argued with Craig until his first cyber-affair, and look how that had turned out. Still, she didn't feel like arguing at the moment. "I'm sure you could make a good case for why it's okay to call white people a derogatory label, but you won't change my mind."

"Then I won't try." He finished his brownie and started in on his second dessert. As a good nephew, he too had chosen a piece of his aunt's pineapple upside-down cake. "I kind of agree with you, but don't tell anyone."

"Your secret is safe with me."

They fell silent again, listening to the band play a more traditional Hawaiian song. Afterward, Kai handed the ukulele to an older man and strolled off to the back of the yard with a very pretty young woman of Japanese heritage. "His girlfriend," said Hinano as they watched the couple disappear into the crowd. "They met at school. I guess they've been dating for five months, and I only found out about her Tuesday, when Kai called to tell me he was bringing a guest home."

"He never mentioned her and they've been dating for five months?" asked Bonnie. "You know what that means."

Hinano nodded grimly. "It's serious."

"She's lovely, and she seems like a nice girl."

"How would you know? You haven't even spoken to her."

"I said she *seems* like a nice girl." Bonnie hoped he wouldn't press her to explain what she based that assumption upon, because she was only trying to reassure him. "Come on, tell the truth. You like her, right?"

"Yeah, I guess I like her."

"I knew it."

"Kai likes her, and that's what's important. He's a smart kid and a good judge of character." Hinano sighed heavily and pushed his empty plate away. "Dis kine ting not easy for an old *makua kane*, you know? It's been just me and Kai for so long. Hey, you want another history lesson?"

"Now?" said Bonnie, caught off guard by the abrupt shift in topic.

"Yeah, now. Now's great. This lesson's topical."

"Okay." Bonnie finished her last bite of cake and took a sip of coffee. "I didn't bring anything to take notes."

"Don't worry. This won't be on the quiz." Hinano settled back in his chair and folded his arms over his broad chest. "American Thanksgiving coincides with an important season for the Hawaiian people called *Makahiki*."

"*Makahiki*?" Bonnie echoed.

He nodded. "The word can mean 'year' or 'new year,' but in ancient times it referred to a four-month season marking the beginning of the new year in the Hawaiian calendar."

"I didn't know you had your own calendar."

"It's based upon the stars, as you might expect of a sea-going island people. There's an important star cluster called Na Huihui o Makali'i that's honored in ancient tradition as the origin of the first Hawaiian people. You probably know it as the Pleiades."

"Or Seven Sisters," Bonnie interjected. "There's a quilt block named after it."

"No kidding." Hinano mulled that over. "You know, I don't think I've ever seen a Hawaiian quilt inspired by the Makali'i. I wonder why not. Maybe too hard to draw." He brushed aside the digression with a wave of his hand. "Anyway, in ancient times, priests of the old religion would watch the night skies from temples on the western sides of the Hawaiian islands. When the Makali'i began to rise at sunset and set at dawn, it marked the beginning of winter, Ho'o-ilo, the rainy season. Ho'o-ilo lasted about four months, until the Makali'i began to rise in the east at sunrise and weren't visible at night, marking the start of Kau, or summer."

"So we're in the rainy season now."

"Yeah, not so you'd notice in Lahaina. We don't get much rain even in Ho'o-ilo." He turned his chair toward hers and leaned forward, resting his elbows on his knees. "These four months were a time of peace and celebration. War was *kapu*, absolutely forbidden. People celebrated with sports and festivals, sometimes with villages competing against one another. As the rains replenished the land, the people were also meant to seek spiritual and cultural renewal within themselves."

"Four months of peace and celebration sounds wonderful," Bonnie remarked. "More societies should adopt that practice."

"Couldn't hurt."

"Midori was right. You *are* an expert on Hawaiian history."

"I didn't even give you the whole picture, just a sketch. And I could be making all of this up on the spot for all you know."

"That's why I plan to verify everything you've told me with Midori before I invite you to come speak to our campers."

"So this was an audition? I thought we were just talking."

"Surprise. I hope you'll play the ukulele for them, too."

"I guess I could do that." Hinano thought it over. "Okay, snowbird. I won't mind entertaining your quilt campers every once in a while."

"Thanks. I'm sure your aunt will be pleased."

"I'm not doing it just for her." His eyes on the night sky, Hinano stood and gestured for her to join him. "Come on. Let's go look for the Makali'i."

She rose and followed him through the tables and clusters of partygoers, hesitating only a moment before taking his hand when he reached back for her. They wove their way to the edge of the party, and then down the gravel driveway, where he abruptly dropped her hand. He had only wanted to make sure he didn't lose her in the crowd, Bonnie realized, still feeling his touch. A reasonable precaution, but nothing more. Which was fine.

How long had it been since a man had held her hand?

He peered toward the east, scanning the sky, and Bonnie tried to follow his line of sight. The dark velvet sky was brilliant with stars, more than she had ever seen. She remembered enough from her Girl Scout days to be able to locate the Big Dipper, Orion, and Cassiopeia if the conditions were right, but she wouldn't have recognized the Pleiades without an astronomy handbook.

"There," he said suddenly, pointing.

"Where? There?"

"No, this way." From behind, he took her by the shoulders, turned her a bit to the left, bent down so that his chin almost rested on her shoulder, and lifted her right arm so that she was pointing into the sky. And then she saw it, a cluster of almost bluish stars high above the tree line.

"I see it," she said with a catch in her voice, conscious of his touch, his closeness. She could feel his breath on her cheek. "Seven Sisters, or— what's the Hawaiian name?"

"Makaliʻi." Abruptly he let go of her arm and stepped away. "It'll be with us for the rest of Hoʻo-ilo, and then, like you, little snowbird, it'll disappear with the coming of summer."

Bonnie could not read his expression in the moonlight. "It won't be going anywhere," she said, "you just won't be able to see it because of the sunlight, because it'll rise in the morning instead of evening. It's still there, it's just—it's just that the timing is bad."

"Right." Hinano nodded, gazed up at the brilliant winter sky for a moment, but then jerked his head to indicate that they should return to the party. "That's what I meant."

Bonnie followed half a pace behind. As soon as they reached the lanai, Hinano bade her good-bye and went off to join the band.

For the rest of the night, until Eric and Claire found her in the crowd and they walked wearily back to the car for the drive home, she saw Hinano only from a distance.

The next morning after breakfast, Bonnie called Elm Creek Manor from her lanai, missing her friends more than she had since their first days apart. Except for Summer, who had remained at the University of Chicago for the holiday weekend, and Judy, who had moved to Philadelphia with her family, the Elm Creek Quilters would gather at the manor for their traditional daylong celebration of the Friday after Thanksgiving. While other people were lining up early outside favorite stores to begin their Christmas shopping, the Elm Creek Quilters would enjoy a day of quilting to mark what Diane called the start of the "quilting season."

Although most quilters pieced and sewed throughout the year, Bonnie understood why Diane had bestowed that title upon the day. When the weather turned colder and forced them indoors, a quilter found it especially appealing to layer a quilt sandwich in a lap hoop, curl up on the sofa, and snuggle beneath the soft folds, enjoying the warmth as she worked the needle up and down in a rocking motion, creating intricate patterns in the soft fabric as the stitches united pieced top, fluffy batting, and smooth lining. The arrival of Thanksgiving also meant that the Elm Creek Quilters had about a month left to complete all the quilts, table runners, garments, and other quilted items they intended to give as Christmas gifts—or in Diane's case, to begin several ambitious projects that she would race to finish by Christmas Eve.

As Bonnie waited for someone to answer her call, she thought wistfully of Thanksgiving Fridays of years past—meeting at the manor in the formal parlor or around the ballroom fireplace, quilting and chatting, sharing advice and suggestions, borrowing thread and trading fabrics. At midday they would gather around the long wooden table in the kitchen to enjoy a potluck lunch, with a special restriction placed upon their contributions to the meal: Each dish had to be made with leftovers from their family feasts the previous day. Sarah usually made a turkey Tetrazzini that couldn't be beat, and Summer always managed to whip up a tasty vegetarian dish that helped Bonnie, a committed omnivore, to understand how it might be possible to refrain from eating meat. Agnes called their dinner a "Patchwork Potluck" and said the meal befit quilters, whose frugality inspired them to find creative uses for leftover turkey, stuffing, and vegetables just as they created beautiful and useful works of art from scraps of fabric.

But more important than the delicious feast—for just as a quilt was more than an assemblage of scraps, so too was their potluck far more than reheated leftovers—and the projects completed during their quilt marathon, was the time spent together with friends. The conversation and company provided a respite from the holiday rush and filled them with a sense of anticipation for the approaching holidays. Bonnie would miss that this year most of all.

Andrew, Sylvia's husband, answered the phone, and after chatting with him a bit, Bonnie spoke with each of her friends in turn as they passed the phone around the circle of quilters. When she found herself repeating the same story to each friend, they put her on speakerphone so they could all talk at once, and when she closed her eyes she could almost imagine herself back at Elm Creek Manor among them. She entertained them with lively stories of the Thanksgiving luau, and they in turn told her about a long-forgotten Bergstrom tradition they had revived. While cleaning out the kitchen cabinets a few weeks earlier, Sylvia and Anna had discovered an old woven cornucopia Sylvia's sister had made as a child. As the Bergstroms had done long ago, the Elm Creek Quilters used the cornucopia as a centerpiece, and into it each placed a symbol of something she was especially thankful for that year. Where the Bergstroms had used pictures, letters, or small trinkets, the Elm Creek Quilters naturally used quilt blocks, each stitching one that either by name or imagery represented something for which she wished to give thanks.

Bonnie was glad to hear that they were having a wonderful time, despite a forecast for heavy snows—but she couldn't help feeling a bit left out that they had established a new tradition without her. But why shouldn't they? Life at Elm Creek Manor went on without her, just as it had after Judy moved away and Summer left for graduate school. The Elm Creek Manor she returned to would not be the same place she had left, and the longer she stayed away, the greater the changes would be.

All the more reason to return home as soon as Aloha Quilt Camp was successfully launched, Bonnie reflected as she hung up the phone and returned it to her purse. Elm Creek Quilts would grow, change, and thrive, and she wanted to be among her friends at the heart of it all.

Just as she was leaving her room, her cell phone rang. One of the Elm Creek Quilters had forgotten to tell her something important, she guessed, hurrying back into the room and snatching the phone from her purse to answer before the caller hung up. Or maybe it was Barry, whom she had been unable to wish Happy Thanksgiving the day before.

"Hello there," she said.

"Hello there," mocked Craig.

Her heart thumped. "How did you get this number?"

"From my mother's caller ID. Where else could I have gotten it now that you've turned my children against me?"

Of course. She had been so foolish to call Linda, and more foolish yet to neglect her own caller ID in her haste to answer the phone. "You know the rules, Craig," she said. "Contact me through my attorney or not at all. I'm hanging up now."

"Wait," he barked, and instinctively she hesitated. "You want revenge. I get that. You want to take every cent from me and ruin my life—"

"That's not what I set out to do," Bonnie broke in. "I only wanted what was right and fair, and this was the only way we knew to get you to see reason."

"Reason? Is that what you call spying and blackmail? Terri has kids, Bonnie. You're going to destroy their lives. Did you even consider that?"

"I'm not the one at fault here," Bonnie snapped. "I didn't make you cheat on me."

"I should have left you years ago."

"You did. In your heart you did. Now it's time for us both to move on and we can start by settling this divorce. The money you spent on those antiques was mine as well as yours—"

"I earned that money."

"I did too!"

"You want to divide up the marital assets? Fine. Let's divide up all the marital assets, yours as well as mine."

"You know very well that there's nothing left of Grandma's Attic."

"I'm not talking about the quilt shop."

"Then what are you talking about? The insurance settlement? You agreed that it was mine as long as I forfeited the profit on the condo. Or have you changed your mind about that too?"

"That's not it. You get a piece of my business assets, then I get a piece of yours."

He wasn't making any sense. "Just say it, Craig. What is it you want?"

"Elm Creek Quilts."

Bonnie went cold. "You must be joking."

"You're a part owner of a successful business. I want my share of your part."

"I'm not a part owner. Sylvia—"

"Sylvia divided the company among you and the rest of those quilters. Did you think I could forget something like that?"

"Craig—"

"You founded that business while we were married. You built that business while we were married. You earned money from that business while we were married. If your income was included in the property settlement, why not the company itself? Why not the manor? And what do you think the judge is going to say when he hears you've been holding out on me? You've got that poor wronged woman act down pat, but after he finds out about your secret fortune—"

"Craig, you can't do this."

"I can and I will. Just wait until I'm a shareholder in Elm Creek Quilts. Believe me, I'll be at every meeting. My vote will be counted. I'd like to make a few changes too. Maybe—oh, just off the top of my head—maybe sell the manor. That's what the old lady had in mind before you talked her into making a quilt camp, right? Maybe if quilt camp becomes less fun than when it was just you girls, she might be convinced to tear the place down and put up some condos after all."

"Craig, don't," she cried, but he had hung up.

Chapter Nine

He can't do this." Then Claire hesitated. "Can he?"

"I don't know." Bonnie folded her arms and rested her head upon the kitchen island. Midori stroked her back comfortingly but it was all Bonnie could do not to weep. "I don't know the law well enough to know if I should worry or if this is just more idle bluster."

"He'll say anything to hurt you," said Midori scathingly. "You can't trust a word that comes out of his mouth. What does your lawyer think about all this?"

"He's out of town for the holiday. I left a message on his voicemail, but I have no idea when he'll get it." Until Darren Taylor returned her call, her stomach would be in knots. "I can't let Craig touch Elm Creek Quilts. I can't. He'll deliberately destroy it just to hurt me."

"You still have us," Claire told her stoutly. "You'll always have a place here. You know that."

"It's not just me and my future at stake. My friends have put their hearts and souls into that business. For some of them, Elm Creek Quilts is their only income."

"They could all come to work here."

In spite of everything, Bonnie had to smile at her impulsive friend's generosity. "You know that's not practical."

"I mean it," said Claire resolutely. "We'll find a way to make it happen."

"We should focus on protecting Elm Creek Quilts from that horrible man," said Midori. "What does he know about the law? If he were entitled to any part of Elm Creek Quilts, wouldn't his lawyer have brought it up earlier? You haven't been hiding that manor under a pile of leaves. They all knew about it."

"I don't know," said Bonnie, too heartsick to think clearly. "I—I remember we agreed not to claim any part of each other's future earnings or retirement accounts as long as Craig kept our children on as the beneficiaries of his life insurance, but I don't know what that means for my share in the business. I swear, if I had ever imagined that Craig could get his hands on Elm Creek Manor—"

"He won't," said Claire.

"—I never would have contested the property settlement. I should have let him keep the money from the auction and considered it the price of freedom."

"You couldn't let him rob you blind," protested Claire. "You did what you had to do for your own financial security."

"Maybe." But what if her security came at the cost of her friends'? "Maybe I was too greedy. Maybe I should have left well enough alone."

Claire threw her hands in the air, exasperated. "Craig says it, therefore it must be true."

Astonished, Bonnie stared at her. "What's that supposed to mean?"

"When friends who love you and care about you tell you that you're a wonderful woman and deserving of all good things in life, it goes in one ear and out the other. When Craig makes some ugly, nasty remark, you grab on to it with both hands and hold it close to your heart."

"I do not."

"You do," remarked Midori, spooning mango preserves into petite serving dishes. "I haven't known you that long, but I've seen it, too. You're one of those people who finds it far easier to believe the bad things others say about you than the good."

"You've been that way as long as I've known you," said Claire.

"You, on the other hand." Midori leveled her spoon at Claire. "You always believe the good you hear and not the bad, which is maybe why you and Bonnie get along so well. Opposites attract."

Claire fixed Midori with a look of injured innocence. "That's not true."

"Actually, it is," said Bonnie.

Claire rolled her eyes. "That's ridiculous. Everyone knows I'm my own worst critic."

Midori raised her eyebrows at Bonnie, who shrugged to show that she too realized that Claire had just proven their point.

"Don't believe a single hateful thing that man says," Midori admonished Bonnie. "Your children are grown. Since he can't threaten you with custody issues, he'll try to use what's second most precious to you: Elm Creek Quilts."

"Midori's right. Don't worry yourself sick over this needlessly," said Claire, squeezing Bonnie's hand. "Put it out of your mind until you talk to your lawyer. He'll know what to do."

Bonnie agreed that they were right. There was nothing she could do at the moment, and worrying wouldn't make Darren Taylor return her message sooner.

But she couldn't drive the fear and worry away. Elm Creek Quilts was in jeopardy, she had brought this danger to their door, and her friends were completely unaware that all they had built could come crashing down around them.

⸎

After breakfast, Claire urged Bonnie to go online and contact her cellular provider about changing her cell phone number. First she had to register on the site, then she had to find the right web page with the right information, and finally she had to call an 800 number, plow through a series of voicemail prompts, and wait twenty minutes to speak to a human being. To her relief, the customer service rep didn't press her for details when she explained that she had been receiving harassing phone calls and had to change her number. Unfortunately, the change wouldn't go through for two business days, so Bonnie faced four days during which Craig could call her constantly if he chose. She hoped he wouldn't, but in the meantime she would put her trust in her caller ID to screen him out and she wouldn't answer any unfamiliar numbers in case he tried to trick her by calling from another line. He hated having his desires thwarted. Ignoring him was the surest way to infuriate him, but she had no choice.

Having closed her quilt shop for the holiday, Claire had intended to spend the rest of the long weekend at home with Eric, but she lingered at the inn, reluctant to leave Bonnie distressed and alone. Only when Bonnie insisted that she would be fine and that Claire shouldn't change her plans did Claire transfer a few files to her zip drive, tuck a bundle of papers into her shoulder bag, and say that she would return on Monday. "Sooner if you need me," she emphasized, hugging Bonnie and glancing back worriedly at her twice on her way to the front door.

After Claire left, Bonnie stayed online to send her kids, the Elm Creek Quilters, and Darren her new phone number, noting that it would not be in effect until Tuesday and warning them, especially Barry, not to give it to Craig. Then she put the computer to sleep and wished she could do the same to the tumult of thoughts swirling through her mind. She had to concentrate, focus, force herself to think of something else. A stack of newly arrived résumés sat on Claire's desk awaiting Bonnie's attention, but the task she had been eagerly anticipating for weeks no longer appealed to her.

"Tending to our guests is enough work for Thanksgiving weekend," Midori advised when Bonnie wandered into the kitchen. "Find something pleasant to distract yourself with instead."

Bonnie nodded and climbed the stairs to her room, heavy hearted. If she were back home, her friends would have their arms around her, offering their sympathy and reassurances. She longed to call them, but how could she ask them to comfort her when she might have put all they had worked for at risk? How could she speak to them without warning them of what might lie ahead, and what good was a warning when she didn't know the extent of the danger or what steps they could take to protect Elm Creek Quilts?

Compelled to warn her friends but reluctant to alarm them needlessly, Bonnie decided her only real choice was to wait. Darren Taylor would know if Elm Creek Quilts was really at risk, and he would know what she could do to mitigate Craig's influence if it came to that.

If she were at Elm Creek Manor she could distract herself with her friends' company and her Christmas quilting projects, but she had left her stash at the manor with her other belongings and had no Christmas projects to work on, since she had planned to buy special Hawaiian gifts for her friends and loved ones instead. But she didn't have to work on holiday quilts to keep the Elm Creek Quilters' Thanksgiving Friday tradition in her own way.

She had not worked on her Pineapple Patch quilt since basting the emerald green fabric to the ivory background. It was still where she had left it weeks before, neatly rolled up and lying on her bamboo bureau. She carried the soft bundle and her sewing tools downstairs and outside to the covered lanai, where soft breezes caressed her and the gentle tinkle of koa wood wind chimes whispered a promise that she must not despair, not until she knew all was lost, and perhaps not even then.

As she spread the quilt top over a table, she glanced up and saw Midori approaching. "Ready for your next lesson?" she asked.

Bonnie wasn't sure she needed one, as she had learned needle-turn appliqué years before. Still, she had never made a quilt quite like her Pineapple Patch before and it was possible Midori knew a different technique to make the stitches finer, curves smoother, and points more precise. So she thanked Midori and obeyed her first instructions: to thread a needle with an eighteen-inch length of green thread and tie a knot at the end. "It is essential to have the right color," said Midori, a hint of warning in her tone. "The thread must match the fabric perfectly so that your stitches will be invisible."

Bonnie, who had heard that tip more than three decades before, smiled and showed Midori the perfectly matched thread she had selected when she had chosen her fabrics at Claire's quilt shop. "Good," Midori said, but only after she held the thread against the fabric and scrutinized both. "Start in the center of your quilt top and work your way out. Take your first stitches on a gentle outward curve. That's much easier than beginning near a point or on the inside of an arc."

Obediently Bonnie slipped the needle through the back of the quilt top near one smooth, gentle curve of her appliqué, tugging on the thread to be sure the knot was secure. The stitch used in Hawaiian appliqué was simply a hemming stitch, Midori explained. Tucking the raw edge of her appliqué under until it met the line of basting stitches, Bonnie brought the needle up through the folded edge and back down through the ivory background fabric where she wanted the appliqué to lie. Then she worked the needle back up through the ivory fabric a fraction of an inch along the line of her design, and again took a tiny stitch through the folded edge of the emerald green appliqué. Again and again she sent the needle through the two paired fabrics, always tucking the raw edge of the appliqué under an inch ahead of her needle. Soon the smooth curve of a leaf emerged, held fast to the ivory beneath it.

"Now you see why it was so important for you to baste one-quarter inch from the edge of your appliqué," remarked Midori, nodding approvingly as she inspected Bonnie's small, neat, practiced stitches. "You cut your appliqué one-eighth of an inch larger than your pattern, all around. When you tuck the edge under, the basting stitches keep the fold to a perfect eighth of an inch."

"The basting stitches guide my seam allowance so I don't have to mark it on the appliqué," Bonnie said.

"Exactly." Midori watched Bonnie a while longer, perhaps to see if she had more questions, perhaps to see if she could catch Bonnie in a mistake, but eventually she declared that she had work of her own to attend to but that Bonnie should come find her if she ran into trouble. Bonnie hid a smile and promised she would.

She sewed the morning away, listening to birdsong, inhaling the fragrance of jasmine and hibiscus, savoring the touch of gentle breezes on her skin. Back home it was snowing; Sarah had mentioned a winter storm alert and thick flurries already falling. Bonnie felt worlds away, and in the benevolent sunlight it was hard to imagine Elm Creek Manor shrouded in winter white, braced against bitter winds.

A far worse storm clouded their horizon, but Bonnie resolved to do everything in her power to divert it.

❖

Bonnie sewed her way through the long holiday weekend, missing her friends, missing her children, and waiting in vain for Darren to return her message. Craig called three times a day, but she refused to pick up when she saw his number in the caller ID window. Apparently he couldn't calculate the time difference very well either because several of his calls came while she was still fast asleep in bed with the ringer silenced. She deleted his voicemail messages unheard and reminded herself that in two business days he wouldn't be able to leave any more.

She took comfort in the emerging beauty of her Pineapple Patch quilt, in pleasant meals shared with Midori in the kitchen, and in knowing that she was helping Claire by seeing to their guests' comfort. Over the past few weeks Claire had noticed an increase in reservations and positive reviews on travel websites, which she attributed to their successful Halloween. Claire often told Bonnie that she couldn't manage without her, and the praise no longer felt like pressure. Eventually Claire would have to manage without Bonnie, but in the meantime Bonnie enjoyed contributing to the fledgling business and feeling appreciated for her efforts. If Aloha Quilt Camp succeeded—*when* it succeeded—she would be proud to know that she had played a significant role in its success.

If only she could be sure that she would not bring about the failure of another business even more dear to her.

At last, on Monday morning, Bonnie checked her phone before leaving for her walk and found that Darren Taylor had called and left a voicemail. After days of anticipation and dread, she felt deflated when he said little more than that he had received her message, he would look into the situation, and he would get back to her as soon as possible. That meant she had another long day of waiting ahead of her, possibly more.

Bonnie was determined not to sit and brood. After exercising and helping Midori with the usual morning chores around the inn, she took the stack of résumés to the central lanai and read each one thoroughly, taking notes on a legal pad. Several of the applicants lived in Hawaii, two in Japan, nine in California, and five more around the rest of the United States. Bonnie ruled out three of the applicants rather quickly, but not without misgivings; although they sounded like accomplished quilters, they had never taught quilting, and Bonnie knew that artistic gifts were not necessarily accompanied by the ability to teach. A demanding, full-time, year-round faculty position at a quilt camp required a seasoned professional, not someone who had no idea what it was really like to think on her feet at the front of the classroom.

The remaining seventeen aspiring Aloha Quilt Camp teachers varied widely in their experience and accomplishments. A few had won ribbons in regional quilt shows and had taught a few introductory courses at their local quilt shops and quilt guilds. Others had had their work displayed at international judged and juried quilt conventions and had led workshops in advanced techniques. There was a clear distinction between those two groups, but most of the applicants fell somewhere in the middle. One quilter had never had her work accepted at a quilt show of national renown, but she was such a popular, engaging speaker that she spent as much time on the road as at home, traveling from one quilt guild to another, teaching and selling her self-published patterns. Another applicant had quilted less than five years and taught less than one, but her stunningly beautiful and innovative creations had appeared in several quilt magazines and her star was clearly on the rise. Yet another quilter had won Best of Show at the American Quilter's Society show in Paducah the previous year, had developed her own system for simplifying complex block construction, and had a book contract pending, but she taught only her own technique, no other subjects. That wasn't to say she couldn't teach other courses, and she lived on the Big Island, which suggested she was serious about the job and would have no problem relocating, but on the other hand—

Overwhelmed, Bonnie pushed herself away from the table and walked out the back gate and down to the beach to clear her head. Weighing one candidate against another when not all factors were equal seemed an impossible task. What was more important: teaching experience or artistic accomplishment? Winning personality or technical skill? Number of published patterns or prizes won? The hiring process had seemed much easier back at Elm Creek Manor, where she and her friends had discussed the different candidates, making suggestions and pointing out issues that the others hadn't seen, achieving consensus, and choosing five finalists to invite for interviews. While it was tempting to interview everyone except for those who clearly weren't qualified, Bonnie knew that wasn't a practical solution, if only because Claire couldn't afford the travel expenses.

The cooling breezes off the ocean soothed her troubled thoughts, and after basking in the sunshine a while, Bonnie returned to the inn with renewed determination—and what she hoped was an acceptable compromise. Claire had asked her to rank the applicants from best to worst, but since that had proven to be next to impossible, she instead divided them into five groups: most qualified, least qualified, and three groups in the middle, each comprised of quilters who were either strong artists, teachers, or designers but had weaknesses in another category.

The applications sorted, Bonnie carried everything inside to the office, where Claire quickly put the computer to sleep and joined her on the sofa. Bonnie arranged the five stacks on the coffee table and sat back while Claire perused the résumés, preparing herself for questions about how she had ranked the applicants.

Claire frowned thoughtfully as she paged through the first pile. "They seem like nice people, but not quite what we're looking for," she eventually said, setting aside the three applicants who had never taught.

"I hate rejecting people," Bonnie confessed. "It pains me to imagine some nice quilter in California or Iowa opening her mailbox, hoping for an invitation to come for an interview and learning instead that we aren't interested. No one wants to be told that they aren't good enough."

"Some people's ambitions are out of line with reality," said Claire, dismissing the first group with a wave of her hand and picking up the second stack, applications from quilters who were exceptional teachers but lacked in other areas. "We said we wanted experienced teachers. If they've never taught before, what are they thinking, applying for these jobs?"

"Maybe they hoped we would be flexible. You can't blame people for dreaming big."

"Yes I can, if it wastes my time."

Bonnie studied her, unsure if she was joking. "That's a little harsh, don't you think?"

"Not really. If they gave our ad more than a cursory reading, they should have known better than to think we're seeking entry-level candidates."

Bonnie sighed. "Maybe. I don't know. Maybe we should have been more specific."

"'Experienced quilt teachers wanted,'" said Claire airily, quoting their ad from memory. "Since unlike me, you don't resent these ladies for taking up your valuable time, I think you're the right person to compose their rejection letters."

"No, you do it. You're the heartless one."

"Which is exactly why you're best for the job. I'm liable to tell them exactly what I think and offend them, whereas you'll be so diplomatic that they'll not only agree that we made the right choice, they'll want to come to Aloha Quilt Camp as students instead."

Bonnie knew Claire was vastly overstating her writing skills, but she agreed and took a seat at the computer. She finished the first draft of a rejection letter—which she knew was much too long, much too apologetic, and much in need of revision—while Claire finished reading the rest of the applications. "Our ad seems to have paid off," Claire later remarked. "I'm ready to invite a few of these applicants for an interview right now, although we should wait to see who else applies."

Bonnie joined her on the couch. "Who's impressed you the most so far?" One glance told her that Claire had kept the very well qualified candidates together just as Bonnie had grouped them, but she had shifted around some of the candidates in the middle three groups. "What did you think about Shelley Stevens, the quilter from Michigan? Doesn't she sound wonderful? I love how she enhances her quilts with embroidery."

"Oh, absolutely. Her work is gorgeous." Claire took Shelley's application and those of the other two well-qualified candidates and placed them on the reject pile with the quilters who had no teaching experience. "Maybe she'd be willing to come as a guest lecturer after we're more established."

"Guest lecturer? But—" Bonnie looked from Claire to the reject pile and back, utterly bewildered. "She wants to be on our permanent faculty."

"That's what she says, but she's unbelievably overqualified. We could never afford to pay her what she deserves, and even if we could, we could never keep her for long."

Bonnie snatched up Shelley's application and paged through it. "How do you know? She doesn't say a word about salary requirements."

"Someone with her experience and status in the quilting world can name her salary."

"Maybe so, but let's at least let her name it before we reject her."

"And go to the trouble and expense of bringing her out here for an interview just to find out she was only angling for a pay increase at her current job?" Claire shook her head in regret, took Shelley's application from Bonnie, and returned it to the reject pile. "We can't afford that. We need to concentrate on recruiting people we could actually hire, not get ourselves tangled up in negotiating for a superstar."

"So we'll ask her during her phone interviews," said Bonnie, exasperation increasing exponentially. "We should at least talk to her. These women applied for the teaching position as described in our ad. Let's assume they want the job and not second-guess their motivations. We agreed to interview our top ten candidates by phone, right? What difference would it make if we expanded that to fifteen?"

"I understand what you're saying, but we have limited time. We have to spend it on the most likely prospects."

Bonnie clasped a hand to her brow. "No, we should aim for the best and compromise if we have to."

"You're too idealistic."

"You're too defeatist!"

"No, I'm realistic."

"Do we want the best faculty or not?"

"We want the best faculty we can afford."

Bonnie took her top three candidates' applications from the reject pile. "We can ask them their salary requirements during their phone interviews. If they're out of our price range, we can thank them and move on, otherwise we can invite them for a second interview here."

"Bonnie—" Claire hesitated, then shook her head. "All right. Fine. All I ask is that you wait a week to see what other applications come in before you call, and that you help me choose a backup top ten, excluding your superstars."

Bonnie agreed, though she suspected Claire had asked for the delay to give her time to make Bonnie see reason. In Bonnie's opinion, Claire was the unreasonable one. How could she dismiss something as too expensive before checking the price tag? And really, how much time would a few additional phone interviews take? Didn't it make good business sense to invest that negligible amount of time and effort into getting all the facts before rejecting the three most impressive applicants?

But who was Bonnie to lecture Claire about good business? Claire ran a successful quilt shop as well as an inn, whereas Bonnie's quilt shop had gone down in spectacular defeat. Her only other business venture, Elm Creek Quilts, thrived because it was a collaborative effort with several other skilled, capable women. Maybe she should ignore her instincts and follow Claire's lead. Maybe part of her past failures had come from setting her sights too high.

Conflicted, she watched as Claire sorted through the applications a second time, reading résumés, admiring photos of quilts, checking for lists of references. Bonnie was on the verge of telling Claire that she should go ahead and interview whomever she preferred, because after all, Claire would have to work with the new hires long after Bonnie departed. Then, just as she was about to concede, a new resolve took hold. Maybe Claire was right, but maybe not, and if Bonnie didn't contact Shelley and the other two most promising applicants, she would never know. If their salary demands were indeed too high as Claire predicted, Bonnie would admit her mistake and learn from it. She would rather blunder that way than act on assumptions that could be entirely wrong.

"So who do you like for our backup top ten?" Bonnie asked, returning her favorite three candidates' applications to their place on the coffee table. "Do we prefer great teachers over great artists, or the other way around?"

"We're hiring two teachers, so if we can't find both in the same person, we'll look for one of each," said Claire, smiling with her familiar friendliness as if the disagreement had never occurred. "We need to strike a balance."

On that, Bonnie couldn't agree more.

❖

It took them another hour to agree upon ten finalists to call for phone interviews, pending any new applications that might arrive in the mail that week. Privately Bonnie composed her own top ten, including her favorites, whom she intended to call the minute the waiting period she had promised Claire expired.

The next day another two applications arrived, including one that expanded their top ten to a top eleven, since Claire and Bonnie could not agree on whom to displace. Later that same day Bonnie's new cell phone number took effect.

She was on the lanai, taking a break from work to sew on her Pineapple Patch quilt when Darren Taylor called. He had investigated Craig's threats and had spoken at length with Sylvia. "Craig can't touch Elm Creek Manor," Darren assured her. "Sylvia owns the house, the grounds, and almost all of the personal property within the manor. None of that was ever identified as an asset of Elm Creek Quilts. Some items purchased since the founding of the business—computers and such—do clearly belong to Elm Creek Quilts rather than Sylvia, but the house and the estate are hers and hers alone."

"Are you sure?" Bonnie wanted to believe him, wanted to be sure that Craig had no power over Elm Creek Quilts and never would. "About two years after we founded Elm Creek Quilts, Sylvia divided up the business among the founding members and Matt, our caretaker. I was sure she had included the manor, the orchard, and the entire estate in that."

"Sylvia told me that she divided the business entity Elm Creek Quilts into shares," Darren explained. "She kept a twenty percent stake for herself, gave twenty percent to Sarah McClure, and gave the remaining Elm Creek Quilters ten percent each. During this restructuring, Sylvia did give away two parcels of land: a lot near Waterford College that she donated to the city for the creation of a skateboard park, and the apple orchard, which she gave to Matt McClure. Everything else remains hers."

"I know Sylvia said something about the manor," Bonnie persisted. "It's been a few years, but I know she made some provision for her family estate. She'd had a health scare and she wanted to get her affairs in order."

"You're probably thinking of the changes she made to her will," Darren replied. "Upon her death, Sylvia's twenty percent of the business, the manor, the grounds, and all her personal property will go to Sarah McClure. I spoke with Sarah, and she intends to continue Sylvia's current arrangement and lease the manor to Elm Creek Quilts for a dollar a year."

"Of course." Bonnie should have made the connection between the lease and Sylvia's ownership of the manor, but in her distress, she had not found a still, quiet moment to parse the details rationally. "You have no idea what it means to me to know that Elm Creek Quilts is safe."

"There is the matter of your ten percent share of the business." Darren's voice took on a compassionate, reassuring tone that immediately filled Bonnie with foreboding. "You established the business during your marriage, and Craig can claim that he supported you financially throughout that time. Therefore your share is considered a marital asset."

Bonnie's heart plummeted. "So he's entitled to half of my share?"

"I'm afraid so. But remember, he can't sell off the lands or the manor. Those were empty threats."

"But he can affect Elm Creek Quilts, the business?"

"He'll have as much influence as a five percent ownership entitles him to."

"What—" Bonnie forced herself to take deep, slow breaths, but the lanai seemed to rock back and forth around her. "What does that mean, exactly?"

"According to your charter, he's allowed on the premises to conduct business and to do whatever tasks are assigned to him."

"We won't assign him any," Bonnie said. "We don't have to, do we?"

"Absolutely not. There's nothing that says you have to give him something to do. He can't demand to teach a class, for example, or redesign your website on a whim. However, he is allowed to attend board meetings, and he is permitted a vote."

"Half of a vote, right?" said Bonnie, thinking quickly. "Because we're sharing the same ten percent. That means that I can always use my half of a vote to cancel out his."

"That's true," said Darren carefully. "But don't fool yourself. He can make your workplace very uncomfortable for you. He can be as annoying and irritating as he chooses, but unless he does something illegal, you can't ban him from the premises."

Bonnie thought her spirits couldn't sink any lower, but then she imagined Craig arguing over trivial details at business meetings, putting his muddy shoes on Sylvia's antique furniture, heckling Bonnie from the back of her classrooms, stuffing himself at the Welcome Banquet and belching loudly whenever Sylvia tried to address the group, laughing derisively when campers bared their hearts at the Candlelight welcoming ceremony. He would ruin quilt camp for guests and Elm Creek Quilters alike, and a business that relied so much upon positive word-of-mouth could not withstand the assault for long.

He had Bonnie trapped, and she knew it.

"I don't know what else to do," said Bonnie, distressed. "Would you ask his lawyer if Craig would give up his share in Elm Creek Quilts in exchange for all the profits from the furniture auction? Would that satisfy him, do you think?"

"I took the liberty of suggesting that to your husband's lawyer this morning."

The tone of Darren's voice conveyed everything. "He refused."

"I'm afraid so."

She couldn't let this happen. She couldn't let Craig ruin Elm Creek Quilts for her friends and for all the wonderful visitors who cherished the manor and the solace and inspiration it offered. "Give him anything. Anything he wants. I don't care. He can't have Elm Creek Quilts."

"He doesn't want anything else," said Darren. "He wants this, because he knows it will hurt you most."

Bonnie closed her eyes, but two tears slipped out. "It's working."

"There is one way to prevent him from having any influence whatsoever," said Darren. "Sell your ten percent before the divorce is final."

"What?"

"I know it's an extreme measure, but it's your only recourse."

"Could I do that, even if I wanted to?" She didn't, not now, not ever. "Isn't it a marital asset? Don't I need his permission? I had to sign papers before he could sell the condo."

"The condo was in both of your names. The share of Elm Creek Quilts is in yours alone. His only claim on it is that he supported you while you were establishing the business. If you sell your share and give him fifty percent of the proceeds, your legal obligation will be satisfied." Darren let out an abrupt laugh. "I had a client who sold her husband's Ferrari on eBay for a hundred dollars out of pure spite. At least you would be acting to save a business and spare your friends a lot of misery."

"I could do something like that," said Bonnie. "Elm Creek Quilts leases the manor from Sylvia for a dollar a year. Why couldn't I sell my share to Sylvia for a dollar and buy it back from her afterward?"

"I'd advise you against it," cautioned Darren. "Judges don't look favorably upon such obvious attempts to circumvent the rules and they tend to adjust the settlement elsewhere to compensate. This would have to be a real sale, Bonnie, or you could find yourself without your share in the Elm Creek Quilts and without the resources to start a new business."

"My friends would never understand." Bonnie could hardly comprehend it herself. Give up her share of Elm Creek Quilts? It was unthinkable. "Even my two friends who moved away didn't sell their shares. The idea never even came up."

"Your friends will understand," said Darren. "I've discussed it with Sylvia and she explained the situation to the others."

"I'm sure Sylvia told you that she would never allow me to sell my share," said Bonnie. "Sylvia would rather face off with Craig every day for a year than see me give up something I've worked so hard for. In fact, I bet she's looking forward to bringing Craig to his knees. Diane, too. And Gwen and Sarah and all of my friends. They won't let him get away with this, five percent owner or not."

"On the contrary, Sylvia believes you should sell."

Bonnie felt as if all the air had been squeezed from her lungs. "What?"

"She was reluctant at first, but after consulting with the other Elm Creek Quilters, she decided that it would be best to bring this matter to a decisive end before Craig has the opportunity to do any damage."

"I don't believe this." That didn't sound like Sylvia, strongwilled, forthright, loyal Sylvia.

"Sylvia wanted me to assure you that you'll always have a place on the faculty, and you're still welcome to open a quilt shop in the manor. Everything will go on as before, except that you'll no longer be an owner."

"They all agree that I should sell?" asked Bonnie, disbelieving.

"From what I gather the vote wasn't unanimous," said Darren, "and of course it's nonbinding. You're free to sell your share or not to sell as you see fit."

"I could never find a buyer in time, not from here."

"Sylvia has already found one."

"Who?" cried Bonnie. "How? I haven't even agreed to sell yet!"

"Anna del Maso stepped up when Sylvia explained the situation."

"Chef Anna?" Bonnie shook her head, flabbergasted. "Chef Anna wants to buy my share of the business?"

"She's offering five thousand dollars cash."

Bonnie blinked away tears of frustration and betrayal. "Is that—is that even a reasonable offer?"

"Fair enough to pass inspection as a real sale. More important, you need a quick decision, the Elm Creek Quilters would prefer to keep it in the family, and it's all Anna has."

Bonnie could not deny the sense of the plan, but the thought of cutting herself off from Elm Creek Quilts was unbearable. "It's not enough." It wasn't the money. Nothing would be worth giving up her small portion of Elm Creek Quilts. "My friends know I plan to come home, don't they? They know this job in Hawaii is only for the winter?"

"They know," said Darren. "That's why Sylvia emphasized that only the ownership has changed, nothing else. You still have your place on the permanent faculty, and I'm sure you still have their friendship. Sylvia said to remind you, 'Once an Elm Creek Quilter, always an Elm Creek Quilter.'"

But it wouldn't be the same, no matter what Sylvia said to the contrary. Bonnie had nurtured the business from its first days, just as her friends had. She knew Anna had been saving up to buy her own restaurant and she was probably sacrificing her life savings to keep Elm Creek Quilts out of Craig's hands. Everyone wanted to do what was best for the business, even though it hurt. Bonnie knew that.

She also knew that she had only one choice, though it broke her heart to make it.

Chapter Ten

Tere must be another way," said Claire, after Bonnie tracked her down to the quilt shop stockroom and told her everything.

Sitting on the floor, Bonnie pulled another tissue from the box on her lap, leaned back against the shelves, and stretched her legs out in front of her. "If there was another way, Darren would have thought of it."

"I can't believe your friends agreed to this."

Bonnie still couldn't either, but she was compelled to defend them. "Elm Creek Quilts has to come first, before any individual Elm Creek Quilter. I understand that."

"I don't," snapped Claire. "What is Elm Creek Quilts, anyway, if it isn't the sum of its parts, if it isn't each of you contributing something uniquely your own to create an amazing whole? You can't let Craig get away with this."

"He's not getting away with anything except for twenty-five hundred dollars. By selling my share, I'm preventing him from destroying everything my friends and I have created."

"One annoying ex-husband couldn't do as much damage as they say," scoffed Claire. "They just don't want to deal with the drama. Fine. You don't need those fair-weather friends. Forget about Elm Creek Quilts. You have a place right here at Aloha Quilt Camp and no one will ever take it away from you."

Bonnie had to laugh. "Don't be opportunistic."

"You mean like your so-called friend Anna, opening her checkbook before you even offered to sell?"

"That's not how it happened."

"You weren't there, so you don't really know, do you?"

"You weren't there either, and you don't know Anna." Bonnie sighed. "But they didn't waste any time, did they."

Claire waved a hand dismissively. "They have to look out for themselves. Whatever. Look, I'm not trying to take advantage of the situation. I just want you to remember that you have options. Everything that you thought you had with Elm Creek Quilts, you can have here with me and Midori and whomever we hire. But there will be three important differences: Craig won't ever get his grubby hands on Aloha Quilt Camp, you'll never face a blizzard in Lahaina, and I would never, ever, not in a million years, ask you to sell your part of the business."

Bonnie studied her, gnawing the inside of her lower lip. "My part of the business? Are you offering me part ownership, or just a faculty position? Because I already have a faculty position waiting for me back in Pennsylvania if I want it."

If I want it. Bonnie could hardly believe she had said the words aloud.

"You've been on the fence for months trying to decide what you should do with your insurance settlement, right? Go into business with me. Invest in the Hale Kapa Kuiki Inn and we'll be partners in the bed and breakfast as well as Aloha Quilt Camp."

Bonnie strongly suspected that her impulsive friend had

given the offer no forethought. "Shouldn't you go over the numbers first, or at least discuss it with Eric?"

"I know Eric will agree with me that this is a wonderful opportunity for both of us. We could use the influx of cash, you would own a business again, and—" Claire smiled at her, suddenly wistful. "And I would really like you to stay. You're not just a consultant; you're my best collaborator and a wonderful friend. Who in their right mind would break up a team that is obviously working so well? That's short-sighted and just plain bad business."

It was true; they were a good team, and success was more likely if they stuck together. Claire encouraged Bonnie to dream big, and Bonnie kept Claire grounded. It was significant, too, that Claire had offered a partnership not only in the quilt camp, but in the inn itself. Therefore even if the quilt camp floundered, Bonnie would remain part owner of a charming bed and breakfast on a beach in Maui.

It was an exciting opportunity, a promising investment that appealed to her more than opening up a small quilt shop within Elm Creek Manor. Sylvia's offer, albeit generous, had always felt like a consolation prize for the loss of Grandma's Attic. Claire wasn't offering her an opportunity out of friendship or sympathy. She needed Bonnie, and the more Bonnie thought about it, she needed Claire.

"We should think this over carefully," she told her friend.

"Don't say no!"

Bonnie threw up her hands and laughed. "Did I say no? I'm not saying no. I'm saying let's think it over."

Claire folded her arms, frowning in almost childlike worry. "That usually leads to no."

"Not this time. In fact, it will probably lead to yes. I just think that you should talk to Eric before you make an official offer, and I want to be sure we do what's best for everyone in-volved." She sighed and shook her head. "I also want to talk to Darren. I don't pretend to know every last detail of the law, but we should probably wait until after my divorce is final before I buy into anything."

"Agreed," said Claire. "Even if Craig can't claim part of anything you take on after you separated, he'll inevitably hear about the deal, and then he'll have your address. Let's post-pone that as long as possible."

"How about forever?" said Bonnie wearily. "It's bad enough that I've had to change my cell phone number and set up all sorts of filters on my email. I'm lucky Craig's too cheap to buy an airline ticket to Maui. He prefers to torment me on a budget."

Claire laughed and flung her arms around Bonnie. "I'm so glad you're staying. I know it hurts to lose Elm Creek Quilts, but I hope you'll soon see that you've gained so much more than you've lost."

"I haven't said yes yet," Bonnie reminded her, laughing as she embraced her friend, blinking back tears when she thought of the friends who seemed all too willing to let her go.

❖

Claire must have called Eric as soon as Bonnie left the quilt shop, for less than an hour later she tracked Bonnie down in the laundry room where she was folding bed linens with Midori and declared that Eric intended to contact their law-yer and draw up the papers that week. Bonnie reminded her that she wouldn't be in a position to buy into a partnership until after the divorce was final and she intended to use that time to consider Claire's offer very seriously. "Don't pressure me," she begged, but when Claire promised she wouldn't,

Midori shook her head, gazed heavenward, and remarked that Bonnie might as well wish for a white Christmas on Kāʻanapali Beach.

Bonnie didn't need snow to spark her anticipation for the Christmas season. Her eldest son, C.J., was coming for a visit, bringing along his wife, Julie; their four-year-old daughter, Alice; and their eight-month-old son, Cameron. Bonnie ached to cuddle her grandbabies again, and with her family around her, Bonnie hoped the pain and disappointment of her most recent losses would ease.

But in the meantime, they weighed heavily upon her heart. She tried to lose herself in preparing for the holidays and in her work—and she certainly had enough to do. As the application deadline approached, each day brought another stack of thick envelopes from aspiring quilt camp faculty. Bonnie and Claire sorted through them, laughing at themselves for their premature ranking of the first eighteen candidates, which had been thrown into shambles by the arrival of twenty-six more applications. In hindsight their disagreement over superstars and salaries seemed embarrassingly silly, and Claire didn't even say "I told you so" when her prediction about Bonnie's top pick proved to be true. Although Bonnie regretted that such a fine quilter had placed herself out of their price range, so many other well-qualified, affordable candidates were eager to come for interviews that her regret was fleeting.

By mid-December they had interviewed twenty candidates by phone and had chosen ten to invite for interviews: five from Hawaii, four from the mainland, and one from Japan. All but one was a woman and each was an accomplished quilter and teacher. Some had written books about quilting techniques or history; others had designed and sold their own original patterns; and all had won recognition for their artistry, either as ribbons awarded in quilt shows or the honor of having photographs of their work published in books, magazines, or calendars. Bonnie was eager to meet them and assess all the intangibles that couldn't be conveyed on paper or over the phone, but she and Claire agreed to schedule the interviews for early January, after the holiday rush. The inn was booked to capacity from the week before Christmas through the first days of the New Year and their finalists were likely busy with holiday plans of their own. Although their launch date was approaching quickly and they had little time to spare, the delay seemed wise since it would offer both interviewers and applicants a better chance to make a good impression.

But the distractions of work and preparing for her son's visit offered Bonnie only momentary solace from her troubles. The divorce proceedings dragged on. Confronted with the evidence of his adultery, Craig had resentfully abandoned his attempt to deny Bonnie a no-contest divorce, but the division of property remained a sticking point. Bonnie dreaded the day Craig would discover how she had evaded his claim upon her share of Elm Creek Quilts, because he was sure to become even more obstinate.

As Darren made arrangements for the sale, several of the Elm Creek Quilters called or sent emails to assure Bonnie that she was as essential to the quilt camp as ever, but their words seemed empty. She could not blame them for putting Elm Creek Quilts first, but she had hoped for something more than a rational business decision from her closest friends. If she couldn't count on her best girlfriends to be irrationally, passionately reckless in her defense, what could she count on?

"What were you hoping they would do?" asked Midori, without a hint of irony. "Let Craig tear down Elm Creek Quilts rather than break up your circle of quilters?"

"Of course not," said Bonnie. "Do you want the whole, embarrassing truth? I wanted my friends to insist that I keep my ten percent regardless of the risk. I wanted them to lock arms with me and dare Craig to bring on his worst. I wanted them to declare that they would rather have us all go down with the ship than cut one of us loose on a leaking dinghy. And then, over a chorus of their protests, I would sacrifice my ten percent to save Elm Creek Quilts."

"I see. You wanted to be the noble heroine."

"Exactly." Bonnie forced a laugh through her tears, mocking her own foolishness. "I know selling my share is the only reasonable option, but I wanted it to be my choice."

"The result would be the same."

"Yes, but it would be my decision. Instead I feel like my friends packed my suitcases for me and left them on the front porch. There's only so much rejection a woman can take."

"Oh, Bonnie." Midori shook her head sympathetically. "You can't take this personally. It was a business decision, nothing more. Your friends haven't rejected you. From everything I've seen, they value your friendship as much as ever."

"In my head, I know that," Bonnie said, "but in my heart, it feels like they've abandoned me when I needed them most. Claire never would have done this to me."

"Not to you, no. I'm sure she wouldn't ever betray you."

"Not just me. Anyone. She's loyal to a fault."

Midori shrugged and began taking mixing bowls and measuring cups from cupboards. "As you say."

"Claire would never betray a friend," Bonnie insisted.

"I doubt your Elm Creek Quilters would, either," said Midori, taking a sack of cornmeal from the pantry. "Once you get beyond your hurt feelings, you'll see that for yourself."

Bonnie tried, but even when the Elm Creek Quilters called

or emailed with what they probably intended as friendly reassurances, Bonnie sensed a widening distance between them.
Anna phoned, bubbling over with thanks and promises to
manage Bonnie's share of the business prudently, but Bonnie could manage only a wooden "You're welcome" in reply.
When Sylvia phoned the day after the documents of sale arrived via overnight mail, Bonnie's first thought was that Sylvia
had called out of concern that Bonnie had changed her mind.
To her relief, Sylvia didn't urge her to sign the papers and return them; on the contrary, she queried Bonnie until satisfied
that she didn't feel pressured to sell and that she understood
she didn't have to. Although she told Sylvia otherwise, Bonnie *did* feel pressured—by Craig and the circumstances if
not the Elm Creek Quilters—and she *did* have to sell. Either
Sylvia didn't realize this, which was unlikely, or she was calling
merely to ease her own conscience, which disappointed Bonnie tremendously.

As the conversation limped to a close, Sylvia suddenly
asked, "Have you given any more thought to opening Grandma's Parlor before the camp season begins?"

Grandma's Parlor—the small quilt shop Sylvia had proposed Bonnie open in the manor, a consolation prize for the
quilt shop Bonnie had lost. "Not really," said Bonnie, surprised. "I've been so busy here that I honestly haven't thought
about it."

"I suppose it isn't necessary to hold your grand opening on
the first day of camp, but if you want to, we should start making plans."

"I can't really think about it now with the holidays coming
up, and we're scheduling interviews for teachers . . ."

"Of course," said Sylvia when Bonnie didn't continue. "Perhaps in January you'll be ready to begin planning in earnest.

In the meantime, should I have Joe take some measurements? You recall he offered to design custom shelves for you. He's eager to begin so that he can be sure to finish everything before opening day."

"I guess it wouldn't hurt to measure the room, if he's not too busy."

"You know Joe. He isn't happy unless he's busy. I'm sure he'll want to speak with you eventually, however. Only you know what you'll need, so he can't start without you."

Bonnie hardly knew what to say. She was no longer certain that she would return to Elm Creek Manor at all, much less open a quilt shop within its gray stone walls. "I'll try not to keep him waiting too long."

"I'll tell him you said so," Sylvia said briskly. "Also, keep an eye out for a package from me. I'm sending you some forms to fill out for the new camp season. Since you won't be here for our planning meetings, I'd like you to turn in your course proposals early so that I can be sure you get your first choices."

"Thanks," said Bonnie, though it sounded like another consolation prize.

The whole conversation made her feel so uncomfortable and awkward that it was a relief when it ended. She brooded about it afterward, turning over certain phrases in her mind, analyzing and reinterpreting them. She considered asking Claire and Midori for their opinions, but she knew that they would hear the same sentences and reach contradictory conclusions. Finally, exasperated with herself, she gave up trying to puzzle out the hidden meaning in Sylvia's words. Sylvia was the least duplicitous woman Bonnie had ever known. If she said she wanted Bonnie to remain on the Elm Creek Quilts faculty, if she said she hoped Bonnie would open a quilt shop in the manor for their campers' benefit, if she said once an Elm Creek Quilter, always an Elm Creek Quilter—she meant every word.

So Bonnie signed the papers and sent them overnight express to Darren Taylor, and with that Anna became the happy owner of ten percent of Elm Creek Quilts—and Bonnie felt as if she had sold away a portion of her heart.

But what was done was done, and there was no going back. She resolved to have no regrets, only satisfaction that she had kept Elm Creek Quilts out of Craig's greedy, grasping hands.

She put a smile on her face for the guests of the inn, mustered up good cheer when any Elm Creek Quilters phoned or emailed to check in on her—and mourned quietly, working on her Pineapple Patch quilt in the peace of the shaded lanai, reminiscing about the early days when she and her friends had worked and planned and worked some more, yet unaware of how they would succeed beyond their wildest dreams.

She wondered if any other venture, even a quilt camp in paradise created with her best friend, could ever replace what she had given up.

✧

Thinking that sharing good news would cheer up her friend, Claire offered to let Bonnie call their ten finalists while she revised the rejection letter and sent it out to those who had already been eliminated. Bonnie gladly agreed to the division of labor. She had experienced enough rejection already and didn't relish the thought of exploring it from the other side.

One day while Claire was working at the quilt shop, Bonnie took over her office and phoned their top ten candidates with the good news. Their reactions ranged from self-assured thanks to shrieks of delight, which lifted Bonnie's spirits and energized her for the difficult task of organizing the interview schedule and arranging the applicants' travel. Working around scheduling conflicts and scouring the Internet for cheap airfares, sending emails back and forth with the finalists and phoning the quilt shop to confirm details with Claire, Bonnie became so engrossed in her work that the morning flew by. Her thoughts rarely turned to Elm Creek Quilts, and she forgot to break for lunch until almost two o'clock.

When she went to the kitchen, she found Midori seated on a stool at the center island, perusing a cookbook as she chatted on the phone. "That's just silly. Ask her yourself," Bonnie overheard her say as she searched the refrigerator for leftovers to heat up, or better yet, some tasty sandwich fixings. "She just walked in."

Bonnie glanced at Midori over her shoulder, surprised to discover herself the subject of conversation. "Who is it?" she mouthed, gathering up sliced turkey, provolone, mustard, lettuce, and tomato and setting everything on the island.

Midori covered the mouthpiece with her hand. "My nephew."

"What does he want?" she whispered, coming around the counter to take a loaf from the breadbox.

"She wants to know what you want," Midori repeated into the phone.

"Don't tell him that," protested Bonnie.

"Here she is." With that, Midori handed her the phone.

Fumbling with the loaf of bread and the handset, Bonnie almost hung up on him. "Hello?" she said, dropping the bag on the counter so clumsily that the twist-tie popped off and a few slices tumbled out. Midori tsked her tongue in disapproval. "Hinano?"

"Eh, howzit, snowbird? My aunt tells me you've been moping around feeling sorry for yourself and scaring the guests away."

Embarrassed, Bonnie forced a laugh. "I find it hard to believe Midori said that."

"Maybe not in so many words. Sorry about Elm Creek Quilts. It must've hurt to sign those papers."

"So much I almost couldn't hold the pen."

"It might not be forever," Hinano said. "You don't know how things will work out."

That was certainly true. Bonnie had given up trying to predict the future, because every time she thought she knew what would happen next, an unexpected twist of misfortune blindsided her. "I still have a job there," she said. "It won't be the same, but at least they haven't fired me. Not yet."

"From what Aunt Midori tells me, I don't think they will."

"We'll see." If Craig had any more nasty tricks planned, they might have to, although they would probably ask for her resignation rather than fire her. She prayed it would never come to that. "Claire's offered me a partnership in the Hale Kapa Kuiki, so at least I have options."

"Yeah, my aunt mentioned that," Hinano said. "But if you don't cheer up, Claire might change her mind. No one wants to work with a grouch."

"I'm trying to recall if we've ever had a conversation in which you haven't deliberately insulted me, and you know something? I can't think of one."

"That wasn't an insult. It was a friendly warning."

"Really. Then thanks, I guess." From the corner of her eye, Bonnie spied Midori fighting to hide a smile. "Is that why you called?"

"No, I wanted to add another item to your list of activities for your campers."

"Oh." Sometimes Bonnie forgot that he could be helpful, on occasion. She glanced around for paper and pen. "I don't have my notebook with me. Could you hold on a moment?"

"I'm not going to tell you what it is. I'm going to show you. Tomorrow."

"Tomorrow?"

"Yeah. My aunt said you need a day off. You aren't afraid of flying in little planes, are you?"

"No." Suddenly Bonnie had an alarming thought. "As long as I get to stay on board throughout the flight."

"Uh, okay, that shouldn't be a problem," he said. "Why? Do you have a habit of falling out?"

"No, I just have this terrible feeling that you plan to take me skydiving."

Hinano burst out laughing. "No. Nothing that exciting. My friend runs a private air shuttle service and he's going over to Oahu for the day. He has room in the plane, so I thought you might like a chance to visit another island."

Bonnie thought it over quickly. "I would, but I'm not sure if it would be practical to schedule evening programs that take our campers off Maui."

"Then don't think of this as a research trip for quilt camp. Come for yourself. Trust me, there's something there you should see. Afterward, if you decide the trip was a big waste of time, you can punch me in the arm. Or yell at me. Or both."

She was on the verge of begging off with the excuse that she had too much work to do when it occurred to her that she hadn't left the inn except for her morning walks in days. She had been in Hawaii for more than two months and she had hardly ventured out of Lahaina. When her trip was over and the islands became a place of warmth, color, and fragrance that she could visit only in memories, wouldn't she regret seeing little more of them than the same few square miles?

"I'd love to go," she told Hinano. "As long as it won't require a parachute or a crash helmet, I'm in."

"I'll save the extreme sports for another time," he said. "Tomorrow at eight too early for you?"

She would miss half of the breakfast service, but she doubted Midori would mind. "Eight o'clock is fine."

"Good, then it's a date. I'll pick you up at the inn. See you tomorrow."

"See you," she said, but he had already hung up.

"Well?" prompted Midori as Bonnie replaced the phone.

"Hinano's taking me to Oahu tomorrow on a top-secret mission to show me something important."

"Wear comfortable walking shoes," Midori suggested, confirming Bonnie's suspicions that she knew exactly where Hinano intended to take her and what he wanted her to see. Perhaps Midori herself had proposed the outing. But if that were true, would Hinano have called it a date?

Of course he would have, Bonnie told herself, brushing off a sudden twinge of worry. People said "It's a date" all the time without meaning that it was a date in the romantic sense. He knew she was still married. She and Hinano didn't even get along very well, at least not all the time.

Hinano was helping her with her research, nothing more. But it was an act of friendship at a time when she felt bereft of friends.

⬧

The next morning Bonnie dressed in light capri pants, a soft cotton T-shirt, and her most comfortable walking shoes. She was helping Midori serve breakfast when Hinano arrived, twenty minutes early. She was flattered until she realized he had come early not for her but to spend time catching up with his aunt over coffee and pineapple pecan muffins.

While Hinano and Midori chatted about family and friends, Bonnie slipped away to check her email, a task she had come to dread since Darren Taylor rarely had any good news and the Elm Creek Quilters' cheerful reassurances rang false. To her relief, that morning she had only a few photos from Tammy, a quilting question from a former student, and two reminders to pay bills. She took her time responding and logged off at five minutes to eight, returning to the kitchen in time to hear Hinano lamenting that his son wanted to spend semester break with his girlfriend on Oahu. "It won't be much of a Mele Kalikimaka without Kai," he said.

Shaking her head, Midori set another muffin on his plate. "Kai has to spend Christmas with *ohana*. Just tell the boy he has to come home."

"Auntie, he wasn't asking for permission. He was telling me his plans." Hinano glanced up, spotted Bonnie, and grinned. "Eh, snowbird. Ready to fly?"

"You haven't finished breakfast," Midori protested.

He patted his stomach and held up his palms in surrender. "Auntie, two muffins are my limit these days."

"You're getting too skinny. You should come around more often and let me feed you."

Bonnie wouldn't have described Hinano's solid wrestler's build as skinny, and apparently Hinano agreed. "I don't miss many meals," he assured his aunt. "But the food's good here and the company's all right. Maybe I'll come back."

Midori swatted him with a dishtowel and said something in a mixture of Hawaiian and Japanese that made Hinano laugh even harder. "We better go before she hurts me," Hinano said to Bonnie. Amused, she retrieved her purse from Claire's office and met him at the front door—but she took her time rather than rescue him too soon.

His car, a ten-year-old blue hatchback that had seen better days, was parked on the street at the end of the block. The door creaked when he opened it for her, but it closed with a solid, reassuring thunk when he shut it after she slid into the vinyl seat. An air freshener shaped like a palm tree dangled from the rearview mirror, giving off the faint scent of orange.

"It doesn't look like much but it gets great gas mileage," Hinano said as he turned the key and released the clutch. Bonnie nodded and wondered if it was too much to hope that it also had functioning air bags.

As they drove south out of Lahaina, Bonnie asked, "What was Midori saying to you back there?"

"She was scolding me."

"I figured that. What was she saying?"

"I don't know. I only understood half of it." Hinano slowed at a stop sign, flicked on the turn signal, and waved a pedestrian across before pulling onto the highway. "The Hawaiian half. I speak only a bit of Japanese, words I picked up here and there, mostly insults and food."

"You're not part Japanese, too, like your aunt?"

Hinano shook his head. "Aunt Midori married my father's brother. Me, I'm *kanaka maoli*, native Hawaiian. Kai has some Japanese from his mother's side, though."

After that, Hinano abruptly changed the subject and began describing some of the more notorious tourist traps as they drove past. His anecdotes were so amusingly preposterous that Bonnie was sure he was making them up, but he swore every word was true. Perhaps to enhance his credibility, he tempered the more outlandish parts of his narrative with historical facts, so Bonnie learned that Lahaina meant "merciless sun" or "a day of calamity" depending upon whom one asked and how one pronounced it; that the town had been the unofficial royal capital of the Hawaiian islands in the early eighteen hundreds; and that Kamehameha the Great in particular had loved Lahaina for its spectacular surfing. Whalers had considered it one of the most important ports in the Pacific, even though they hunted whales far to the north rather than in Hawaiian waters.

"They wintered here, making repairs, replenishing stores," Hinano explained as they turned on to the main highway that wound through lush mountains as it cut across the island. "After the whaling era ended, Lahaina made its money off the sugar industry, the pineapple plantations, and," he gave Bonnie an acknowledging nod, "tourism."

"Why do you indicate me when you talk about tourism?" said Bonnie. "I'm more than a tourist. I work here, and—"

She was about to add that she might be staying, but she halted before the words tumbled out.

"I wasn't calling you a tourist," said Hinano mildly. "I only meant that you make your living from tourists. You're in that industry as opposed to pineapple or sugar or whaling, unless you've been moonlighting without telling anyone."

"Oh." She thought of herself as belonging to the quilting industry, but she supposed he had a point. "I see."

He shook his head. "This'll be a long day if you're going to be so sensitive."

"I was going to say the same about you, except instead of sensitive, I was going to say insulting."

"Insulting?" Hinano protested. "I've been on my best behavior."

Bonnie hid a smile. "I don't dispute that."

"Now you're just teasing me."

She shifted in her seat to better admire the view out the side window. "Maybe a little."

From the corner of her eye, she saw his grin widening. "You pretend to be annoyed, but I think you like me."

Bonnie hesitated. "Maybe a little." Before he could reply, she added, "You're a fairly good tour guide."

He mulled that over and shrugged. "That's a start."

Bonnie kept her face turned toward the window, smiling.

Hinano fell easily into the tour guide role as they drove across Maui, naming mountains and native plants, relating legends and histories. Before long they reached the Kahului Airport, but instead of parking near the main terminal, he turned off farther down the road, passed through a security checkpoint, and pulled to a stop at a private hangar. As they climbed out of the car, Hinano called out a greeting to a pilot standing at the foot of the stairs to a Cessna propjet. The pilot responded with a brief wave before returning his attention to the two men in business suits boarding the plane, briefcases in hand.

Bonnie followed Hinano on board, ducking her head as she passed through the doorway and quickly counting eight seats. She had never been on such a small plane before, not even for short hops from the Elm Creek Valley regional airport to Pittsburgh or Philadelphia. She hid her nervousness as she settled into her seat at the back of the plane across the aisle from Hinano, tested her seatbelt with a sharp tug, and glanced around for the nearest life vest and air sickness bag.

Soon they were under way, and after a smooth liftoff and a breathtaking aerial view of an exquisite, emerald green Maui, Bonnie began to relax. It was too loud for comfortable conversation, so she gazed out the window admiring the dazzling blue of the ocean. When a bump of unexpected turbulence made her instinctively clutch her armrests, she started at the touch of a hand upon hers. "Don't tell me a snowbird doesn't like to fly," Hinano said over the drone of the engines.

"I guess this snowbird is a penguin," she said weakly, and Hinano threw back his head and laughed. His hand lingered on hers for a moment, surely just to reassure her. She felt the warmth of his touch long after he let go.

Less than an hour later, they touched down at the Honolulu airport and parked at another private hangar not much larger than the one they had departed from on Maui. Hinano had arranged to borrow a car from a friend who worked at the airport, so they hitched a ride on the businessmen's shuttle to the terminal, walked to the parking garage, and searched the right floor, section, and row until they located the car, a brown Honda in slightly better condition than Hinano's. Hinano found the keys hidden exactly where his friend had promised, within the fold of a newspaper lying on the back seat.

"Everyone checks the floor mats and the sun visor," Hinano explained as he started the engine. "Car thieves aren't usually big readers."

As they left the airport, Bonnie was surprised by how much more urban everything seemed in comparison to Maui. "Welcome to Honolulu," said Hinano as they pulled onto a busy freeway. "Biggest city in Hawaii both in size and population."

"And in the number of tourists," Bonnie guessed. "Weren't you stationed on Oahu?"

"Near Pearl Harbor. That's worth showing your quilters, but they'll need a day for it. Maybe you should think about adding day trips to their schedule. There's too much of Hawaii to see to try to squeeze it into a few evenings. They won't want to quilt all day long."

"You'd be surprised. How long will it take us to get to Pearl

Harbor?" Bonnie inquired casually, but Hinano recognized her attempt to trick him into revealing their destination and merely smiled.

They left the freeway and drove through a part of the city that to Bonnie seemed more like an office district than a tourist hotspot. Puzzled, Bonnie wondered why they seemed to be circling the same few blocks until she realized Hinano was searching for a parking place. Whatever their destination was, they were close.

Eventually he found an unoccupied meter on a side street and quickly pulled into the spot before someone else could beat him to it. "We have a bit of a walk," he said as they climbed out of the car.

Bonnie nodded and opened her purse. "I think I have change."

"Put that away. This day is on me." He fed coins into the meter. "All right. If we aren't done in two hours, I'll run back and put more in. Or I guess I could stick my friend with a parking ticket."

"He won't stay your friend long that way."

"She. And you're right, she probably wouldn't ever speak to me again."

The news that Hinano's friend was a woman left Bonnie feeling oddly unsettled. "Why didn't you invite her to join us?" she asked.

"It didn't occur to me."

A strange obstinacy compelled her to say, "You could call her."

Hinano gave her an inscrutable look. "I guess I could, but she's seen it before, and she's at work, remember?"

"Of course," Bonnie murmured. She fell in step beside him as he headed down the sidewalk.

They walked down the block, crossed a broad intersection, and suddenly came upon an oasis of green lawns and sprawling banyan trees in the middle of the skyscrapers and busy streets. Surrounding the green expanse was a coral block wall topped with an iron fence, and through the branches of the banyan trees, Bonnie glimpsed a tall, white building. Mystified, she followed Hinano along the outer wall until they came to an elaborate gate.

"The Hawaiian coat of arms," Hinano noted, indicating a plaque on the gateway. Two men in red robes, one holding a tall feathered staff and the other a spear, flanked a heraldic badge displaying motifs reminiscent of the Union Jack and topped by a red-and-gold crown. Along the bottom was a curved blue banner bearing Hawaiian words in gold letters.

"'Ua mau ke ea o ka'aina i ka pono,'" read Hinano. "'The life of the land is perpetuated in righteousness.' The motto of the Kingdom of Hawaii, and now the state motto."

Bonnie's gaze traveled from the open gates down the driveway to the stately white building, Italianate in design, with verandas on the first and second stories boasting arches supported by columns. A broad tower in the center flanked by two smaller towers on either end extended the building to the third story. A grand stone staircase climbed to the lower veranda, and although it appeared to be cordoned off to forbid access to the tourists milling about at the foot, Bonnie could imagine elegant men and women in traditional Hawaiian and Victorian attire ascending the stairs to enter the building through the double doors.

"What is this place?" she asked, but as she spoke, she guessed.

"This is 'Iolani Palace," Hinano said.

"This is where your wife—"

"Yes." A shadow fell over his face and his gaze involuntarily darted somewhere beyond the gate, a patch of grass in the shade of the banyan trees. Then, somehow, Hinano managed a small, rueful, heartbreaking smile. "But that's not why I brought you here."

He beckoned her forward and reached for her hand. Too overcome and saddened to think twice, she gave it to him.

While making halting conversation about the history of the palace—built in 1882, it had been the official residence of the last two monarchs of the Kingdom of Hawaii—Hinano led Bonnie down the driveway past an elaborate domed pavilion. As they drew closer to the palace, Bonnie spotted another structure behind it and off to the side; considerably smaller than the palace, it was built of coral block and resembled a fortress.

"This was the *halekoa*, the barracks of the Royal Guard," Hinano explained, leading her toward it. "It's served many different purposes through the years, but now, among other things, it holds the gift shop and ticket booth."

Hinano purchased tickets for them both, pointedly ignoring her offer to pay her own way. Then they reported to the back entrance of the palace, where they received instructions about proper behavior within the historic building—no photography, no cell phones, no touching the priceless antiques—and how to operate the mp3 players that would provide the audio tour.

When a docent dressed in Victorian attire opened the door and allowed them and a handful of tourists to enter, Bonnie found herself in a grand hall facing the back of an elegant koa wood staircase that split into two flanking staircases on the second floor. Portraits of dignitaries lined the walls above arched niches displaying exquisite vases and other art. The

black marble floor gleamed beneath natural light that fil-
tered through the crystal doors of the main entrance on the
opposite side of the hall. The streaming sunlight illuminated
images of women dancing with flower garlands etched into the
glass.

And there the tour began. As they had been instructed,
Bonnie, Hinano, and the others in their group put on their
headphones and slipped the straps of their mp3 players around
their necks. Bonnie and Hinano synchronized the start of their
tours by counting to three and pressing play simultaneously so
that one of them wouldn't be sent on to the next room without
the other.

The narrator guided the listeners through all the first floor
state rooms—the Blue Room for smaller receptions and
the state dining room on one side of the Grand Hall, the re-
splendent Throne Room on the other. In each room Bonnie
admired art and furnishings from the era of Hawaii's last monarchs and discovered more about the members of the royal
family who had called the 'Iolani Palace home. She learned
how King David Kalakaua, elected in 1874 and known as the
"Merrie Monarch" for his patronage of arts, music, and culture,
had received dignitaries from around the world at the palace,
which had been not only the official residence of the royal family but also the center of political and social life for the Kingdom of Hawaii. Beautiful and luxurious, it had been furnished
with the most modern conveniences of the era, including in-
door plumbing; gas chandeliers, which were soon replaced
with early electric lights; and a remarkable new invention to
improve communications, the telephone. But King Kalakaua
was as diligent in preserving Hawaii's traditional culture as he
was eager to embrace modern marvels, for he had supported
the revival of the hula, long forbidden by the missionaries, and

had promoted the transcription of Hawaiian language and oral traditions.

After Kalakaua's death in 1891, his sister Lili'uokalani, who had served as Princess Regent during her brother's voyages abroad, succeeded him as Queen of Hawaii. Resolving to strengthen the political stature of the monarchy, she proposed a new constitution, earning her the enmity of an opposition group comprised primarily of businessmen, foreign nationals, and sugar plantation owners. Over the objections of an ailing President Cleveland but with the assistance of the United States Marines, Queen Lili'uokalani's political enemies staged a coup and instituted a provisional government that granted them positions of power and influence.

In the Blue Room, Bonnie read the carefully preserved letter of protest the betrayed queen had written when faced with the threat of invasion by armed forces. "I, Lili'uokalani, by the Grace of God and under the Constitution of the Hawaiian Kingdom, Queen," she had begun the protest of the actions against her and her nation. With poignant eloquence, she had acknowledged that she could not confront a superior military force without risking her people's lives, and therefore she yielded her authority to the government of the United States, trusting that when the situation was reviewed, the United States would recognize the wrongdoing and reinstate her.

Her words were proud, strong, and just, but Bonnie could read the pain and loss between the lines.

She felt a touch on her arm. Hinano waited until she removed one of her earpieces before saying in a low voice, "Note that she yielded her authority to the United States, not to the provisional government, not to the men who overthrew her."

Bonnie nodded, understanding that this was significant,

but unsure how or if it truly mattered. Queen Liliʻuokalani had lost a kingdom. Did it really matter to whom she had yielded her power? Or was her choice a courageous act of defiance, as well as a sign of the greater trust she placed in the United States government?

As she replaced her earpiece, Bonnie wondered how much of the tour Hinano already knew by heart. Probably every word. She almost wished that she could hear him tell the history of the palace rather than listen to the anonymous narrator on the audio tour.

After marveling at the impressive beauty of the Throne Room—and feeling her heart sink a little lower when she learned that Liliʻuokalani had been tried for knowledge of treason there two years after her abdication—Bonnie followed Hinano to a discreet elevator and up to the second floor. The koa wood staircase was not used, to better preserve it.

Upstairs, Bonnie and Hinano visited King Kalakaua's bedroom, his impressive library full of priceless volumes and works of art, and the music room, which must have been a favorite gathering place for the family of composers and performers. As they returned to the upper hall, Hinano again gestured for Bonnie to pause the recording. "You know the tune, ʻAloha ʻOe?ʼ"

"I don't think so."

"I bet you do. If you've never heard any other Hawaiian music, you've heard this song. It's part of the show at the Old Lahaina Luʻau." Quietly, so not to disturb the other visitors, Hinano sang a few bars in Hawaiian, his rich baritone a soft rumble. Just as he had said, she immediately recognized the melody. "That was Queen Liliʻuokalani's most famous composition."

"Such a remarkable woman," Bonnie mused, following Hinano across the upper hall. "Educated, musically gifted, and a stateswoman."

"She had other talents you'll appreciate too," said Hinano cryptically, putting his headphones back on and gesturing for her to do the same.

Hinano and Bonnie synchronized their mp3 players as they had done before and moved on to the next room, identified on the map as Queen Lili'uokalani's Imprisonment Room. Bonnie was preparing herself to hear the heartbreaking story of the queen's downfall when she caught sight of a large glass display table and stopped short. Then she drew in a sharp breath and hurried forward to confirm what her first glance had suspected.

Within the glass case lay an elaborate crazy quilt about eight feet square, a mosaic of multicolored fabrics stitched together apparently at random, undisciplined and heedless of symmetry. A closer look revealed that the quilt possessed a subtle, appealing order, for it was actually composed of nine distinct sections arranged three by three. Dark maroon satin sashing strips separated the ostensibly haphazard patchwork blocks, with pairs of crossed flags embroidered at each junction. The irregular scraps of silk, velvet, and satin had been lavishly framed and embellished with a variety of stitches worked in silk thread, ranging in difficulty from simple to painstakingly intricate. Bonnie's gaze flew over the quilt, taking in fanciful embroidered pictures, names, dates, silk-screened ribbons, inked images—as well as sections where only a few threads of shattered silk remained, hinting at other beloved names, other precious details that had been lost to time.

So transfixed was Bonnie by the unexpected treasure before her that she had not heard a word of the narration. She skipped to the beginning of the track and listened as the narrator told of the events leading to the creation of the Queen's Quilt, for it was indeed Lili'uokalani's own.

Two years after Lili'uokalani was forced to give up her rule of the Hawaiian Kingdom, a group of loyal supporters tried to restore her to power. When the attempt failed, Lili'uokalani was arrested and forced to sign a document relinquishing her claim to the throne forever. Soon thereafter, she was tried before a military tribunal in her own former throne room and convicted of knowing about the royalist plot. A heavy fine was levied against her, but a sentence of five years of hard labor was commuted to imprisonment in an upstairs room of the palace—the very room in which Bonnie stood.

Listening, spellbound, Bonnie took in the room, turning slowly in place, trying to imagine confinement within the same four walls for an indefinite future. Tears came to her eyes when she learned that Lili'uokalani had been permitted only a single companion during her long imprisonment, a devoted friend named Eveline Wilson who had shared the queen's sentence, except that she had been released one day each week to visit her family.

How many women would sacrifice their own liberty to offer comfort and companionship to a friend? How many women possessed such courage, such compassion? Bonnie wondered if she could have relinquished her freedom for anyone but her own children, her own mother, her own most beloved friends. She wanted to believe that she could have done it for any of the Elm Creek Quilters, but she knew she would never be tested in such a dramatic fashion and it was easy to offer what would never be required. She wondered if any of the Elm Creek Quilters could have given up so much for her. Then she remembered how quickly they had urged her to sell her share of Elm Creek Quilts, and she had her melancholy answer.

Forcing the unpleasant reflections from her mind, she studied the quilt again, making her way around the entire case to view the astonishing masterpiece from all angles, stepping politely around the other visitors who were as engrossed in examining it as she. Only one of the nine large blocks bore embroidery stitches but no names or pictures; the others each preserved at least a few initials, names, or images.

The center block and focus of the masterpiece, divided into four quadrants by narrow bands of white satin, preserved the history of the quilt and the rise and fall of the last queen of Hawaii. The first quadrant of light blue silk displayed an embroidered crown surrounded by a wreath of leaves worked in gold thread, and beneath it, a proud testament:

Lydia Kamakaeha Liliuokalani
Born, Sept. 2nd. 1838.
Proclaimed Heir Apparent, Apr. 10th. 1877
Ascended the throne,
January 29th 1891.

The second quadrant put forth an ominous message in light thread on shattered red silk: "Dethroned January 17th 1893. Uprising January 6th 1895."

Continuing clockwise, the third quadrant of ocean blue silk recorded a fateful day, the embroidered words flanked by blossoming branches: "H. M. Queen LILIUOKALANI abdicated on the 24th of Jan. 1895." A list of eight witnesses followed, and then the poignant addition, "Companion, Mrs. E. T. K. K. Wilson, Iolani Palace, May 24th 1895."

The fourth and last quadrant, the red silk almost completely deteriorated, offered the provenance of the quilt in copper-plate script worked in gold silk thread:

Her Majesty Queen
Liliuokalani
Imprisoned at Iolani Palace
January 17th 1895
Companion
Mrs Eveline Melita Kilioulani Kaopaokalani Wilson.
Released Sept 6th 1895
We began this quilt there.

Bonnie wondered where the two women had finished it.

Where the four quadrants met at the very heart of the quilt was a circle of white satin with an image drawn or painted upon it. Bonnie leaned over as far as she could without touching the glass case and was able to make out a rendering of the Hawaiian coat of arms, almost but not quite identical to the emblem Hinano had shown her upon the front gates of the palace. Even after her abdication, conviction, and imprisonment, Queen Lili'uokalani had considered Hawaii the center of her creation.

Bonnie drew away from the quilt to allow others to gather around it, her gaze traveling around the room. She imagined the queen and her faithful friend sitting quietly by the window, stitching irregular shapes to muslin foundations, sharing scissors and spools of silk thread, reminiscing about happier days in the palace, encouraging each other with hopeful words of better days to come. Prayer, reading, companionship, and artistic expression had seen them through the long, sorrowful days of their confinement, when their movements were restricted and only their imaginations could take flight.

When the narrator prompted Bonnie to continue on to the next room, she quickly paused the recording. As other visitors stepped away, Bonnie returned to the glass case and gazed again at the quilt, marveling at the exquisite detail, reflecting upon the women who had created it. The quilt was a treasure of both art and history, for it was a tangible link to the imprisoned queen and her companion, a testament to their friendship and forbearance. Bonnie was grateful for whatever act of chance or wisdom had preserved the quilt through the ages so that it could speak to generations to come. So that it could speak to her.

Suddenly she became aware of Hinano standing quietly at her side. With tears in her eyes, she thanked him for bringing her to the 'Iolani Palace.

"It would have been tragic for you to come all the way to Hawaii and leave without seeing the Queen's Quilt," he said. "My friend had room in his plane, so I thought, why not?"

He made it seem so simple and clear, as if it weren't obvious how moved she was by the queen's story and how grateful she was to learn it. Bonnie smiled at him, and together they resumed the audio tour. The remaining few rooms were as lovely and interesting as those they had already toured, but Bonnie's thoughts remained in the queen's imprisonment room with the priceless treasure preserved there.

After the tour concluded, they returned to the old barracks building so that Bonnie could browse through the gift shop. She was delighted to find a small booklet with beautiful photographs of the Queen's Quilt as well as a more detailed history than had been included on the audio tour. She quickly snapped up ten copies, one for her and one for each of the Elm Creek Quilters, to include with their Christmas gifts.

Near the checkout counter, she spotted a poster of another antique quilt much different in style from either the Queen's Quilt or the traditional Hawaiian appliqué quilt. Four rectangular Hawaiian flags, each pieced with a Union Jack canton on a field of eight red, white, and blue stripes, framed a central white square bearing the Hawaiian coat of arms in appliqué. Above the coat of arms was an appliquéd scroll with the embroidered words *Ku'u Hae Aloha.*

"'My Beloved Flag,'" Hinano translated. "After Queen Lili'uokalani was overthrown and Hawaii became a republic, many Hawaiian quilters made flag quilts like this one to commemorate the monarchy, and maybe also to mourn its passing. I always considered these quilts a form of rebellion, but maybe rebellion is too strong a word for it."

"A remembrance?" Bonnie offered. "A protest?"

"A protest," Hinano agreed. "A quiet, eloquent, resolute protest. The men of the provisional government brought down the Kingdom of Hawaii, but they couldn't make the people forget it."

Bonnie nodded, studying the poster. For generations mainland quilters had expressed their political beliefs in patchwork and appliqué. It did not surprise her that Hawaiian quilters had also taken up needle and thread to articulate what must have been strong and intensely personal feelings about the upheaval in their nation.

"My grandmother made a flag quilt much like this one, except the Hawaiian coat of arms is more detailed and on a navy background instead of white," continued Hinano. "My sister has it, but it's fragile and she rarely takes it out of climate-controlled storage. I'll have her show it to you someday."

Bonnie thanked him, honored that he would consider allowing her a rare glimpse of the precious family heirloom. She wondered, though, when she would have the opportunity, or if she ever would.

After Bonnie made her purchases, Hinano drove them to Waikiki, where they walked along a beach crowded with sunbathers, families, and surfers. The sidewalks were packed with tourists, most of them Japanese as far as Bonnie could tell, and the streets were lined with restaurants, clubs, convenience stores, and high-end retailers. After the contemplative reverence of the 'Iolani Palace, Waikiki seemed too crowded and bustling to suit Bonnie and she found herself leading Hinano down the beach away from the throng.

"Look there." When Bonnie failed to glance in the right direction, Hinano took her by the shoulders and steered her toward the southwest, to what seemed to her to be a low, jagged mountain jutting out into the sea. "That's Diamond Head, one of the most recognizable images of Hawaii."

"I don't recognize it," Bonnie said. "It can't be that famous."

"I guess you must be right and millions of other people are wrong."

"I guess so. It's sad for them, isn't it?"

"It's probably the most famous volcanic crater in the world," he said, sighing with infinite patience. "Is there some reason you're giving me a hard time about this?"

Yes. Because she was nervous, because his hands had lingered on her shoulders much longer than necessary to turn her in the right direction to see the landmark. Fortunately, her back was to him, and he could not see the conflicting emotions written plainly upon her face. "Sorry. Continue the lesson, professor."

"I don't know if I want to now."

She risked a glance over her shoulder at him. "Please?"

"All right," he relented, and he gave her shoulders a gentle squeeze as if in reproach. She returned her gaze to Diamond Head as if she found it endlessly fascinating. "In the nineteenth century, British sailors who spotted the crater from a distance saw calcite crystals in the lava rock glimmering in the sunlight. They assumed the soil was full of diamonds."

"I bet they were disappointed when they discovered the truth."

"Maybe not too much. The great view alone is worth the climb."

She shrugged, but even then his hands remained on her shoulders. "You and I might think so, but most people would prefer a mountain made of diamonds."

"After the United States took over Oahu, they built a strategic defense post up at the top. You can still walk through the underground observation deck at the summit. We should go there sometime. You like to walk. Want to go for a hike next time my friend has room in his plane?"

"I thought you said it was a volcano."

"I said it was a volcanic crater. Eh, your voice is shaking! What are you scared of?"

"Nothing."

"You really think I'd drag you up the side of an active volcano?"

"I don't know. You might."

"Diamond Head's been extinct for more than a hundred and fifty thousand years."

"It must be safe, then," she said, willing indifference into her voice, wanting to step away from his hands on her shoulders, wanting to hold perfectly still so he would keep touching her.

It had been a long time since a man had touched her in kindness, in friendship, in desire.

"It's safe. You sure you're okay?" Hinano spun her around and lifted her chin with his finger. "This sun too much for you, snowbird?"

"Don't be silly," she scoffed. "I can handle a little Hawaiian sun. I'm tougher than you—"

Then she stopped speaking because he was kissing her, his lips warm and gentle as they lingered on hers.

Suddenly he released her and stepped away. "I know you're tough," he said quietly. "You say it like a joke, but you're strong. Stronger than you know."

Speechless, she stood frozen in place for a moment after he inclined his head down the beach the way they had come. He was already a few yards ahead before she shook off her astonishment and caught up with him.

They returned to the bustling streets. Hinano suggested lunch at a noodle shop with a view of the ocean, small and off the main thoroughfare. The entire menu was in Japanese, but Hinano translated enough of it for her to choose a dish that she thought she'd like. Hinano offered her a taste of his shoyu ramen in exchange for a bite of her miso ramen, and as they placed small samples on each other's plates, Bonnie couldn't help but think of all the times Craig had asked, "Are you going to eat that?" and then helped himself to food off her plate without waiting for a reply—at restaurants, at home—from the time they were in college through their last futile attempt to reconcile.

Craig. She really didn't want to think about him at the moment.

They returned the borrowed car to the airport parking garage, hid the keys in the folded newspaper, and met Hinano's pilot friend back at the hangar. The original passengers had not returned, but three new business travelers, a man and two women, joined them for the flight back to Maui. The din in the cabin restricted conversation, but Bonnie was relieved to gaze out the window, as alone as she could be with her thoughts. Over lunch their conversation had been light, restrained, and Bonnie couldn't help wondering if Hinano regretted the kiss, if he wished he could take it back. If he apologized for it, she didn't know what she would do. She couldn't bear to think that he might be sitting on the other side of the aisle chagrinned and embarrassed, wishing he had never invited her to Oahu.

They were halfway back to the inn in his old blue hatchback when the words she had dreaded finally came. "Eh, snowbird, I'm sorry about that back there."

"Sorry about what?" she said indifferently, but her heart sank.

"I was out of line. I know you're going through some stuff now—"

"Don't worry about it. I know we're just friends."

"Oh." He kept his gaze fixed upon the road ahead. "Okay. Friends."

"I mean, if that's what you want to be."

"If that's all you want—"

"That's not all I want but—" She wrung her hands in her lap. "I'm still married."

He was silent for a long moment. "I thought you were separated."

"I am, but—" She didn't know how to explain it. "I can't do to him what he did to me."

"Okay. I get that." Hinano nodded, but he didn't look at her. "You'll be leaving soon anyway, so I guess it's just as well."

"I'm not leaving until the end of March." Months away, plenty of time for—for what? Bonnie wasn't sure what he wanted, what she wanted.

"Eh, well—" He shrugged and sighed, and she understood what that meant. What did it matter whether she was leaving in four months or four days? She was leaving, so what was the point of getting involved and setting themselves up for heartache?

There was nothing more to say, so they rode in silence the rest of the way back to the inn. Hinano walked her to the door, but when she thanked him for the wonderful day, he grinned and said it was his pleasure, but he didn't put his hands on her shoulders again, he didn't kiss her, and he said nothing more to suggest that they might make that second trip to Oahu so he could show her the beautiful view from the summit of Diamond Head.

Chapter Eleven

For days afterward, Claire and Midori pressed Bonnie for details about her excursion to Oahu with Hinano. Bonnie shared every detail about her impressions of the Queen's Quilt—which her friends had already seen—but said nothing of the kiss, nothing to imply that the sightseeing trip had been a date in the romantic sense, nothing to suggest it was an outing that might ever be repeated. They drew their own conclusions. Midori eyed her curiously for a few days and had one heated phone conversation with her nephew that she abruptly ended when Bonnie entered the room, but otherwise she never mentioned Hinano. Claire, naturally, was less able to conceal her expectations for the aftermath of the date, which she insisted upon calling it. "Do you think you'll go out with him again?" she asked one evening.

Bonnie furrowed her brow as if she had not considered it until that moment. "I guess so, if he thinks of something else I should add to the campers' itinerary."

Claire fell into the habit of looking up expectantly whenever Bonnie's cell phone rang, frowning in puzzlement each time she learned that the caller wasn't Hinano. Over time, her

frowns turned into scowls. "He still hasn't called?" she demanded a week later.

"Who hasn't called?" Bonnie asked.

"Hinano, of course."

"He's called his aunt."

"What about you?"

"Why should he call me? We're friends, that's all. I'm not
sure where you got the idea that there's anything more going
on between us. I'm still married, Claire."

"In name only."

"But that's enough. I'm married, and I'm not dating anyone
until I'm not."

Bonnie wasn't sure whether she was fooling anyone, but
she was determined to try. Claire insisted upon being indignant on her behalf. Once Bonnie even caught her exploring
the revenge websites again, although as usual Claire closed her
web browser the moment Bonnie stepped into the office.

"What are you trying to hide?" she teased to deflect attention from her own issues, but when Claire blanched and
fumbled to explain, Bonnie assured her she was only joking.

Sometimes she was tempted to call Hinano with the excuse
that she needed more information about some of the items
on his list of must-see Maui attractions, and once she almost
stopped by his music shop to ask him about his grandmother's
antique Hawaiian flag quilt. Each time she managed to talk
herself out of doing anything potentially embarrassing. Hinano was right. They were better off as friends. She couldn't
pretend that she didn't find Hinano attractive, that she didn't
wish she could spend more time in his company getting to
know him better, that she didn't imagine what it would be like
to be in his arms—but she was still married, and that meant
something to her. She hadn't been with anyone but Craig in

more than thirty years, and it was unsettling to find herself dealing with emotions and desires that she had never expected to feel again, and wondering what Hinano felt and wanted. And not knowing. And being both eager and afraid to find out.

But in the end it didn't matter. She wouldn't be in Hawaii long enough for anything real or lasting to develop between them. And yet she couldn't be sorry that she had fallen for him or that he had, maybe, fallen for her. She had assumed that she was long past the time in her life when anyone would find her attractive or desirable, and it felt good to be proven wrong, to be admired by a man who possessed so many qualities that she herself admired. His absence and the thought of what might have been pained her, but she knew in time those feelings would pass and she would learn to think of him fondly and without regret.

In the meantime, it was better not to see him, which made a sad joke of the idea that they were friends.

Christmas approached, and at last C.J. and his family arrived for their much-anticipated visit. Claire gave them the best rooms in the inn, and Bonnie enjoyed showing them all of her favorite places in Lahaina. The children loved the beaches and the stories Midori told them of Christmas in Hawaii— of Santa arriving in an outrigger canoe instead of the sleigh he preferred for colder climates, of children leaving sushi and juice for him on Christmas Eve instead of cookies, of Hawaiian residents buying Christmas trees shipped from the mainland in refrigerated containers while others decorated backyard palm trees, and of celebrating with *kanikapila*, informal parties with music, after church services. Midori taught them how to say *Mele Kalikimaka* instead of Merry Christmas, to make the *shaka* sign, a fist with thumb and pinky extended, to say *aloha*.

On Christmas Eve, Bonnie called family and friends back

on the mainland and phoned Elm Creek Manor to ask Sylvia to pass along her good wishes and thanks to the other Elm Creek Quilters. They had sent her a Christmas box full of treats to remind her of home, including Anna's delicious quilt block cookies, a new CD from her favorite Pennsylvania folk ensemble, Simple Gifts, and a bundle of fat quarters with the pattern of her beloved homespun plaids but in delightfully bright tropical colors. Bonnie felt her heart softening toward her estranged friends as she unwrapped each small treasure, reminded anew of how well they knew her and how much they still cared.

Perhaps if she returned to Elm Creek Manor in the spring, things between them could be as they had always been.

On Christmas Day, Claire, Midori, and Bonnie hosted a Christmas luau for their guests, with a delicious buffet and a succulent roast pig cooked in the new underground *imu* Eric had built. Hinano and some of his friends came to celebrate and provide the musical entertainment, but Kai did not accompany them. When the band took a break and Bonnie managed to catch Hinano alone, she asked him how he was managing without his son. Hinano managed a smile and said that he was doing okay but he planned to smother his sorrows with his aunt's fantastic cooking. It was their first conversation since their trip to Oahu, and after they ran out of things to catch up on, they exchanged a few awkward smiles before Hinano said, "This is stupid. Come here." He wrapped her in a bear hug, planted a kiss on her cheek, and murmured, "Mele Kalikimaka, snowbird."

It felt wonderful to have his arms around her, and yet sad, because he released her so quickly and he could have made the same gesture to any other woman at the party. She was indeed no more than a friend to him, and she would have to content herself with that.

Aside from those moments, Bonnie enjoyed spending the holiday week with her son and his family, but all too soon the days passed and the time came to prepare for their return journey. On his last day in Hawaii, C.J. asked Bonnie if he could accompany her on her morning walk. Since her tall, athletic son typically began each day with a brisk, eight-mile run, rain or shine, Bonnie knew he was more interested in talking to her alone than the exercise.

They had not spoken about Craig during C.J.'s visit except on Christmas Day, when Bonnie had urged him to call his father. C.J. had flatly refused, and seeing Bonnie's distress, Julie suggested that she have the children call and wish their grandfather a Merry Christmas instead. C.J. had settled for that, but he brushed off Bonnie's protests that he couldn't refuse to speak to his father forever. "We have nothing to say to each other," C.J. told her while Julie took the children out to the lanai where the reception on her cell phone was better. "What he did is unforgivable and I've lost all respect for him."

After all Craig had done, how could Bonnie persuade her son otherwise?

They had almost reached Courthouse Square when C.J. abruptly changed the subject from his travel plans to his father. "Dad's pressuring all three of us to give him your address and new phone number," he said. "Tammy tells him not to put her in the middle anytime he brings any of this up, but Barry's wavering. Last time I spoke to him, he told me he feels sorry for Dad and thinks that all you two need is a chance to talk and you'll work everything out."

"Barry can't really believe that," said Bonnie, astonished. "I've told him we passed that point long ago."

"But that was before Terri dumped Dad," said C.J., rushing through the other woman's name as if to minimize the sting.

Bonnie stopped short. "She did what?"

"She broke it off after she was subpoenaed. You knew about that, right?"

"Yes, she was going to testify about Craig's adultery. But the hearing was cancelled when Craig stopped claiming he was trying to reconcile with me."

"The damage was already done. Her ex-husband heard about the subpoena and the truth came out. He's taking her to court to get sole custody of their children."

"Oh, those poor kids, to have their home thrown into such chaos." Then she had another thought. "How do you know all this?"

"Dad told Barry and Barry told me. Terri told Dad that their relationship is over, she has to put her children first, and that he shouldn't contact her ever again."

Bonnie resumed her walk at a brisker pace. "It's too bad she didn't put her children first from the beginning. All this ugliness could have been avoided."

"Dad's frantic," said C.J., catching up to her in two quick strides. "He's tried everything to reach Terri short of showing up on her front porch, but she won't have anything to do with him."

"So even though your father clearly prefers his other woman, Barry assumes now that your father's single, so to speak—"

"He'll come running back to you."

Bonnie sighed. Her poor youngest baby, so hopeful, so mistaken. "Could you talk some sense into him?"

"I've tried and so has Tammy. He won't listen. I thought you should know."

Bonnie thanked him and resolved to send Barry a loving but firm email as soon as they returned to the inn. He had to accept the hard, bitter truth that she and Craig were finished.

And so, apparently, were Craig and Terri. Bonnie wanted not to care, but she couldn't help a tiny glimmer of satisfaction that their passionate romance had fizzled as soon as reality had dumped a cold bucket of water upon it.

⟡

After C.J. and his family departed, the inn seemed quiet and lonely without her grandchildren's happy patter and their inexhaustible supply of hugs and kisses and questions. The new year came, and once the holiday bustle had subsided, Bonnie again found solace and contentment in her Pineapple Patch quilt. Every day, no matter how busy she was preparing for the upcoming teacher interviews, she made time to add a few stitches to her quilt, joining the emerald green appliqué to the creamy ivory background. Midori often complimented her on her progress, as did the Laulima Quilters. Soon, they assured her, she would be ready to layer and baste the finished top, and they would be ready ro assist her with threaded needles.

A few days into the new year, Bonnie and Darren had a long phone conference to discuss the divorce proceedings, which were at last back on course. Any relief Bonnie might have felt was quashed when Darren told her about Craig's reaction to the news, given to him in a meeting with their lawyers, that Bonnie had sold her share of Elm Creek Quilts and that he would receive only $2,500 as his half of the profits. He had overturned a chair, thrown a glass of water against the wall, and lunged across the table at Darren shouting threats. Security had come running to escort him from the building.

"I'm so sorry," Bonnie said, horrified.

"You don't have to apologize for his behavior," Darren said. "I've seen worse. I'd advise you to stay off his radar, however. No phone calls, no emails, don't check in on him, don't discuss matters about the kids, and definitely don't apologize. His actions are not your responsibility, and there's no reason for you to expose yourself to contact that will only upset you."

"Don't worry," said Bonnie. She had absolutely no desire to speak with Craig, especially with his temper clearly out of control.

Darren ended the call with a reassuring prediction that since Elm Creek Quilts had been removed from the equation, the property division could be settled soon, and perhaps the divorce could be made final within a month. Bonnie thanked him, relieved to hear that the end could be in sight. She had feared that Craig would come up with an endless supply of obstacles and drag out the divorce forever.

In the second week of January, Bonnie and Claire began interviewing the ten finalists for their new faculty. After much discussion and debate, they decided to hire three teachers and to alternate their course offerings so that one week would be focused on making a Hawaiian quilt top from start to finish—or as close to it as each quilter could come, depending upon her skills and diligence—and the next week would offer two different classes each day, one in the morning and one in the afternoon, focused on different techniques or methods rather than one particular project. Bonnie preferred the Elm Creek Quilts model and her concerns about varying their schedules lingered until Claire pointed out that their schedule *would* follow a regular pattern, just one that covered two weeks instead of one. Bonnie finally relented when Claire pointed out that the variety would keep their teachers from getting bored and might encourage campers to book two-week stays rather than a single week, allowing them to fit in day trips to other islands on the weekend between. Certain that their guests would enjoy seeing the Queen's Quilt as much as she had, Bonnie agreed that Claire's proposed schedule had advantages that she hadn't considered. Perhaps she had been so intent upon re-creating Elm Creek Quilts that she had closed her mind to other possibilities.

The rest of the month was a whirlwind of interviews, reference checks, and long, private discussions about the candidates' qualifications and personalities and their balance of skills and experiences, as Claire and Bonnie worked to assemble the best possible team of teachers. Nearly every day brought a different aspiring quilt teacher to the Hale Kapa Kuiki, and at least half of the candidates brought along their husbands at their own expense.

Upon each applicant's arrival, Claire provided a tour of the inn that ended at the courtyard lanai, where Bonnie took over. There, in the outdoor classroom, she described the ideal quilt camp experience as well as the general structure of the day from classes to evening programs. After a delicious casual lunch on the lanai courtesy of Midori, the candidate would have a break, which most used to settle into their rooms or call family back home. Afterward, Claire, Bonnie, and Midori met on the shaded lanai for the formal interview. With more practice they became more adept at asking questions that encouraged the applicants to share openly about their strengths and weaknesses, their experiences and career aspirations, their ideal working environments and potential conflicts, and most especially, why they wanted to teach for Aloha Quilt Camp. Some provided well-rehearsed, flawless answers, while others spoke more frankly, with less polish but more feeling. Bonnie took copious notes, concerned that under pressure she would begin to confuse one applicant with another, mixing up their responses and giving one credit for another's achievements.

Bonnie found the applicants' responses to the question of why they wanted to teach for Aloha Quilt Camp to be the most intriguing. Some wanted to give up the itinerant teaching life and have students come to them instead of traveling from quilt guild to quilt guild offering lessons. Others thought of the faculty position as a retirement job, and they could think of no better place to retire to than Hawaii. One spoke movingly about longing to pursue her passion for quilting as her livelihood rather than a hobby she squeezed in after the demands of another, less compelling career. Almost everyone spoke of wanting to make dramatic changes in their lives, to undertake something out of the ordinary, to surround themselves with people who understood their passion for the art, history, and rich heritage of quilting.

Bonnie understood exactly what they meant, and she knew that this passion for the art of quilting was an unquantifiable quality that would distinguish an outstanding teacher from a merely competent one. She also knew that it marked a kindred spirit, and she could not imagine hiring anyone who did not possess it.

The applicants came prepared with questions of their own, of course: what benefits Aloha Quilt Camp offered, how much opportunity teachers would have to design their own courses, if housing and meals were included or deducted from their salaries, and—a question posed delicately—how certain Claire and Bonnie were that their business venture would succeed. Bonnie understood their caution. It required a particular entrepreneurial spirit to move to Hawaii to work for a business that was far from established. Claire responded frankly, mak-

ing no promises about guaranteed success, but not discourag-
ing the applicants from taking a chance, either.

After the formal interview concluded, the applicants were
encouraged to explore Maui for a few hours with their spouses.
Bonnie or Claire offered to acompany them if they had traveled
alone. Most preferred to sightsee on their own, but one candidate from upstate New York asked Bonnie to show her around.
To Bonnie's astonishment, the quilter confided that she had
applied for a job at Elm Creek Quilt Camp the previous year,
but she had not been invited for an interview. She asked Bonnie whether new positions might become available there soon,
because in all honesty, she would much rather work in Pennsylvania, closer to her extended family in New York. When Bonnie told her that she didn't think Elm Creek Quilts would be
hiring new faculty in the foreseeable future, the woman looked
so crestfallen that Bonnie regretted that she must tell Claire
and Midori about their conversation. This applicant had been
one of their favorites, but if Aloha Quilt Camp was not her first
choice, she might become homesick and resign within a few
months, leaving them understaffed and in disarray.

When evening came, Claire and Eric took each candidate
out for a nice dinner and one last chance to make a good impression. Then it was back to the inn for coffee or tea and
relaxed conversation in the kitchen. Bonnie and Claire privately agreed that they learned more about how their candidates would fit in from these late-night chats than from any
other part of the formal interview process. Then, after a good
night's sleep and a delicious breakfast on the lanai, the candidate would depart and the next would arrive. Occasionally the
arrivals and departures overlapped, and Bonnie noticed the
applicants taking each other's measure, sometimes nervously,
sometimes in the cheerful spirit of friendly competition.

As far as Bonnie could tell, each candidate left the Hale Kapa Kuiki certain that she would enjoy working for Aloha Quilt Camp—even the woman from New York who secretly wished to become an Elm Creek Quilter instead. "They've set the standard," she said as Bonnie helped her carry her luggage to a waiting taxi. "But I have to say, you and Claire are going to give them some competition in the years to come."

Bonnie couldn't disagree, and she decided not to hold the woman's preferences against her. After all, Elm Creek Quilts was Bonnie's first choice too. So was a loving, enduring marriage with a good man rather than divorce. But as she had recently learned the hard way, she couldn't always have everything she wanted.

After the last aspiring teacher departed, Claire, Bonnie, and Midori compared notes, reviewed files, and had endless discussions about the merits of one applicant over another. Bonnie pointed out that they shouldn't consider the teacher in isolation but approach the selection as if they were assembling a team. One teacher's strengths could balance another's weaknesses, and some personalities might clash where others would harmonize.

On the first day of February, with one month before their soft opening, they settled upon three wonderful instructors: Kawena Wilson, a master of the Hawaiian quilt from the Big Island; Arlene Gustafson, a traditional quilter from Nebraska and author of three best-selling pattern books; and Asuka Fujiko, an innovative quilt artist from Tokyo who specialized in machine quilting techniques and had won numerous awards for her breathtakingly intricate quilts.

Bonnie insisted that Claire enjoy the privilege of notifying the finalists. As the dreamer who had bought the dilapidated Hale Kapa Kuiki and had transformed it into a wonderful place suitable for Aloha Quilt Camp, she deserved to be the one to share the good news.

Bonnie was not at all surprised when Kawena, Arlene, and Asuka gladly accepted their invitations to become the first Aloha Quilters.

✣

With the pressure of selecting their faculty off their shoulders, Bonnie and Claire tackled their remaining preparations for the soft launch with renewed energy and excitement. One activity at a time, Bonnie finished investigating the remaining items on Hinano's list, reflecting wistfully that she would have enjoyed herself more had he accompanied her. She should have been able to invite him along—as a friend—but something held her back.

After she had seen the recommended sights and had begun to make arrangements for group discounts and guided tours with those she thought their campers would most enjoy, she threw caution and embarrassment aside and stopped by the music shop to thank Hinano for his help. He seemed pleased to see her and invited her to go for coffee. They chatted as easily as before, so two hours flew by before Bonnie remembered that she had work awaiting her back at the inn and she shouldn't have kept him away from his store for so long.

"Let's do this again, snowbird," Hinano said as they parted on the sidewalk. "If you have time before you fly home."

She assured him she wanted to and invited him to meet her there in a week, hiding her annoyance that once again, he had emphasized her impending departure instead of making the most of the time that they could enjoy together. But she supposed she couldn't blame him.

Just as the plans for the soft opening of Aloha Quilt Camp

were falling into place, Sylvia called to remind Bonnie of other responsibilities far away. "Maggie Flynn arrived last week and she's settling in nicely," she said. Bonnie had forgotten that the newest Elm Creek Quilter was expected so soon, and she had to remind herself that Maggie wasn't early but right on schedule. It was Bonnie who had lost track of time.

"She'd like to teach a week-long class in sampler design," Sylvia continued. "Would you be willing to offer your quilted garment seminar at the same time so it will be easier to assign classroom space? It wouldn't be for the entire summer, just the first two weeks of camp until the end of the college semester when Gwen can begin her workshops on color theory."

Bonnie agreed, but not without misgivings. Sylvia and the Elm Creek Quilters expected her to return in less than two months. Sarah was trying to finish the master schedule before she went into labor. Friends were choosing which courses to teach based upon Bonnie's preferences. But only Bonnie and Claire knew there was a chance that Bonnie wasn't coming back.

"Sylvia," she said, "I need to tell you something, in strict confidence."

"Of course, dear. What is it?"

"Claire has offered me a partnership in the Hale Kapa Kuiki Inn and Aloha Quilt Camp."

"Oh." Sylvia fell so completely silent that Bonnie heard distant conversation that must have come from another room of the manor. Perhaps the Elm Creek Quilters had gathered for a quilting bee or business meeting. Suddenly Bonnie felt a pang of longing to be there among them, although they didn't seem to miss her.

After a moment, Sylvia inquired, "What would this partnership mean for Elm Creek Quilts? I don't suppose your friend has offered you the sort of honorary position allowing her to keep your name on the company letterhead without requiring you to do any actual work."

"No," said Bonnie, laughing in spite of herself at Sylvia's dry humor. "I'd need to be here, teaching classes, organizing curricula, and planning evening programs, and that's not the sort of work I could do from a distance."

"I see." Sylvia sighed quietly. "Have you accepted Claire's offer?"

"Not yet. I'd like to wait until the end of the month to decide, if you can bear with me that long. I know it'll be difficult to plan for the entire summer if you don't know whether I'll be on the faculty."

"Difficult but not impossible. I'll hope for the best, assume that you'll be returning to us, and plan our summer accordingly. If you decide to remain in Hawaii—and frankly with the weather we've been having lately I'm tempted to join you— we'll adjust our schedule as necessary."

"Thank you, Sylvia. I know it's a lot to ask, but if there's any way you could keep this to yourself until I decide—"

"Of course. It wouldn't do to worry our friends unnecessarily. Bonnie, dear, I know it was an ugly business back in December, recommending that you sell your share of Elm Creek Quilts—"

"I understand. It had to be done."

"But it might not be forever."

"What do you mean?"

"It's best not to say anything more until your divorce is final. As far as Craig is concerned, your share in Elm Creek Quilts is gone forever."

As far as *anyone* was concerned it was gone forever, Bonnie thought, but her emotions were too raw and she didn't want to discuss it. "I'll let you know my decision by the end of February," she promised. "But whatever happens, I'll always admire you, Sylvia."

"And I will always be your friend, Bonnie. Remember that."

Bonnie promised she would.

How could she choose between Elm Creek Quilts and the Hale Kapa Kuiki, between Claire and the Elm Creek Quilters? Aloha Quilt Camp offered an exciting opportunity, something new and promising, but she had put her heart and soul into Elm Creek Quilts. Even though she was no longer a part owner, she cherished the business she and her friends had created together. Maui was indeed a paradise, but her children and grandchildren were back on the mainland and travel expenses would limit them to infrequent visits. Claire wanted her, needed her, and seemed to believe that Aloha Quilt Camp would fail without her, but if Bonnie didn't return to Pennsylvania, Elm Creek Quilt Camp would continue on as successfully as ever, her absence scarcely noticed.

She told herself she was fortunate to be blessed with two wonderful choices, but she knew that whatever she decided, she would be both happy and sad.

Her conversation with Sylvia left her with such mixed feelings that when she tracked Claire down in the stockroom of the quilt shop to have her sign some paperwork, Claire regarded her with concern and asked if she was coming down with something. "Just a case of frazzled nerves," Bonnie said, trying to smile. "I finally told Sylvia about your partnership offer."

Claire winced in sympathy. "How did she take it?"

"As she always takes bad news, rationally and calmly but with assurances that things will work out for the best." Bonnie knew, too, that Sylvia would not divulge her secret to the other Elm Creek Quilters, even though it would be easier to plan for Bonnie's potential resignation with their help. "I thought it would be unfair not to give her some advance notice just in case I don't return."

"What do you mean, just in case?"

"What do you mean, what do I mean? You know I still haven't made up my mind."

"I thought you had." Claire's brow furrowed. "You've been working so hard, we've been having such a great time together—"

"Of course," said Bonnie, so astonished she laughed. "But that would be the case whether I'm staying on or just finishing up the consulting job you originally hired me for. Do you think I'd slack off because I might be leaving in a month?"

Claire waved her hands as if to ward off an unimaginably unhappy future. "Don't even say it. I can't bear to think of launching Aloha Quilt Camp without you."

"I'll definitely be here for the soft launch," Bonnie reminded her. "If I leave, it won't be until two weeks after that, so we'll have time to work out any problems that come up during our dress rehearsal."

Claire clasped a hand to her forehead, distressed. "I can't believe you're still thinking about leaving."

"I haven't made a secret of it," protested Bonnie.

Claire paced down the narrow aisle between the shelves, tears in her eyes. "Are you going back to Craig?"

"What?"

"Are you going back to Pennsylvania because you want to reconcile with Craig?"

"Are you out of your mind? Of course not! He betrayed my trust. He's killed any love I ever felt for him. Don't you think I have any self-respect at all? Craig has nothing to do with this decision, absolutely nothing."

"That's what you say," Claire murmured, her gaze distant. "That's what they always say. They always go back to their cheating husband. He can treat her like dirt again and again and again, but she always takes him back."

"You're not making any sense." Suddenly Bonnie had a sickening thought. "Claire, has Eric cheated on you?" She couldn't believe it, but Claire seemed to know too much not to have gone through the nightmare herself. "Is that what this is about?"

"No, no, you've got it all wrong."

"Claire." Bonnie embraced her friend, held her at arm's length, and looked her in the eye. "I know what it's like to be betrayed by someone you love. I know what it's like to feel as if you're all alone. You can tell me. I've been there. I understand."

"No, you don't. Eric would never do that to me."

"Then why are you so upset? Why are you so sure that I'll take Craig back? How do you know anything about it?"

"Because I cheated on Eric," Claire burst out. "That's how I know. Because I cheated on Eric."

Bonnie stared at her. "What?"

"It was a long time ago." The words tumbled out like rocks down a steep hillside, dangerous and unstoppable. "Eric was deployed when it started, I was lonely, we were having problems, and so was my—my friend, he and his wife—"

"I can't hear this." Bonnie forced her frozen fingers to uncurl from around Claire's shoulders. "I can't hear this."

"Bonnie—"

Bonnie held up a palm. "No. Don't. No more." She shook her head slowly, ears ringing. "How could you? Eric adores you. He's a wonderful man, a wonderful husband. How could you do such a thing?"

"It's complicated. I—I don't even know—"

"How could you do to Eric what Craig did to me? How could you do to some other woman what Terri did to me?"

"This happened long before Craig cheated on you," Claire pleaded, as if it made any difference. "I thought I was in love with this man. I didn't know how it was for you, for the wife. I never thought about her. I only thought about myself. Don't you think that if I'd known then what I know now, I would have made better choices?"

"Choices? You mean the choice between living a life of integrity and betraying the people who love and trust you? If you wanted out of your marriage—"

"I never wanted to lose Eric."

"Oh, so you wanted them both? You wanted a good, responsible husband to provide for you, and some other woman's husband for fun on the side?"

Claire flinched. "You think it was fun for me? I was miserable every day of that affair. You don't know how it was. The lying, the deception, the fear, the guilt—"

"Then why do it? If it was so awful, why not end it? Was the sex that good? Was it worth it?"

"Bonnie, please, it's been over for a long time—"

Another thought flared. "Is that why you close your web browser every time I come into the office? Are you still in contact with this man? Because if you are, then you're still having the affair, even if he never touches you."

"Bonnie—"

But Bonnie couldn't bear to hear another word. She stormed from the stockroom and out of the quilt shop, ignoring the curious, anxious glances of Claire's employees. She strode across the street, the usually benevolent sunlight suddenly harsh and unyielding upon her shoulders. Stumbling up the front stairs to the Hale Kapa Kuiki, Bonnie realized that even the inn was too small to contain her, her former friend, and the horrible secret that now lay revealed between them. Choking back an angry sob, Bonnie hurried to her suite, packed her suitcase, slung her purse over her shoulder, and rolled her Pineapple Patch quilt into a tight bundle that she tucked under her arm. Hearing the commotion on the stairs, Midori met her in the front foyer. She asked what was wrong but Bonnie brushed past her without a word and left the inn. Let Claire explain. Let Claire offer her skewed version of what had happened and see if Midori accepted it.

Bonnie couldn't accept it and she couldn't stay. Nothing Claire could possibly say could justify what she had done. So many people she loved and thought she knew—Craig, the Elm Creek Quilters, and now Claire—

When she stumbled into the music shop, arms aching from hauling her burdens across Lahaina, Hinano's expression swiftly changed from pleased surprise to worried concern.

She couldn't stay under Claire's roof any longer, and aside from Midori, Hinano was her only other friend on Maui. He had to help her.

"I hear you know Lahaina pretty well," she said, fighting back tears. "Could you recommend a cheap hotel for a homeless tourist?"

Chapter Twelve

Hinano insisted that Bonnie take Kai's room. "There aren't any cheap hotels on Maui," he told her when she demurred, and that settled it. He helped her carry her things upstairs to his apartment and into a small bedroom with a twin bed, a dresser cluttered with soccer trophies, and posters of rock bands she had never heard of decorating the dark blue walls. A Hawaiian quilt covered the bed, deep green on blue, four sea turtles swimming serenely in the midst of waving kelp. The Hawaiian quilts at the Hale Kapa Kuiki had become so familiar to her that she quickly recognized Hinano's design technique and Midori's fine handiwork. She looked up from the beautiful quilt as Hinano brought her a folded pile of clean sheets. He apologized for leaving her on her own, but he had no one to watch the shop. She didn't mind. It was a relief to be alone and she was thankful that he had given her a place to stay without interrogating her about why she needed it.

She shoved her suitcase into a corner and piled her other things on top of it, stripped the bed, made it up again with the fresh sheets, and left the others in a hamper beside a small stacked washer and dryer she found in a hall closet.

Then she stood in the hallway with no idea what to do next.

She heard her cell phone ringing in her purse back in Kai's room, but she ignored it and eventually it fell silent. Dullness of spirit rather than curiosity compelled her to make a brief tour of the small apartment: two bedrooms, a narrow galley kitchen with a breakfast bar that opened into a dining room, a family room with comfortably worn sofas and chairs littered with books, magazines, and ukulele parts. Framed photos of Hinano, Kai, and a beautiful, laughing Japanese-Hawaiian woman who must have been Nani sat on every shelf and table-top. Bonnie picked up one photo of Hinano and Nani seated on grass mats on the beach, laughing as they tried to hold a squirming, eager two-year-old Kai long enough for the photo to be taken. They looked so happy. They had no idea what was coming.

Pained, Bonnie returned the photo to the shelf and clasped a hand to her forehead. In the other room her cell phone rang again. Surely it was Claire. Bonnie strode back to Kai's bedroom, confirmed her suspicions with a glance at the caller ID, and turned off the ringer. Tossing the phone back into her purse, her gaze fell upon the Pineapple Patch quilt top. She gathered up the bundle and her sewing kit and carried them back to the family room, where she cleared off part of the sofa, spread the quilt top over her lap, and took up her needle. Claire had given her the fabric, thread, and needles, sharing gener-ously from her quilt shop. How could that beloved friend be the same woman who had betrayed Eric?

Bonnie couldn't bear to think about it. She cleared her mind of everything but emerald green appliqué, ivory background, smooth thread and slender needle, losing herself in the medita-tive, repetitive motion of the stitches.

She was sewing still when Hinano came upstairs at half-past six gripping a few plastic bags by the handles. "You hungry?" he greeted her, setting the bags on the dining table and unpacking a few take-out containers. "I brought plate lunch."

Bonnie was somehow both famished and too heartsick to contemplate eating, but he had already gone to the trouble, so she rolled up her quilt top and joined him. He set out white rice, macaroni salad, pork lau lau wrapped in *ti* leaves, and something that looked like raw salmon in a marinade, enough food for at least four people. From another bag Hinano produced a six-pack of beer and a bottle of Chardonnay; without asking what she preferred, he opened a bottle of beer for himself and poured her a glass of wine.

He paid attention, she thought, remembering the number of times he had brought her coffee prepared exactly the way she liked it. She dug around in another bag until she found paper napkins and plastic utensils, which she set out for them. She felt his eyes upon her as they took seats on opposite sides of the small, round table and served themselves, but before he took a bite, he set down his fork and said, "When do you plan to tell me why you moved out of the Hale Kapa Kuiki?"

Bonnie made herself sample the raw fish; it was sweet and savory, with a hint of ginger and spice. Delicious, or it would be if she could forget that it wasn't cooked. "You mean you weren't on the phone with your aunt five minutes after you returned to the music shop?"

He grinned, took a bite of pork lau lau, and let her figure out the answer while he ate. "Four minutes," he replied before taking a second bite. "All Auntie said was that you and Claire had one kine *paio*."

"If that means fight, then you already know the story."

"Not the whole story," Hinano said. "Must've been some fight to send you running from a lifelong friend."

For a long moment, Bonnie ate in silence. "I learned something terrible about Claire, something I can't forgive. I can't—" She shook her head and poked at her macaroni salad with her fork. "I don't want to talk to her. I can't even look at her."

Hinano's brow furrowed. "What did she do, kill someone?"

"She cheated on Eric."

His eyebrows shot up. "So that's what it was—unless you're talking about something recent?"

"Recent?" Bonnie echoed before understanding struck. "You mean you knew?"

He shook his head, loading up his fork with rice and salmon. "Not if it's something new."

"She said it happened a long time ago."

"Okay, that I knew about. Or guessed, anyway. About eight years ago, they were going through some rough times. I knew Eric was upset—"

"Eric knew?" exclaimed Bonnie. "Did he catch her in the act?" She fervently hoped he had been spared that.

"He never said. I knew they were having trouble, that's all. Eric was drinking more than usual, angry one minute and depressed the next."

"You never asked him what was wrong?"

"If he'd wanted me to know, he would have told me. I took him fishing a lot, pushed him to join our soccer league—eh, if we were quilters maybe he would have bared his soul while we stitched squares but we men do things differently, snowbird." He ate in silence for a long moment. "There was this one time. He showed up here furious and told me he needed a place to stay for the night. So I gave him the sofa—Kai was still in the house then—but I woke him up before dawn and took him to see the sunrise at the Haleakala Crater."

"What's that?"

"Something I should've put on your list. It's a dormant volcano more than ten thousand feet above sea level at the summit and one of the most amazing places in Maui, maybe in all Hawaii. Nothing I could say would prepare you for that first look into the crater, for what you feel when you see the vastness of that landscape and try to grasp the creative and destructive power of God's creation." Hinano inhaled deeply, frowning, remembering. "Eric hardly said anything the whole way there, just looked out the window at the night sky while I drove. It was almost dawn when we reached the summit. We waited in the cold, shivering, until the sun rose and light touched the edge of the crater. There's nothing like it in the world. Dawn hits you like a physical force, stuns you. You realize how finite you are. You can't help realizing it."

Bonnie nodded, but his thoughts had turned inward, and she wondered if he had forgotten she was there.

But after a long moment, Hinano resumed his story. "We hiked into the crater when it grew light enough to see. Eric didn't say much until we reached the turnaround point. 'I love her,' he told me. 'I know I'll love her for the rest of my life. But I don't know if I can stay.' So I asked him if he thought he could leave her. Which would be harder? He made a sad kine smile then and said that was the real question."

Bonnie drew in a shaky breath, Eric's confusion and anger painfully familiar. She had struggled with the same question, to leave or stay with the man she loved after his cruel betrayal. She had given Craig a second chance, and all it had done was delay the inevitable.

"We talked more the rest of the way as we climbed up the switchbacks out of the crater, and then on the return drive, but not about Claire, not about the trouble at home, whatever it was. But when we got back to Lahaina, Eric thanked me for spending the day with him, and he seemed at peace." Hinano shrugged and took up his fork again. "He didn't leave, so they must have worked things out."

"How could anyone cheat on a good man like Eric?"

"I don't know. How could anyone cheat on a good woman like you?"

"That's exactly my point," countered Bonnie. "What Claire did makes her no better than Craig."

"You don't know that," said Hinano. "It might have been a one-time thing. One huge mistake that she's regretted ever since. Craig was calculating, deliberate, and from what you said, he's only sorry he got caught. Craig won't ever change, but Claire seems remorseful. Claire and Eric's troubles happened years ago and from what I've seen she's been a good wife to Eric ever since."

"As far as we know," said Bonnie, thinking of Claire shutting down her web browser whenever someone interrupted her while she was online. What if the affair wasn't in her past?

"Eric must think so or he wouldn't have stayed." Hinano reached for her across the table, but stubbornly she pulled her hands onto her lap. "Eric knows what happened and he stayed. Maybe if you knew the details, you'd understand too."

But Bonnie didn't want to know the details. She didn't need to know.

❖

Bonnie slept poorly that first night, woken by bad dreams of Claire weeping, of Claire and Craig together. Of course it had never happened that way, but her dreams made a sort of twisted sense since they had both deceived her. Once awake, Bonnie found it difficult to fall back asleep. Kai's bed was comfortable enough, but Bonnie was all too aware of Hinano sleeping only one room away, and then, thinking of Claire, she became too angry to sleep.

In the morning she slipped out of the house at sunrise for her morning walk and returned to find Hinano in the kitchen preparing breakfast. After a transient awkwardness faded, she found herself chatting easily with him while they ate, and she could almost believe that she could content herself with remaining just friends. Then he would say something to make her laugh or grin lazily at her as he stretched and yawned, and she would find herself imagining how it would feel to go around to his side of the table, sit on his lap, put her arms around him, and rest her head on his chest. It was impossible to be friends with someone she wanted so badly to kiss.

Either she would have to change her airline ticket and leave Maui sooner than planned or find somewhere else to stay.

As the days passed, Claire's phone calls tapered off until they ceased altogether. Bonnie went for her morning walks and spent the rest of the day quilting. She met Hinano for plate lunch and turned the leftovers into supper for them both when he came upstairs after closing the shop at the end of the day.

But after the friendly bustle of the inn, Bonnie found the isolation of Hinano's apartment lonely whenever he was not there. On the fourth day, she returned to the music shop with him after lunch, hinting that she would like something to do. Hinano eventually asked if she would help with some accounting chores he'd been putting off too long, and when Bonnie finished that assignment, he found another task for her. The work was easy but engrossing, almost like being back in the office of her lost quilt shop. On the fifth day, Bonnie accompanied Hinano downstairs after breakfast and got right to work. Over lunch Hinano remarked that she was almost as useful as Kai.

"Almost?" Bonnie retorted.

Hinano made an apologetic shrug. "He knows ukuleles better than you do."

Bonnie couldn't disagree. She wondered when Kai would next return home from college. She would lose both her informal job and her bed.

A week after her arrival, Bonnie and Hinano were cleaning up the kitchen after supper when Hinano said, "Eh, snowbird, my auntie says they're hurting at the inn without you."

"Is that so." Bonnie had suspected that Hinano was keeping Midori informed about her, and that Midori most likely shared what she learned with Claire. Bonnie didn't like it, but at least that kept them from worrying and calling.

"Yeah, that's so," he said. "They need you to get this quilt camp going. You should go back and finish what you started."

"You just want your bachelor pad all to yourself again," said Bonnie. "You're afraid people are going to talk, what with a sort-of-married woman staying with you."

Before she knew it, he drew her to him and kissed her.

When their lips parted, he said, quietly, "Is that what you think?"

"Yes," said Bonnie, though she didn't think so anymore. Her heart pounded and she found herself drawing him closer to her, pressing herself against him.

He kissed her again, his mouth lingering on hers. "Still think so?"

She couldn't speak. Eyes closed, she nodded.

He kissed her again, and when she finally found her voice, she said, "I thought we were going to be just friends."

"If that's what you want, I guess—"

"Don't say it," said Bonnie. "No more one step forward, two steps back. But—I'm still married. For now, there are limits to what we can be to each other. I know it might seem silly since my marriage is all but over—"

"No, it's not silly." Hinano held very still for a moment, and then, almost imperceptibly, his embrace relaxed though his arms still held her close. "All right. There are limits, for now. And you're leaving soon. I'm fine with that, but I'm done with missing out on what I could have with you because of all the things I might never have."

Overwhelmed, she could not find the words to express the wonder, the hope, the thankfulness his admission evoked, so she poured all of her feelings into a kiss and hoped he understood what she could not say.

❖

Later, he returned to the subject she hoped he had forgotten. "They need you," he told her. "You can keep Kai's room if you want. I'd like that. But Aloha Quilt Camp won't get off the ground without your help. It's too much for Claire and Midori, especially now that they're scrambling to get ready for the practice camp."

Bonnie knew he was right, and her conscience nagged her for abandoning her responsibilities. Claire had hired her for a job and she was obliged to complete it. Even if Bonnie didn't care how Claire might be affected by her departure, Midori and their new teachers were counting on her, and the success of Aloha Quilt Camp depended upon her efforts. Bonnie had put too much into Aloha Quilt Camp to sit back and watch it fail—and she and Claire had been friends too long for Bonnie to wish her any misfortune.

She let another day pass, and then another. Hinano could

have refused to let her help him around the music shop so that she would return to the Hale Kapa Kuiki out of boredom, but he didn't.

One morning, he surprised her by announcing that he had arranged for a friend to mind the store so he could show her more of Maui. They packed a picnic lunch, stuffed sweatshirts and jackets into a duffel bag, and set off in his old blue car for Haleakala National Park. They drove past neighborhoods, fields of sugarcane, and pineapple plantations and gradually began to climb a winding road full of hairpin turns and switchbacks. They passed ranches, signs warning of cattle on the road, and markers alerting them to the increasing altitude—8,000 feet, 9,000, 10,000. They drove through a cloudbank that misted the windshield and brought on a false twilight but dissipated almost as quickly as it had appeared.

The sun shone brightly by the time they pulled into the lot near the visitors' center, but the temperature was a good twenty degrees colder than in Lahaina because of the altitude. Bonnie shivered into her sweatshirt and jacket before leaving the car, glad that she had worn jeans instead of shorts. But once outside in the clear, brisk air, Bonnie forgot the chill, captivated by the view of the coastline miles away and far below, land kissing ocean, emerald and azure, white cotton clouds above. Somewhere in that idyllic scene, too distant for her to discern, was the Hale Kapa Kuiki. With a pang she turned away and forced a smile when Hinano beckoned her to follow him to what he promised would be an even more breathtaking view.

Nothing he had described could have prepared her for her first astounding glimpse of the crater—the starkly beautiful volcanic landscape, the sweep of red sands down the sides of the crater, the sculpted rocks, the dramatic scattering of cinder cones, the majestic billowing of clouds shrouding the distant peaks. Hinano had said that the entire island of Manhattan could fit within the crater, but even knowing that and measuring the distance with her gaze, she found herself struggling to grasp the scale and the scope of what she observed. Everywhere she looked she discovered new wonders, new astonishments. She could have been on another planet, so different was the slumbering volcano from any other place she had visited on Maui, from any place she had ever seen.

After a time, Hinano and Bonnie hiked down the Sliding Sands trail into the crater and around the nearest cinder cone. Bonnie often paused to take photographs and marvel at the rich, dramatic reds and browns of the soils, the intense frosty-white of the silversword that thrived impossibly in the harsh environment, the sudden and dramatic shift to soft dusk as clouds billowed over the rim of the volcano and enveloped them. As they backtracked along the trail and began the far more difficult ascent, Bonnie was overwhelmed with wonder and with gratitude that she had been able to experience the embrace of the clouds, but that the changeable weather had held off until she had filled her senses with the whole, illuminated, unobscured landscape. She felt humbled to think that she had looked upon one of the most amazing and awe-inspiring places on earth, that she had seen what most people in the world could only imagine, and that their imaginations could only approach but never equal the richness of what was real.

It was early evening when they finally returned to Lahaina, passing the two-hour drive back discussing geology and natural history facts, which Bonnie read aloud from a book she had purchased at the visitors' center, and reliving the hike, which had left them pleasantly fatigued. Bonnie doubted she would have made the climb out of the crater before nightfall if she were not accustomed to regular exercise, but even so, she suspected her calves would ache throughout her walk the next morning.

As Hinano parked in the private lot behind his building, Bonnie spotted someone lingering near the darkened back door of the music shop. When the headlights illuminated his face, Bonnie recognized Eric. A quick measure of Hinano's complete lack of surprise told Bonnie the two men had arranged the meeting.

"I'll see you upstairs," Hinano told her as they left the car. He greeted Eric briefly and disappeared inside the music shop as Eric hesitantly approached. Bonnie's heart went out to him, knowing how he had been hurt, and yet she was bewildered and angry. How dare Claire send her betrayed husband to speak to Bonnie on her behalf? How dare Claire ask anything of him?

"Claire needs you," Eric began without preamble. "Think you might consider coming back?"

Bonnie shook her head and studied a pattern of cracks on the sidewalk. "I don't know if I can. She's not the person I thought she was."

"She made a terrible mistake, but she's still your friend."

"A mistake? A mistake is accidentally giving a customer a ten instead of a one when you're counting out change. A mistake is mixing a red T-shirt in with your whites when you're doing laundry. Claire made a choice, a terrible, destructive choice, and frankly I don't understand why you aren't more angry."

"Believe me, I was angry," said Eric, grim. "Angry and hurt and confused. I wanted to kill the guy. Sometimes I still get these pictures in my head, the two of them together, and I want to punch someone. But life's too short, Bonnie. I love Claire. She's sorry for what she did. We had to put it behind us."

Incredulous, Bonnie said, "She betrayed you."

"The blame isn't hers alone." Eric sighed and dropped onto a bench near the curb, resting his elbows on his knees. "That guy—he was almost like a predator. He wanted her, he sensed a vulnerability, and he took advantage of it."

"Vulnerability? Are you kidding me? Claire is not the victim here."

"That's not what I'm saying, but I made choices too. I checked out of our marriage long before I was deployed."

"Please don't tell me you're going to take responsibility for this."

"I'm not excusing what she did, but we both made mistakes. I wasn't paying attention to her. She told me she was unhappy, but I didn't hear her. She begged me to go to marriage counseling, but I insisted that we were fine, that we didn't need it. We were the perfect couple, remember? We had the perfect marriage. I couldn't admit that we had hit a rough spot, even with Claire standing right in front of me, telling me so."

"All marriages go through doldrums now and then. An affair isn't the solution."

"Obviously not, but it sure got my attention."

"Are you trying to tell me that Claire's affair was a cry for help?"

He shrugged sadly. "That's how I see it, all these years later."

"Unbelievable."

"I've had a lot of time to think about it, Bonnie, and Claire and I have talked about what happened and what went wrong. Not so much recently, but back when we were rebuilding, trying to hold our marriage together." Eric sat back against the bench, stretching his long legs out in front of him, folding his arms. "You know what I finally figured out? That relationship was hell for her, just as finding out about it was for me. She never wanted that guy. She didn't want affection and intimacy and romance with him. She wanted them with me. That's why the affair was doomed to fail from the beginning. It was never going to work. It was never going to get her what she really wanted."

Bonnie shook her head. "By that logic, Craig and I—"

"People cheat for different reasons. I'm not saying you neglected Craig and all he wanted was your attention. Craig's a jerk and he wanted to play around. That's not Claire. She's truly remorseful. Yes, she did something terrible. Yes, she hurt me. But she hurt, too. I was with her every day after the affair ended, and I saw what she went through, the depression, the self-loathing—"

"She's only sorry that she got caught."

Eric's brow furrowed in puzzlement. "She didn't get caught. Didn't you know? She couldn't take the lying and the sneaking around anymore, so she ended it."

Claire had ended it? "I . . . I didn't know." If Bonnie hadn't fled the inn, if she had let Claire explain, she would have known.

"The guy didn't take it well. For months he tried to get her back, but she wouldn't see him, wouldn't speak to him. Finally he showed up at her office and demanded that she come back to him. When she refused and begged him never to contact her again, he tracked me down and told me everything."

"What?"

"It was in the parking lot of a grocery store. I had just picked up some things for a cookout—" Eric shook his head as if to clear it of the memory. "At first I didn't believe him. I didn't want to believe him. But when I came home and told Claire what had happened, all the blood ran out of her face and I knew it was true."

"I'm so sorry, Eric." Bonnie sank down onto the bench beside him. Somehow she had never imagined the events unfolding that way. "Why would he do such a thing?"

"Maybe so I'd throw Claire out and she'd have no choice but to go back to him. Maybe for revenge. His marriage was ruined, so why not ruin hers?" Eric let his head fall against the back of the bench. "Claire had to pick a nutcase."

"She didn't have to pick anyone. How can you joke about this?"

"Sometimes that's all that gets me through."

"How do you know she won't do it again?"

"I just know. I trust her. It took years, but she finally earned my trust back."

"I'm amazed that you can be so forgiving, so tolerant."

"I'm not tolerant," said Eric, suddenly forceful. "If she ever does it again, she knows it's over. But I am forgiving. I had to forgive her to save the marriage. It was worth saving, Bonnie. I know that. We're happier now than we were before that whole mess happened. We don't take each other for granted anymore. We've seen what can happen when you get lazy in a marriage and we won't repeat our mistakes." He laughed shortly. "I'm not saying I'm glad it happened. I'll never say that. But I will say that we recovered from something that could have destroyed us, and for that I'm thankful."

Bonnie nodded, eyes on the sidewalk. Eric was right; Claire's affair bore little resemblance to Craig's ongoing deceptions and cruelty. If he had cheated, but had returned to her remorseful, ashamed, and determined to undo the damage he had done, maybe she could have learned to forgive him, too.

But she couldn't ignore the fact that the difference between what Craig and Claire had done was only a matter of degree.

Eric broke the silence. "I think what's most important at this moment is that Claire betrayed me, not you. She's been nothing but supportive and loyal to you for as long as you've been friends, and you know it." He touched her on the shoulder. "If I can forgive Claire, maybe you can too."

✧

The next morning Bonnie thought it over on her morning walk, the intensity of her emotions fueling her pace so that she completed her route ten minutes early. Over breakfast, when Hinano casually asked her what her plans were for the day, she said, "What you really want to know is whether your plan worked and I experienced a Haleakala epiphany as Eric did all those years ago."

"Well? Did you?"

"In a sense," Bonnie replied. "I realized that I made a commitment to Aloha Quilt Camp, and I don't have to forgive Claire to work with her."

She could tell from Hinano's frown that he had hoped for more, but it was all she could give at the moment. It would be enough to get her through her last weeks in Lahaina. Perhaps in time she would be able to offer Claire more.

Breakfast service was already underway when she arrived at the Hale Kapa Kuiki. She found Midori alone in the kitchen arranging slices of banana bread on a serving plate. Her eyebrows rose when Bonnie entered, but she said only, "We're out of juice. Squeeze some oranges for me?"

Bonnie got right to work, relieved that Midori greeted her with little fuss and no questions. She doubted she would receive the same reaction from Claire.

Sure enough, when Claire arrived and came to the kitchen for her usual cup of coffee before retreating to her office, she stopped short at the sight of Bonnie wiping down the countertop. "Bonnie?" she said tentatively. "You're back?"

"Just to work. I'm not staying." She hadn't meant to sound so cold and abrupt, but she couldn't take the words back. "I couldn't leave you shorthanded with the soft launch so near."

"Thank you." Claire regarded her sadly, eyes filling with tears. "I'll keep your room ready for you just in case."

"Don't bother. I won't need it."

Bonnie heard Midori muffle a sigh as she carried the plate of banana bread outside to the lanai. Suddenly ashamed of her coldness, she busied herself cutting oranges and pressing the halves in the juicer.

"As much as you hate me," said Claire, voice quavering, "you'll never hate me as much as I hated myself."

Bonnie set the knife down on the countertop, a small cut on her finger stinging from the orange juice. "I don't hate you. I just . . . I don't think I can trust you."

"If Eric can—"

"Maybe he shouldn't."

Claire frowned, incapable of accepting criticism unchallenged, even when she was indisputably wrong. "Whatever you might think of me, I'm not a serial cheater."

"Then why the secrecy?"

"You mean why didn't I confess to you earlier? You, the most judgmental person I know?"

"It's not judgmental to disapprove of adultery."

"I disapprove of it too! Don't you get it? It's in my past. Every day I regret what I did. Every day I thank God that Eric was able to forgive me."

"If it's in your past, then why do you password protect your computer? Why do you shut down your web browser every time I walk into the office when you're online?"

"I keep my guests' financial information on my computer," said Claire. "It would be irresponsible of me not to use a password. As for the web browser—fine, I admit I haven't wanted you to see what sites I've been visiting."

"Because you're still communicating with that man."

"No, because I'm the co-administrator of an online support group for women who are involved in affairs."

"Be serious."

"I am. There's a real need whether you believe it or not. We offer them support, encouragement, and tough love when it's called for. These women are desperate and despondent, Bonnie. They want to end their affairs, but they feel trapped and they have nowhere else to go. Some of them face violence from their husbands or lovers or both when they want to leave the affair or if the truth comes out. These women need help, but they can't turn to their friends, because what would their friends think of them if they confessed the truth?"

"You know who deserves help?" Bonnie countered. "The betrayed spouses."

"They have online support groups too, but obviously I'm in no position to run them. I learned my lesson the hard way and now I try to help other women stop the lies and betrayal, for their own sakes as well as that of everyone whose lives they touch. Every day I try to atone for what I've done by being the best possible wife I can to Eric and by helping other women end their affairs—" Abruptly Claire fell silent and inhaled deeply. "But I understand if after all you've been through, that's not enough. Forgiveness isn't something you can demand, or even earn. I get that. If our places were reversed—"

"Our places could never be reversed," Bonnie broke in with more force than she felt, for most of her anger had drained away. "I never could have done what you did."

Claire regarded her for a long moment. "Probably not," she

finally said, "but nine years ago, I would have insisted the same thing about myself."

She poured herself a cup of coffee and left the kitchen, leaving Bonnie speechless and staring after her.

✧

With two weeks to go before the soft launch of Aloha Quilt Camp, Bonnie and Claire raced to prepare, working separately whenever possible, together when absolutely necessary. Bonnie wasn't sure which of them was trying harder to avoid the other, but at least they managed to be civil. She missed their old friendliness and wished Claire had never impulsively blurted out her guilty secret.

"She can't win," Hinano remarked one evening after Bonnie returned to his apartment after a long day setting up the outdoor classroom. "You condemn her for lying and you hate her for telling you the truth."

"I don't hate her," Bonnie replied automatically. "I hate what she did."

"Eh, snowbird, I'm sure Claire finds that very comforting."

In the days that followed, their new teachers arrived and began settling into their rooms at the Hale Kapa Kuiki. Asuka Fujiko, a strikingly beautiful and vivacious art quilter, had brought only two suitcases with her on her flight from Tokyo, one packed with clothing and the other stuffed full of sample projects for her quilting workshops. When Claire could not disguise her concern that Asuka's lack of luggage meant that she didn't intend to stay long, Asuka cheerfully explained that she preferred to travel lightly, but she intended to go on a shopping spree in Waikiki after she received her first paycheck.

Bonnie was especially eager to become better acquainted with the second new teacher to arrive, Arlene Gustafson, a

twice-divorced traditional quilter in her late fifties who looked
as if she would be equally comfortable seated at a sewing machine or on a tractor. When Bonnie expressed her dismay that
she had left her copies of Arlene's three pattern books back
home in Pennsylvania and would miss the opportunity to have
them autographed, Arlene pulled pattern book number four
out of her denim knapsack, signed the title page with a flourish, and announced that Bonnie was the only other person
beside her own mother to receive a copy a month before the
official publication date. "It's hot off the presses," she explained
as Bonnie, Midori, and Asuka admired the book and Claire
wondered aloud why Arlene hadn't mentioned it during her
job interview. "Not that I'm a pessimist, but I didn't want to say
anything until I held a copy in my hands and it was too late for
my publisher to cancel production."

Last of all came the teacher who had the shortest distance
to travel, Kawena Wilson, who had lived all her life on the Big
Island. She and Midori struck up a fast friendship over their
mutual love for traditional Hawaiian appliqué as well as other
native arts of the islands of the South Pacific. Before Kawena
had even unpacked, she and Midori began brainstorming plans
for a weeklong seminar in the making of traditional kapa cloth
by soaking and pounding the inner bark of the paper mulberry
tree.

"Not for next week," Claire said, alarmed. "The schedule's
set and we couldn't possibly squeeze anything else in."

Kawena and Midori laughed and assured Claire that they
were willing to wait until well after the official launch of Aloha
Quilt Camp before they overhauled the curriculum. With a
pang of regret, Bonnie realized that she would be far away by
that time. Not only would she miss out on the chance to learn
an intriguing traditional art, she would also be unable to watch

Aloha Quilt Camp grow and evolve over time as she had with Elm Creek Quilts.

For three days the founding faculty of Aloha Quilt Camp prepared for the arrival of their first students, organizing the outdoor classroom on the shaded lanai, discussing the daily schedules, finishing display samples, and planning for emergencies. In the midst of the whirlwind of activity were the usual tasks of the Hale Kapa Kuiki, and Bonnie was pleased to see that the new teachers volunteered to help out however they were needed, once they realized how much work needed to be done.

"Now that I see everyone working together, I know we chose the best of the best," Claire confided to Bonnie as they overheard Midori, Arlene, and Kawena folding linens in the laundry room, laughing and commiserating as they confessed their worst sewing disasters.

"They remind me so much of the Elm Creek Quilters," Bonnie said. "If a task needs to be done, they pitch in and take care of it, regardless of what's in their actual job description."

"It's all about teamwork, not competition," Claire agreed. "If we can keep this up, I think we have a chance to make it."

"You have more than a chance. Aloha Quilt Camp will be a huge success. I know it."

Bonnie and Claire exchanged smiles full of hope and anticipation, and for a moment Bonnie remembered the Claire she had long known and long believed in, the impulsive but loyal friend who sometimes acted without thinking but never failed to support Bonnie staunchly whenever she faced a crisis. Suddenly Bonnie wondered why Claire had not come to her when her marriage had faltered eight years before. She searched her memory but could not recall a single sign that Claire had been unhappy or lonely. Why had she hidden her troubles from her oldest and dearest friend?

Or had she hidden them?

Was it possible that Claire had dropped hints, hoping that Bonnie would encourage her to open up, but Bonnie had been so caught up in her work and new friendships that she had missed the signs completely? Or worse yet, had she seen the signs but had dismissed them as nothing of concern? With a shock of realization, Bonnie recalled odd catches in Claire's voice over the phone that she had attributed to fatigue, puzzling asides about Eric in letters that she had decided were meant as jokes, tearful questions about what comprised a "normal" marriage that Bonnie had teasingly answered and forgotten. She suddenly remembered one particular phone conversation in which Claire confessed that Eric hadn't touched her in three months, even when she put on provocative lingerie and threw herself at him, and since she hadn't lost her looks as far as she could tell and she knew his equipment still functioned, she could only assume he was getting it somewhere else. Bonnie had laughed it off, assured Claire that she was as pretty as ever, insisted that Eric adored her, and teased her about watching too many daytime talk shows when she should have been working. Claire thanked Bonnie for her reassurances, but her voice had been oddly subdued. She had never mentioned her concerns again, so Bonnie assumed Claire and Eric had overcome the bump in the road—if there ever had been a bump, since Claire was prone to exaggeration—and soon forgot the whole matter. Or she had until Claire's terrible secret forced the memories to emerge and hindsight revealed Claire's worries for what they truly had been.

Claire had come to Bonnie at her most desperate hour, but Bonnie had brushed off her worries, as reluctant as Eric had been to believe that her friends' iconic, happy, stable marriage was as fragile as any other. If Bonnie had listened, if she had truly heard Claire, she could have encouraged and supported her as she tried to figure out where her marriage had taken a wrong turn and how she and Eric could get back on track. If Bonnie had been a better friend, perhaps Claire never would have turned to another man for what she was missing in her life.

Claire was still ultimately responsible for her bad choices—but, Bonnie admitted, she *had* accepted responsibility for them. It would have been better if the affair had never happened, but Claire had ended it, she was remorseful, and she was atoning by committing herself to her marriage and helping other women find their way free.

If that was good enough for Eric, it ought to be good enough for Bonnie.

When the day's work was done, the staff of Aloha Quilt Camp would gather outside on the lanai in the flickering light of tiki torches drinking iced tea spiked with pineapple juice, listening to the waves crash on the beach beyond the trees and chatting about the week ahead and the months to come. Each night Bonnie lingered later into the evening, hurrying back to Hinano's apartment for a kiss hello, a late supper, and a few delightful hours enjoying his company before bed. Then one evening Claire excused herself from what had become their customary way to relax after a busy day, explaining that she had piles of registration forms to sort through and coordinate with those she had received online. The three newcomers protested that they couldn't possibly enjoy the gorgeous Maui sunset knowing that Claire was toiling away in her office, and they insisted that she bring her paperwork and laptop outside so they could all share in the work as well as the pleasant company. Bonnie and Midori pitched in too, but it was very late by the time they finished and Bonnie was too weary for the walk through Lahaina to Hinano's apartment.

She had left behind some extra clothes in her haste to leave the inn, so she called Hinano and told him she was thinking about sleeping over at the Hale Kapa Kuiki instead of coming to his place.

"I'll miss you," he said, "but it's late and you should stay. I have some projects to work on anyway."

"It's just for one night. I'm coming home tomorrow."

"Home?"

"You know what I mean."

"Eh, I guess I do."

She smiled. "I'll see you tomorrow."

"I'm counting on it. I want to see you as much as possible before you fly back to the mainland, snowbird."

Bonnie felt the same way. How ironic it was that just as Claire had made it easier for her to leave Maui, Hinano had made it more difficult.

Claire couldn't contain her delight that Bonnie had decided to stay over. "Maybe I should spend the night here too," she said, trailing Bonnie upstairs to her old room on the transparent mission of bringing fresh towels for her bathroom. "I'd be able to get an earlier start tomorrow morning."

Bonnie almost laughed. "Claire, it isn't a slumber party. Go home to Eric."

Reluctantly, Claire switched the towels and bade Bonnie good night. Alone, Bonnie took in the room, the turquoise-and-white Breadfruit quilt spread upon the cozy bed, the view of the moonlit ocean from the lanai, the framed photographs from their college days Claire had arranged on the dresser, her favorite comfortable chair. Over the past few months the room had come to feel like home, but winter was almost over and soon she would depart.

She would be leaving, and yet she wouldn't be returning home. Where was home for her anymore? The condo she had shared with Craig and the children was gone. She was now only a faculty member and not a part owner of Elm Creek Quilts. Sylvia had welcomed her into the manor, but did Bonnie belong there any more than anyplace else?

She missed Hinano, but she slept well that night in the room she had come to think of as her own.

Bonnie had been so focused on the approach of their weeklong dress rehearsal that another significant date completely slipped her mind until Darren Taylor phoned to inform her that her divorce was officially final.

"That's it?" she asked, wondering how she could have been too preoccupied to mark her last day as a married woman when she had been married for more than half of her life. "I don't need to appear in court or sign some paperwork or something?"

She had already signed the paperwork, Darren reminded her. They had only been awaiting Craig's acceptance of the property settlement, and once he realized that he had gotten the most advantageous division he was going to get, he acquiesced.

"He signed the documents?" Bonnie asked, skeptical. After so much belligerence and so many threats, it was hard to believe that Craig had finally given in, that it was finally over.

But Darren assured her Craig had and it was. "He wasn't happy about it," he acknowledged, "but his lawyer managed to convince him it was for the best. Now you're both free to move on with your lives."

Bonnie thanked him for his hard work on her behalf, knowing that without Darren she would have lost all the money from the furniture auction, Elm Creek Quilts would have had a nasty new part-owner determined to ruin them, and other even more dire consequences might have befallen her.

As she hung up the phone, she felt a strange mixture of sadness and relief. It was good to have it over and done, and yet it was unfortunate that a marriage begun with so much love and hope and high expectations had ended so miserably. Bonnie wondered why she didn't feel more celebratory, especially since she had once feared she might never untangle herself from the snarls of their failed marriage. She decided that she was simply too busy to weigh the consequences and contemplate her future as a single woman. After she returned to Pennsylvania, to the places that retained so many memories of Craig and of happier times when the children were young, full awareness of her dramatic life change would no doubt sink in. For now, she was caught up in the excitement of the launch of a promising business with wonderful new friends, and she meant to enjoy every moment.

Chapter Thirteen

The moment they had been anticipating and preparing for finally arrived on Sunday morning of the last week in February. Bonnie hardly slept the night before, her thoughts churning through all the last-minute details she must race to wrap up before their eighteen carefully selected quilt campers came to the Hale Kapa Kuiki. Some were Maui residents—Laulima Quilters or long-time customers of Plumeria Quilts—while others were flying in from all corners of the world, quilting friends Claire had met in her travels while Eric was in the service. They were sure to be the friendliest, most receptive, and most tolerant group of campers the Aloha Quilters were ever going to welcome to the inn.

But they would also be the group to observe Aloha Quilt Camp at its unpolished, unpracticed worst. Claire had made them promise to provide thorough, unsparing evaluations at the end of the week. "We can take your toughest criticism," Claire assured each camper at registration, where each received her room key, information packet, and a beautiful *lei* made of plumeria blossoms. "It's the only way we'll improve, so let us have it."

"Maybe let *her* have it," Arlene chimed in on more than one occasion. "As for me, I want to hear only praise, as lavish as you can get. Lie if you have to."

Everyone laughed whenever she said this, but Bonnie found herself hoping that at least a few of their guests would take her seriously and be gentle—however, she reminded herself, that would defeat the purpose of having a soft opening and not help Aloha Quilt Camp in the long run.

As their guests arrived and settled into their rooms, Bonnie observed them going from room to room, knocking on doors, eager to meet their fellow campers. Many of the quilters from Maui were already acquainted, which gave the inn the festive air of a friendly reunion. Throughout the afternoon, quilt campers greeted one another with hugs and exclamations of delight and introduced new roommates to old friends in impromptu gatherings that spilled into the hallway.

"You were right to assign the quilt campers to the same floor," Bonnie told Claire. "Otherwise they'd be disturbing vacationers and interrupting honeymooners."

Claire's bleak expression revealed that they had avoided such conflicts by luck and not foresight. "I'll keep doing that as long as we host both quilt campers and regular guests. I hadn't considered that one group might disturb the other."

"Don't worry," Bonnie said. "No one's complained, so everything's fine, right?"

Although Claire nodded, Bonnie knew they shared the same sudden realization: They had avoided their first potential disaster by chance, but what other unforeseen problems awaited them like traps ready to spring?

But the quilt campers were so cheerful, so eager to begin a week devoted to friendship and fun, that Bonnie couldn't dwell upon whatever unanticipated obstacles might await them. As an Elm Creek Quilter she had learned to adapt to unexpected quilt camp disasters, and she had to believe that the Aloha Quilters would as well.

As evening approached, the faculty and the first campers of Aloha Quilt Camp gathered on the central lanai for a Welcome Luau, full of all the delicious flavors Bonnie had come to love: *kalua* pork cooked all day in the *imu*, steamed chicken *laulaus*, vegetable long rice, lomi lomi salmon, and taro rolls, with coconut pudding *haupia* for dessert. Hinano and three friends provided the music, and often Bonnie caught herself watching him, enchanted, instead of paying attention to her guests.

"You're a terrible distraction," she scolded him teasingly when the band took a break.

"Me?" His eyes widened in injured innocence. "What about you? You're a worse kine distraction. I haven't struck so many wrong notes since I was a *keiki*."

Bonnie had to laugh. As far as she was concerned Hinano couldn't hit a wrong note if he tried.

When everyone had eaten their fill, Claire called them together and led them through the gate at the back of the garden down to their private beach, where she and Eric had arranged grass mats around a bonfire. As the campers took their seats, Midori offered a brief history of the hula while two of her nieces performed the graceful, swaying dance accompanied by Hinano on ukulele and another man on drums. After a round of applause, Midori brought forth her *'uli 'uli*, gourd rattles topped by red and yellow flowers, and demonstrated how dancers shook them in the hula. Bonnie, who had never seen Midori dance the hula before nor suspected she knew how, was so delighted and impressed that her cheers rang out above everyone else's.

Then Claire stood and raised her hands for silence. "Now

I invite you each to take some time to reflect upon the significance of our gathering." Firelight cast a glow on the campers'
upturned faces as Claire gazed around the circle. "One of our
traditions is to conclude the first evening of quilt camp with
a ceremony we call Ho 'ā Ahi," she told them. "It means 'to
kindle fire.'"

"Traditions?" one of the guests spoke up, muffling a laugh.
"I thought this was the first night."

A ripple of quiet laughter went up from the circle, and
Claire allowed a smile. "We're hoping it becomes a tradition,"
she clarified. "We were inspired by a similar tradition at Elm
Creek Quilt Camp, but we've adapted it to make it especially
Hawaiian."

Bonnie detected a ripple of expectation passing through
the group at the mention of Elm Creek Quilt Camp, and her
heart stirred with pride. Perhaps someday Aloha Quilt Camp
would also be held in such high esteem by quilters from around
the world.

"At its simplest," Claire continued, "the Ho 'ā Ahi is a way
for our guests to introduce themselves to us and to one another. Since we'll be living and working together closely this
week, we should feel as if we are among friends."

Claire paused, allowing the expectant silence to grow
before she explained the ceremony. The campers would pass
the 'uli 'uli around the circle, and as each woman took her turn
to hold the feathered gourd rattles, she would explain why
she had come to Aloha Quilt Camp and what she hoped to
achieve that week. When she was finished speaking, she would
shake the 'uli 'uli as Midori had shown them and pass them on
to the woman seated beside her.

"But there's another equally important reason for our ceremony," Claire went on. "It helps us to get to know one another,

true, but it also helps each of us to know ourselves better. It encourages us to reflect on our goals and hopes for the week to come, and the better we understand our dreams, the more likely we will be to make them come true." Claire found a place on one of the woven grass mats and joined the circle. "I'll begin."

"She's improvising," Midori murmured for Bonnie's ears alone. Too surprised to reply, Bonnie merely nodded and seated herself among the quilt campers. When Bonnie had described the Elm Creek Quilters' Candlelight ceremony to the Aloha Quilters, she hadn't mentioned that the teachers joined in the sharing—because they never had. They led the ceremony, but didn't participate. Apparently Bonnie had forgotten to explain that to Claire, but as Claire held the 'uli 'uli reverently and described how the creation of Aloha Quilt Camp was the fulfillment of a long-cherished dream, Bonnie wondered if it was better that she had not. At the Candlelight ceremonies back at Elm Creek Manor, there was always a moment of nervous silence after Sylvia asked for a volunteer to speak first, and whoever accepted the challenge set the tone for the rest of the ceremony. If the first to hold the candle spoke quickly and vaguely in an anxious rush to get it over with, the other campers usually did the same. By taking the first turn, Claire not only encouraged the others to speak thoughtfully by doing so herself, but also showed that she was one of them, that she hoped to learn and grow from the camp experience just as her guests did.

Perhaps the Elm Creek Quilters should adopt this variation of the tradition when their new camp season began. Until that moment, it had not occurred to Bonnie that the more experienced camp staff would have anything to learn from the new. Perhaps Bonnie would have more than souvenirs to bring home to her friends at Elm Creek Manor.

Around the circle the *'uli 'uli* went, hand to hand, quilter to quilter. Most of the campers explained that they had come to quilt camp for fun and to help their friends on the staff prepare for the real campers. "You *are* real campers," Claire said after the third time someone expressed some variation thereof. "There's nothing fake or artificial about any of you."

Several quilters added that they hoped to learn a particular technique, or perfect an essential skill, or make new friends, or complete an old project that had been too long neglected. One woman declared that she wanted to be able to brag that she had been one of the first quilt campers at Aloha Quilt Camp, because she was confident that the camp would become so successful that Claire and her staff would soon have a waiting list a mile long. "Who knows if you'll have space for me in the future?" she asked with comic sadness. "I wasn't going to miss this chance knowing that it might be my last."

"We'll always make space for our first campers," Claire promised. "Everyone here tonight will automatically go to the top of the registration list whenever you want to join us for camp in the future."

The quilters cheered this declaration, but Midori shot Bonnie a look across the bonfire that warned her to prevent Claire from any more improvisation before she did something dangerous. Bonnie smothered a laugh, but she knew Midori was correct. Claire was the boss, but the staff should discuss such things before making a public announcement they couldn't retract.

Bonnie knew that in the weeks to come, the quilt campers around the fire would offer more heartfelt revelations about why they had come to quilt camp. Women who could barely sew would seek their first lessons; accomplished quilters would hunger to work uninterrupted on masterpieces they could as yet only envision. They would come to sew quilts for brides and for babies, to cover beds and to display on walls, for warmth, for beauty, for joy. Through the years, Bonnie had heard many tales from many women at Candlelight ceremonies on the cornerstone patio of Elm Creek Manor every summer Sunday of quilt camp season. Although each story had been unique, common threads joined all the women who came to Elm Creek Manor. Those who had given so much of themselves and their lives caring for others—children, husbands, aging parents—were at last taking time to care for themselves, to express themselves creatively, to pursue their passion for the beloved art of quilting, to spend time with new friends and old far from the cares of ordinary life.

Bonnie knew that in time, the same would happen at Aloha Quilt Camp. Whether in a grand manor in Pennsylvania or a historic inn on Maui, quilt camp offered its guests a glimpse of the world as it could be, and ought to be. Women of all ages and from widely varied backgrounds would come together in harmony to create objects of beauty and comfort. Differences would be not merely tolerated, but accepted and even admired. For one week the troubles and disappointments of the world would fall away, the stress and monotony of daily routines could be forgotten, and they could quilt—or read, or stroll the beach, or soar along a zipline, or relax on the lanai, or stay up all night laughing with friends—as their own hearts desired. Teachers and more experienced campers would willingly pass on their knowledge, while friends would offer companionship and encouragement. Confidences would be shared at mealtime and in late-night chats in cozy suites or on moonlit beaches. Quilters could take artistic and emotional risks because they would know they were safe and unconditionally accepted, whether novice or master quilter.

Bonnie knew Claire would create this wonderful haven for quilters because despite the mistakes of the past, her heart was in the right place. Guests of Aloha Quilt Camp would leave refreshed and renewed, and they would return to their homes with a new resolve to stay in touch with the rediscovered artist within each of them. When the plumeria-blossom *leis* had been pressed into scrapbooks and the music and flavors of the luau were only a memory, they would remember the soul-enriching experience of creation and artistic expression, and they would make time for it in their regular lives, even if for only a few precious minutes a day.

Or so Bonnie hoped. It was her wish for each of their guests to take part of Aloha Quilt Camp home and return to it often in thought, especially when the cares of ordinary life weighed most heavily upon them.

As far as Bonnie was concerned, Claire, Midori, and their new teachers were off to a wonderful start.

After the bonfire ceremony, the guests returned to the Hale Kapa Kuiki, tired but exhilarated. Bonnie knew that anticipation for the week ahead in the company of new friends would keep many of them up for hours, until the most sensible among them would remind the others that they needed rest for the marathon of quilting awaiting them the next day.

Hinano had left the fireside with the drummer and dancers after the hula performance, but Bonnie found him waiting for her on the lanai, his ukulele packed away in a case resting on the table. "You were wonderful," she told him, sitting down beside him and accepting the glass of wine he had poured for her. "I could listen to you play for hours."

He feigned disappointment. "Only hours, not all day?"

She reached across the table and took his hand. "All day."

"That's better." He leaned over and gave her a quick kiss as curious quilt campers passed by on their way indoors. "You coming back with me tonight?"

She wanted to, but it was late and she had to be up and ready to go first thing in the morning. "I don't think I can," she said. "Do you miss me?"

Hinano laughed. "What do you think?"

"I think—" She hesitated. "I think maybe you do."

He shrugged and made a face to suggest that maybe he did and maybe he didn't, but she knew he was only teasing her. She also knew that he would miss her much more after she left Maui—and that she would miss him.

The first breakfast of Aloha Quilt Camp went off smoothly, just as it did every morning at the Hale Kapa Kuiki, with friendly service in the aloha spirit and Midori's excellent cooking. Their first real test came afterward, when the campers gathered on the shaded lanai for their first class, a rotary cutter workshop based upon an innovative technique from Arlene's new book. Bonnie observed the class discreetly from the back of the lanai, noting how the students used the workspace and how they might need to rearrange some of the tables to improve their view of the teacher's design wall. After a break for Hawaiian plate lunch provided by a local restaurant, campers indulged in a bit of free time before Kawena took over with a class on needle-turn appliqué. Many campers used the two hours of free sewing time that followed to work on projects they had begun in their workshops, but others changed into swimsuits and headed for the beach.

Inspired by the example Claire had set at the welcome ceremony, Bonnie joined the campers on the shaded lanai and worked on her Pineapple quilt top while they sewed and chatted and swapped fabric. The Laulima Quilters in the group, who had observed her progress at their weekly meetings, praised her handiwork and asked her what she planned for her next Hawaiian quilt. Quilters who were less familiar with the style looked on, intrigued, and asked her about her methods and inspiration. Bonnie modestly referred questions about the history and traditions of Hawaiian quilting to the more knowledgeable quilters in the group, and Claire seized the opportunity to inform them that during the regular season, Aloha Quilt Camp would offer programs in Hawaiian quilting every other week. Before the afternoon passed, several campers had taken Claire aside and asked to register for sessions, and to Bonnie's amusement, Claire could hardly contain her delight. If she could high-five herself, Bonnie thought, she would.

After the last class of the day, Bonnie invited the campers to her first evening program, a night at the Old Lahaina Lu'au. As they awaited the start of the show, they strolled through the grounds admiring the demonstrations of traditional crafts and gathered around to watch the opening of the *imu*. The feast was as delicious as Bonnie remembered, and the music and dance even more captivating. The performances traced the tradition of the hula from its origins in sacred ritual, to its adaptations under the influence of Christian missionaries, to its preservation and re-emergence under King Kalakaua, and its continuing practice and evolution in the modern era. As an elegant Hawaiian woman in a batik gown sang a flawless, haunting rendition of Queen Lili'uokalani's "Aloha 'Oe," it occurred to Bonnie that the history of the hula mirrored the consequences of the Hawaiian people's contact with outsiders, for better and for worse. This was the real Hawaii she wanted guests of Aloha Quilt Camp to experience, the sunlight as well as the shadow.

Bonnie couldn't have asked for a better start to quilt camp

than that first, glorious day, and though she was thankful everything had gone so smoothly, she doubted it would last. Sure enough, during a precision machine piecing workshop the next day, they blew a fuse and lost power to the entire west wing of the inn. It was two hours before an electrician could arrive to fix the problem, so Asuka raced off for her laptop and improvised with a slideshow of the most recent Tokyo Great International Quilt Show. Fortunately, most of the inn's regular guests were out sightseeing, so few people other than the campers noticed the disruption.

"We've never run all the sewing machines at once," a chagrined Claire said to Bonnie later, after showing her the exorbitant bill for upgrading the power supply to the shaded lanai. "I should have thought to test everything last week."

"We couldn't think of everything. That's what this dress rehearsal is for," Bonnie reminded her, but Claire seemed little consoled. Despite Claire's insistence that she welcomed constructive criticism, Bonnie knew she had wanted the week to go perfectly so that their first guests wouldn't have any complaints.

Fortunately, as the days passed, no other dire emergencies threatened to ruin the campers' fun. Arlene ran out of handouts during one class, but Bonnie simply hurried off to Claire's office and photocopied more. Kawena discovered in the middle of a workshop that she had inadvertently omitted a particular color of fabric from the supply list she had distributed to her students in advance, but Claire ran across the street to Plumeria Quilts and soon returned carrying a bolt with enough yardage for everyone.

A thornier issue they had not anticipated was the interest the campers' activities provoked from many of their regular guests, some of whom turned out to be quilters or aspiring quilters. After two women separately asked if they might join in the workshops the next day, Claire and Bonnie deferred their decision, explaining that they must ask the teachers first. In truth, they were buying themselves time until they could decide how to handle the situation. Bonnie was inclined to let the newcomers join in, since quilters always made room for one more chair around the quilt frame. And after their last-minute campers sampled a class, they would be more inclined to spread the word about the new quilt camp to their friends back home and perhaps even return for a full session themselves. For her part, Claire understood the value of good public relations and referrals, but she didn't want to set a precedent of allowing people to register as regular guests but take advantage of Aloha Quilt Camp activities they hadn't paid for. After some discussion, Bonnie and Claire decided to allow other guests to participate in quilt camp activities as long as they paid a workshop fee above the cost of their lodgings, there was space in the classroom, and the teacher permitted.

Other than that, the week passed so swiftly and so enjoyably that Bonnie began to regret that she would not be around to see how wonderful Aloha Quilt Camp would become once they had a chance to iron out a few wrinkles. She was so happy and relieved and delighted with their first successful week that, almost without noticing it, she felt her anger at Claire ebbing away. She could almost forget the divorce, too, except for a few brief phone calls from Darren Taylor to wrap up some final details and one unhappy, cryptic email from her younger son. Barry had typed "Dad," in the subject line and the message itself was almost as brief: "I'm sorry."

Sorry for what, exactly? Sorry that Craig had betrayed her? That his love had turned to contempt? That living with him had demoralized and degraded her? Or sorry that they had divorced? Bonnie regretted that she had not been able to live happily ever after with the man she had promised to love and cherish until death parted them, but she no longer regretted the divorce. Instead she felt an unexpected sense of relief and freedom she had not known in years. Sometimes she felt a shiver of apprehension as she peered ahead into the uncertain, unknowable future, but those anxious moments had become few and far between since she had come to Maui. Craig had forced her to find her own way, and she had. No longer would she shy away from adventure, or from the chance at new love—or from finding the courage to forgive a friend.

Or so she hoped. Every day she tried to restore the old warmth and closeness she and Claire had once known, but Claire's deception stood between them like an iron gate through which they could only regard each other sadly. The key and the lock were on Bonnie's side, if only she could bring herself to use them.

Saturday arrived, the last day of the first week of Aloha Quilt Camp. When the campers came downstairs for breakfast, Claire greeted each one with a bright smile and an evaluation form, which she asked them to complete while they ate. "It's perfect timing to ask them how they enjoyed camp while they're indulging in Midori's fabulous cooking," Claire had told Bonnie as they prepared the forms. "It's hard to be overly critical when your tummy's full of Maui coffee and the best pineapple scones you've ever tasted."

Claire arranged for the campers to deposit their completed forms in a box covered with bright green batik fabric set on a classroom table on the shaded lanai. From the many glances Claire threw the box while the last campers took their time thoroughly answering each question, Bonnie knew she wanted to snatch it up and race off to her office. There she would pore over the forms, noting the insight and intelligence of everyone who praised her and expressing surprise anytime anyone suggested that Aloha Quilt Camp had fallen short of complete perfection. Bonnie would patiently listen while Claire explained why all the negative comments were entirely wrong, and later, after Claire calmed down and could think more rationally, they would study the evaluations together with unflinching honesty and devise clever ways to improve Aloha Quilt Camp before their official launch.

Or at least that was how Bonnie had expected events to unfold, but now they both knew Bonnie would not always tolerate Claire's emotional side trips, that she would not always be there to assure Claire that everything would be all right. Their review of the campers' evaluations would be more restrained and formal than they would have supposed weeks ago, which would perhaps be more efficient and productive—if not nearly as comfortable and not at all fun.

They would find out in a few hours, but first Claire had one more rite of passage to introduce to their guests, another ceremony borrowed from the Elm Creek Quilters. At midmorning, after most of the campers had finished packing and the inn's regular guests had cleared the lanai, the campers and staff gathered in the side garden, where Bonnie and Kawena had arranged bamboo chairs in an oval on the coral brick patio. Like the Ho 'ā Ahi ceremony that had marked the beginning of the week, the Aloha ceremony would give each an opportunity to speak, to share her thoughts and feelings about her time at quilt camp.

Claire—not unexpectedly this time—found a place in the circle among her guests and gestured for the staff to seat themselves, patting the chair beside her and beckoning for Bonnie to take it. "Since coming to Hawaii, you've heard a very special word spoken many times," Claire began when everyone was seated. "Aloha. It has been said to you in greeting and in fare-well, and I'm sure you've all heard that it also means love."

A chorus of murmurs of agreement rose from the circle.

"It seems impossible that one word should convey so much meaning, and yet we've only scratched the surface." A few of the Hawaiian quilters nodded knowingly. "If you break the word down to its roots, you will find that it is made up of the words *alo*, which means presence, front, or facing. And of course if you wish to greet someone properly, you do it fac-ing them, don't you?" All the quilters nodded. "The word *ha* means breath. Together, *aloha* means 'the presence of breath' or 'the breath of life.' But it means even more than that. To say *aloha* is to invoke the divine, to say to another person, 'I recognize the divine in you.' It acknowledges a way of living that calls us to treat one another with love and respect, to offer caring and concern to all, for we are all the children of God." Then Claire broke into a smile. "If you break the word into dif-ferent roots, *aloha* also can mean, 'to share joyfully.' Any and all of those meanings speak to the heart of what we hope to create here at Aloha Quilt Camp."

Claire explained that each quilter in turn would display something she had made that week and describe what favorite memory she would take with her when she left the Hale Kapa Kuiki. "I'll go first," she said, and held up a complex patchwork block Arlene had demonstrated in one of her workshops. "I was spying from the back of the room," she confessed, evoking laughter from the circle of quilters. "She made it look so easy that I decided to try her technique. My block isn't perfect, but I think my next one will be better." She paused. "As for my favorite memory, it will be seeing all of your faces as I look around the circle. You seem so happy with the week that we've spent together and very reluctant to leave—which is very good news to me!"

As the quilters chimed in their agreement, Claire invited the camper seated on her other side to take the next turn—and Bonnie realized that Claire had arranged things so Bonnie would speak last. With rising trepidation, Bonnie wished she could switch places with another quilter without drawing anyone's attention, but that would be impossible. As the last speaker, it would be her responsibility to conclude the ceremony in a grand fashion, but she was no great orator. What had Claire been thinking?

Her thoughts raced as she tried to compose something suitable while the other quilters proudly showed off their new creations and shared favorite memories. The Ho'ā Ahi on their first evening together was remembered fondly, as were the late-night chats with roommates, the engrossing and productive workshops, the Old Lahaina Lu'au, the walking tour of historical sites in Lahaina, and lazy, carefree hours spent lolling on the beach. Ordinarily Bonnie would have been pleased and proud to hear so many of her evening programs praised so highly, but she was too anxious to take much pleasure in their rave reviews.

Just as she realized divine inspiration was not going to fill her head with the perfect words, the woman to her left finished her turn and beamed at Bonnie expectantly.

She took a deep breath and plunged ahead. First, the easy part. "Most of you have seen me sewing this throughout the week, and some of you have watched me work on it even longer." She reached into the tote bag she had set at her feet and unfolded her Pineapple Patch quilt top, standing with arms outspread when a chorus of voices urged her to give them a better look. "This is my first quilt in the Hawaiian style," she said as the campers admired the graceful curves and precise points of the emerald green appliqué, glowing on the rich ivory background. "Midori coached me along every step of the way, from designing the pattern and purchasing the fabric, to basting and taking my first needle-turn appliqué stitches. Yesterday I sewed down the last arc, and now my top is complete."

"It's beautiful," one quilter exclaimed.

"Will you teach us to make one just like it?" another asked. "If we sign up for another week of camp?"

Bonnie had to laugh. "We have far more qualified Hawaiian quilters on staff to teach you. In this style I'm still a novice."

"What are you going to do for your next Hawaiian quilt?" a third quilter inquired.

"I don't know," Bonnie admitted. She definitely wanted to make another, but she had been so busy preparing for the launch of quilt camp that she had not had time to sketch any designs. "I want to finish this one first, though, and since I haven't even layered and basted the top yet, I have time before I'll need to decide."

"We should talk about the quilting before you leave," said Midori. "Traditional Hawaiian quilters prefer echo quilting, stitching around the outline of the appliqué in concentric forms, like ripples in a pond after a stone is tossed into it."

"It would take forever to mark all those quilting lines," remarked one of the youngest campers.

Midori shook her head in mild rebuke. "It shouldn't be necessary. Hawaiian quilters use their finger as a guide. The lines of echo quilting should be no wider apart than the width of one's index finger and no closer than the width of one's pinky." Turning back to Bonnie, she added, "You should also quilt in the ditch all around your appliqué so its shape will be visible on the back of the quilt, and use definitive quilting to create details on the appliqué—stems on leaves and scales on the pineapples, for example."

The youngest camper's brow furrowed as if she couldn't quite picture how it would be done, but just as Bonnie was beginning to enjoy the friendly exchange, Claire said, "What favorite memory would you like to share with us, Bonnie?"

All eyes turned to her and every word of her half-composed closing speech vanished from her thoughts. Bonnie dropped her gaze and bought herself a few moments by folding her quilt top, slowly and methodically. There was so much to choose from: shaking the 'uli 'uli at the Ho 'ā Ahi ceremony on the beach, watching the campers enjoy themselves at the evening programs she had so carefully planned, finishing her Pineapple Patch quilt top and chatting with the campers during free sewing time, seeing the fledgling business take flight. She would take away so many wonderful memories from her time at the Hale Kapa Kuiki that it was impossible to single out only one.

Yet perhaps there was one that encompassed all the others.

"Discovering the aloha spirit," Bonnie said. "I'd heard the phrase before and I thought it meant simply a hospitable welcome, but that's just a phrase from a tourist brochure. After coming to Maui, I've learned that the aloha spirit is so much more. It's a way of living rightfully in the world, of seeking harmony with others, of acting generously, of caring for the natural world that sustains us, and of caring for one another. If my months here in Hawaii have taught me nothing else, they've shown me that if all of our words were spoken and actions conducted in the aloha spirit, the world would be a more joyful and peaceful place. I hope that everyone who comes to Aloha Quilt Camp will experience the aloha spirit here and take it home to share with friends and loved ones around the world."

Bonnie's voice trembled at the end, and she quickly sat down. She barely heard as Claire made a few closing remarks, thanked everyone for helping the Aloha Quilters with their dress rehearsal, and invited them to come back soon.

And then the first week of quilt camp was over. Wistfully, in pairs and alone, the quilters made their way inside to retrieve their luggage and to exchange tearful hugs as well as addresses with new friends before departing for the bus stop, airport, or, for a very fortunate few, homes in Maui.

Midori caught up to Bonnie as they passed from the lanai into the kitchen. "That was a fine way to wrap up the week."

"Claire set the right tone when she explained the different meanings of the word *aloha*."

"Yes, she remembered almost everything I told her," Midori remarked. "Your speech at the end was quite nice too."

"I think Claire set me up."

"And you rose to the occasion just as she knew you would." Midori regarded her speculatively. "Perhaps you can put your words into practice and extend the aloha spirit to Claire."

"Midori, if you knew what she did—"

"I do know, and I don't approve, but I admire her for the honesty she's shown since that terrible time and everything she's done to atone for her mistakes. Do you know how many marriages she's saved since almost losing her own? At least two dozen I know of. Probably more, but Claire doesn't tell me about all of them because she doesn't want to brag."

"You knew?" exclaimed Bonnie, and then, "Since when doesn't Claire want to brag?"

"Believe it or not, she doesn't, not about that support group. That should tell you how seriously she takes her role as advisor.

She's been there, done that, as she says, and she gives others the benefit of her hard-earned wisdom. I'll tell you something else. She doesn't coddle anyone who refuses to accept responsibility for their bad choices. And she's as tough on herself as she is on them, so you don't need to pile more guilt on her shoulders. She's carrying enough as it is."

"If I had ever done anything so terrible—"

"Claire would have been the first person to hold you and comfort you and tell you that everything would be all right. And after a while, she'd order you to dry your tears and get busy making things so."

"I know," admitted Bonnie. That was Claire, staunchly loyal but also pragmatic. Imagining Claire at her computer, advising scores of unhappy, unfaithful women the world over, Bonnie suddenly remembered a website Claire had seemed particularly familiar with.

"Did Claire ever seek revenge on her old lover?" Bonnie asked.

"She didn't tell you?" Midori feigned disapproval, but her mouth quirked in a smile. "She wouldn't do such a thing now, and in fact she specifically advises her Internet friends never to seek revenge, but her emotions were all over the place after that man confronted Eric in the grocery store parking lot. I think she wanted revenge for Eric more than for herself."

Bonnie was almost afraid to ask. "What did she do?"

"She had a box of elephant dung mailed to his office." As Bonnie exploded with laughter, Midori added, "Anonymously, of course."

"Of course." Bonnie could hardly speak for laughing. "That's the only way to send elephant dung."

"I'm not sure, but I think it might be illegal."

"If it's not, it should be."

"Maybe you should give Claire a break," Midori said. "Forgive others as you wish to be forgiven. If she had fooled around with Craig, I could understand if you couldn't do otherwise but hate her forever. As it is, she betrayed Eric, not you. If he can forgive her, maybe you can find it in your heart to do the same."

Bonnie's heart softened to hear the echo of Eric's own words. Was it worth abandoning a decades-long friendship over a sin long past and long since forgiven by the one who had been truly wronged? Would Bonnie's righteous indignation comfort her in the years to come, when her friendship with Claire was nothing more than a memory?

The aloha spirit made the answer plain.

Bonnie quickly thanked Midori, set her Pineapple Patch quilt top safely out of the way, and hurried off to Claire's office. She found Claire in the front foyer instead, bidding farewell to the last of the quilt campers.

"Claire—" Bonnie fell silent as Claire threw her an inquiring glance as she closed the front door. How could Bonnie explain that she still loathed what Claire had done, but forgave her anyway? How did she express her shame that she had not been there for Claire in her time of greatest need? How did she confront the ugly truth about herself, that too often she found it far easier to see the world in black and white than to accept all the shades of gray in between?

But Claire, who did not know what Bonnie was struggling to say, smiled. "It was quite a week, wasn't it?"

"Yes," said Bonnie. "Quite a week. Are you—"

Words failed her.

Claire studied her quizzically. "Am I what?"

"Are you ready to read those evaluation forms?" Bonnie managed a laugh. "Maybe we should have a stiff drink first."

"Don't be silly. Everything's going to be fine. We won't need anything stronger than a couple of glasses of iced tea."

Promising Bonnie that they were sure to read much more praise than censure, Claire led Bonnie off to the kitchen for iced tea, then on to her office to study the evaluation forms, to celebrate their accomplishments and reflect upon their weaknesses, to brainstorm and debate and devise a plan to make Aloha Quilt Camp a haven for quilters, a place that put the aloha spirit into practice every day.

An hour later, they were engrossed in a camper's lengthy description of additional workshops they should consider offering when they were startled by a loud pounding upon the front door.

"Bonnie," a man bellowed, "I know you're in here! Don't make me come looking for you!"

Frozen with alarm, Bonnie looked at Claire and saw her own shock and fear mirrored on her friend's face.

Craig had found her.

Chapter Fourteen

W hat is he doing here?" Claire asked in dismay as Craig shouted again. Both women jumped as the front door banged open.

Bonnie shook her head, heart plummeting. Suddenly Barry's cryptic email apology made perfect sense. He must have told his father where to find her. "I'm sorry, Claire." Shakily, she forced herself to stand. "I'll go out there and try to get him to calm down."

"Absolutely not. I'll talk to him. You stay here." Claire bounded up from the sofa. "Lock the door behind me and call the police."

"I can't call the police on him. He's my children's father."

"He's dangerous!"

"Then you shouldn't confront him either. Stay here." But what about their guests and Midori?

They heard hard, deliberate pacing in the foyer. "I'll tear this place apart if I have to," Craig shouted, followed by a shattering of glass and a splintering of wood as if a table had been overturned. They heard light running and Midori berating Craig in a mixture of English and Japanese. Quick footsteps sounded on the floor above, guests startled by the outburst below.

Bonnie couldn't let it go on. "I have to talk to him," she said, her stomach in knots as she forced herself to the door.

"Not alone you won't," said Claire, following her into the hallway.

They rounded the corner just in time to see tiny Midori trying to block the passage from the foyer to the rooms beyond. Viciously Craig shoved her out of the way and sent her sprawling to the floor. Bonnie gasped and Craig looked up sharply at the sound. His face was covered with a week's growth of beard, his eyes bloodshot and furious.

"You thought you could hide from me," he glowered. "You didn't count on my one loyal son, on the one child you couldn't turn against me."

"Craig." Bonnie held up her hands, appealing for calm. "I didn't turn the kids against you. I tried to keep them out of it. They saw what was happening and they made up their own minds. I tried—"

"Shut up," Craig bellowed. Bonnie flinched and drew back.

Then Claire's arm was around her. "This is private property, Craig," she told him, quiet but firm. "You're disturbing our guests. Leave now and I won't call the police."

"Maybe you won't, but I will." Midori gingerly pushed herself to her feet. Instinctively, Bonnie and Claire reached out to help her, but Craig stood between them and Midori. "What kind of man knocks down an old woman? You have no respect. You deserve every bad thing coming to you."

Craig spared her a baleful glance before turning his rage back upon Bonnie. "You thought you could run away and hide. You thought you could ruin my life and get away with it."

"You need to go now," Bonnie said shakily, backing away as Craig strode toward her. "You're trespassing."

"I'm going, but you're coming with me." He lunged forward and seized her by the upper arm. Bonnie cried out in pain as his fingers dug into her flesh and he wrestled her toward the door.

Suddenly Bonnie felt Claire's arms about her waist. Claire tried to dig in her heels, but they slipped on the polished wood floor and Craig dragged them both ever closer toward the open doorway. Frantic, Bonnie clawed at his fingers but could not peel them from her arm. Swearing, Craig grabbed Claire's wrist, flung her arm aside, and yanked Bonnie from her grasp. As Claire fell backward to the floor, Craig forced Bonnie outside, slamming her shoulder against the doorframe. Stunned, she stumbled and flailed about for an anchor, knocking over a chair and grabbing hold of a post on the lanai. Locking her elbow around it, she brought Craig to an abrupt halt, gasping in pain as he yanked her so hard she thought he might pull her arm from the socket.

She knew she couldn't hold on for long, but she was desperate not to go anywhere with the enraged stranger her ex-husband had become. "What do you want?" she cried, stalling for time, praying that Midori was even now on the phone with the police.

"You're coming back to Pennsylvania with me." Roughly Craig worked to break her hold on the post. "Then you're going to tear up our property settlement and give me everything I want. Then you're going to tell that judge you made up everything. You faked those pictures of me and Terri. You wrote those emails yourself. You never saw us together."

"No one would believe it," Bonnie choked out. "It's not my word against yours. The detective saw you at the hotel. You'll never get him to lie too."

Craig wrenched her arm free from the post and dragged her down the front stairs, but she stumbled and fell, tearing herself from his grasp. She scrambled backward out of arm's reach and up the stairs, just as Claire raced outside.

Claire darted between Bonnie and Craig. "Listen, Craig," she said, hands on his chest, barely holding him off. "You're not thinking things through. This isn't going to work and you know it." Claire's arms trembled from the strain of holding Craig at bay as he lunged around her for Bonnie. "How are you going to strong-arm her all the way to Pennsylvania when you can't even get her across the street? Do you think airport security will let you drag her through the terminal? Do you think the judge won't know you're coercing her? Do you think your kids won't find out? Do you think they'll be okay with this?"

For a moment his rage seemed to waver. "I want my life back."

"That old life is gone. You can't unkindle a fire, and putting it out won't restore what you burned." Claire planted her feet and pushed him so hard he staggered backward a few paces. "You aren't helping yourself by coming here like this, scaring people, acting like a monster."

Craig shook with rage. "That's the same thing *she* said. I am not a monster." He lunged for Bonnie, but Claire wedged herself between them again.

"Bonnie never called you a monster," said Claire.

"Not Bonnie! Terri."

Suddenly Bonnie understood, remembered—Craig's visit to Terri's home, how she had ordered him to leave her and her children alone.

"Do you really think this will get Terri back?" Claire asked, forcing Craig back another few inches. "Think it through, Craig. How will forcing Bonnie to tear up the settlement and telling the judge she faked the detective's photos change anything? You'll be a little bit wealthier, but wealthy enough for

Terri to risk losing custody of her children for you? Do you really believe that?"

Craig began pacing the length of the lanai. Behind him, a black SUV screeched to a halt at the curb and Eric leapt out. Faint with relief, Bonnie groped for a support and found the doorframe. Claire made the smallest gesture to her husband, asking him to hold off; Eric slowed his pace but his jaw was set and he looked ready to tackle Craig if he made the slightest threatening move.

"This is not the way." Claire took a step toward Craig, waving sharply behind her back for Bonnie to go inside, but Bonnie couldn't leave her alone on the lanai, not even with Eric only a few yards away. "You can't have your old life back, but you can build a new one."

"How am I supposed to do that?"

"That's for you to figure out," retorted Claire. "You've got a home, a job, your health—other people have managed with a hell of a lot less than that. All I can tell you is that you're going to do it without Bonnie. She's not going anywhere with you, and you're never going to bother her again."

"Who are you to tell me what I can do or say to my wife?"

"She's not your wife, not anymore. As for me, I'm the best friend you've got within thousands of miles, so if there's even a fraction of the Craig Markham I once knew still in you, you'll listen to me."

Craig suddenly seemed to become aware of the tourists who had paused on the sidewalk to watch the events unfold, of the guests who had come out onto their lanais and were looking down upon him with alarm or contempt, of Claire's stern resolve. His rage seemed to flicker and fade. With so many former friends and even strangers arrayed against him, he could not compel Bonnie to go with him. Not that it mattered. Claire was right. His misguided quest had been doomed to fail from the moment he conceived it, and watching his expression shift, his shoulders slump, Bonnie knew he finally understood that.

"You're going to let me and Eric drive you to the airport, and you're going to take the next flight back to the mainland," Claire said, her gaze traveling past Craig to her husband. Craig whirled around and spotted Eric, feet planted, an arrow fit to a bow. "Where you go after that is up to you, but you're never going to bother Bonnie again."

With one last flare of defiance, Craig retorted, "How do you know I won't catch the next flight back?"

"I'm counting on you to have at least a shred of self-respect left," Claire snapped. "But if I'm wrong and you show up here again, you'll find the police waiting for you."

Craig seemed rooted to the spot, his face twisted in consternation. Eric stepped toward him, and only then did Craig turn his back on the Hale Kapa Kuiki and follow Eric to his SUV. Pausing only long enough to touch Bonnie reassuringly on the shoulder, Claire dashed after them. Bonnie watched as Eric escorted Craig into the front passenger seat before taking his place behind the wheel. Claire climbed in the back, and as the vehicle pulled away, Claire pressed her hand to the glass and nodded to Bonnie through the window. Bonnie raised a hand to show her friend that she was all right, that everything would be all right.

When they were gone, Bonnie's legs gave way and she sank to the floor, trembling.

❖

Soon after Eric and Claire drove away with Craig, the police arrived at the inn. After Bonnie and Midori gave them a full report, the officers advised Bonnie of her legal options. Bonnie thought that since Craig had decided to go away on his own, it would be best to let him. As a precaution, one of the officers called dispatch and arranged for security to meet him at the airport and make sure he boarded the plane.

The police were gone by the time Eric and Claire returned from the airport. Claire and Bonnie embraced, and Bonnie breathlessly thanked her again and again. "If you hadn't been here—"

"You would have managed fine on your own. But I *was* here, and so were Midori and many of our guests. Craig wouldn't have done anything stupid in front of all those people."

Bonnie was less certain of that. "How did you know what to say to him?"

"He's hardly unique." Claire waved a hand dismissively. "They all think their illicit affairs are unique in the universe, so special, so rare, and yet they're all the same. All sordid and all false. I should have known he would come here, but you said he was too cheap to pay the airfare."

"Maybe he used frequent flyer miles," suggested Midori, and the friends' disproportionate laughter was a release of tension that soon gave way to the sober realization that they had been lucky. Bonnie had been left with rattled emotions and bruised arms, but the afternoon could have taken a far more tragic turn.

At Eric's urging, Bonnie contacted Darren Taylor and told him all that had happened. Darren took down Craig's flight information and promised to arrange for another police escort to meet him upon his arrival in Pennsylvania. He also urged Bonnie to obtain a protection from abuse order from the county. When Bonnie hesitated, worried that more legal action might provoke another violent outburst, Claire and Eric persuaded her that it was a necessary precaution. Craig had left Maui and Bonnie would be safe at the Hale Kapa Kuiki for the rest of her visit, but Bonnie needed to think ahead to the days and weeks and months that would follow her return to Pennsylvania. Craig was not entirely unreasonable, as his willingness to leave Maui indicated, but a deterrent against future contact was appropriate and warranted.

So Bonnie agreed, knowing that she would feel safer returning to the Elm Creek Valley knowing that Craig had been officially warned to keep his distance.

For she would return soon.

That evening, when she told Hinano about Craig's unexpected appearance, he was as wary as Darren had been that Craig's rage was not completely spent and that he might cause trouble for her upon her return to Pennsylvania. He was also unfairly upset with himself that he had not been there to help her.

Touched, Bonnie nonetheless teased, "That would have been an entertaining sight for Claire's guests—my new boyfriend slugging it out with my ex-husband on the front lanai."

"I wouldn't have slugged him unless absolutely necessary," said Hinano, and then added, "Is that what I am, your new boyfriend?"

"You're certainly not my old boyfriend," she said lightly. "I don't know, Hinano. It's been so long since I've dated that I have no idea what to call you."

"You're my lovely snowbird," said Hinano, embracing her, but his smile was sad. "I only wish you weren't flying back to the mainland so soon. I wonder when you'll fly back."

Bonnie wondered, too.

❖

In the days that followed, Bonnie and Claire returned to the task Craig had so brutally interrupted. They studied each camper's evaluation, mulled over which changes were immediately necessary and what could be postponed until later seasons, and devised a plan for fine-tuning their program in time for the official launch of Aloha Quilt Camp, now only days away.

"I wish I could be here to see it," said Bonnie wistfully. "If only to mark that historic first day. If only to experience one more Ho'ā Ahi ceremony on the beach."

"You could change your ticket," Claire suggested, as she had done several times before. She didn't wait for the answer Bonnie invariably offered, that she would love to stay but she was expected back at Elm Creek Quilt Camp and couldn't delay any longer. "I'm glad you stuck around this long. After everything that happened . . ."

"You had to have known that I wouldn't have left you without finishing the job."

"I know," said Claire. "Unlike some of us, you stand by your commitments."

"Don't say that," said Bonnie. "You've had your commitments tested in ways I can only imagine. You could have given up and started over somewhere else, but you held your head high, stuck it out, and saved your marriage. You deserve my admiration, not all this unfair judgment and condemnation I've been slinging at you ever since you told me the truth. And after the way you stood up for me to Craig— All I can think of is that I've let you down and I'm sorry."

"I don't want your admiration, just your friendship."

"You have it." Bonnie embraced her, tears in her eyes. "You always will."

"I know."

"It's so hard to leave the Hale Kapa Kuiki now," Bonnie confessed. "I can't bear to leave without seeing how everything turns out. I know you're going to be a huge success, but I feel like I'm walking out of an exciting movie after the first few scenes."

"It doesn't have to be that way," said Claire. "Maybe you're only heading to the lobby for intermission."

Slowly Bonnie smiled, her heart lifting. "What did you have in mind?"

⬦

On Bonnie's last day, Eric and Claire offered to take her to the airport, but Bonnie explained that Hinano had asked to see her off. With tearful hugs and promises to be in touch soon, Bonnie bade Claire, Midori, and Eric good-bye, took one last, long look around the Hale Kapa Kuiki, and met Hinano outside. They loaded her bags into the trunk of his old blue car and headed east across the beautiful island of Maui.

She would miss the endless blue ocean, the lush green mountains, the soft caress of gentle breezes. She would miss her morning walks along Front Street on the ocean, watching glorious sunsets from her lanai, and sleeping beneath the turquoise and white Breadfruit quilt Midori had made.

She would miss the new friends she had made, and the old friends she had almost lost.

She would miss Hinano.

She wanted to take his hand, but he needed it free to change gears. She rested her head on his shoulder instead, thinking that if she were in the way, he would ask her to move.

He didn't.

He cleared his throat a few times as they left Lahaina behind, as if he wanted to speak but couldn't find the words.

Bonnie knew exactly how he felt. Eventually they fell into conversation, obscuring the painful subject of their separation with a light flurry of questions about Kai's plans for spring break, whether Bonnie had remembered to pack everything, how well she might sleep on the red-eye flight, Hinano's next upcoming gig with his band.

All the while Bonnie wished he would ask her to come back soon. She had an answer ready on her lips, but unless he asked, she would say nothing. He had made her no promises, no commitments. All along he had assumed that she would be leaving, and perhaps that's what he secretly wanted. Thousands of miles would separate them for a very long time and she could not expect him to wait for her. He might not even remember her by the time she returned to Maui. Perhaps to him she had been nothing more than a diversion, a light romance to pass the winter, easily forgotten with the coming of spring. He meant more to her than that, so much more, but her heart had been broken before. If he wanted a future with her, any sort of future, he would have to let her know without any prompting from her.

They reached the Kahului Airport. Hinano parked the car and helped her inside with her luggage. Before long she stood at the security checkpoint and he could accompany her no farther.

She hardly knew how to say good-bye.

They embraced. She blinked back tears and tried to smile.

"Bonnie," Hinano said, holding her at arm's length, searching her face as if memorizing every feature. "You're going to laugh, and you're going to say no. But I have to ask."

"What?" Bonnie could scarcely breathe. "Ask me what?"

"Don't go." He smiled helplessly as he said it, knowing what he asked was impossible. "Stay here in Maui. I think I'm falling in love with you and I'd like you to stick around long enough for me to figure it out."

His words were so unexpected and yet exactly what she needed to hear. She burst out laughing, and after regarding her in puzzlement for a moment, Hinano grinned.

"So you did laugh," he said. "Now do we come to the part where you say no?"

"I have to say no," she told him as gently as she could, quickly adding, "but I'm coming back."

He forced a pained smile and nodded, pulling away.

"No, you don't understand," she hastened to add. "I'm not talking about coming back on some future vacation that might never happen. I'm coming back at the beginning of September."

He hesitated as if waiting for the punch line. "September of this year?"

"Yes, September of this year and every year after that." Bonnie threw her arms around him, bright with happiness. "As the new part-owner of the Hale Kapa Kuiki Inn, I'll be coming back every winter to help run quilt camp and look after my investment."

"New part-owner?"

Bonnie nodded. "Claire offered me a partnership months ago. I was considering it until we had our falling out. But now I see that Claire is a true friend to me and has always been, and I couldn't bear not to be a part of Aloha Quilt Camp after all the work I've put in to it. When Claire assured me the offer was still on the table, I took it. We signed the paperwork two days ago."

"Congratulations, snowbird!" Hinano swept her up in a hug. "Any chance the thought of how much you'd miss your favorite ukulele player influenced your decision?"

"It influenced me a lot," said Bonnie. "I think . . . I think I need to figure out if I'm falling in love with him too, and I can't do that from thousands of miles away."

"We'll have to, for the next few months."

She forced a smile to keep tears at bay. "I know. But I'll be back at the end of the summer and then we'll have all the time we need."

He nodded, but she could tell that he was thinking that the beautiful Hawaiian summer would pass too slowly to suit him. "I have a present for you," he said, reaching into his back pocket. "Something to keep you busy so you aren't pining away for me. Something so you won't forget me."

"I could never forget you," Bonnie said, but she fell silent at the sight of the small triangle of paper Hinano was carefully unfolding before her. She knew at once that it was a pattern for a Hawaiian quilt, and as she took in the cascade of arcs and graceful curves he had drawn, she saw a small bird alighting upon a bird of paradise stem surrounded by a full *lei* of bird of paradise flowers so lifelike and graceful that they appeared tossed by a garden breeze.

"I left the paper square whole because I wasn't sure if you liked to pin the pattern to your fabric or cut on a drawn line," Hinano explained, handing her the intricate pattern he must have spent days creating.

Bonnie held it up and admired it, her breath catching in her throat. "Hinano, this is beautiful. It's so much more complex than any quilt I've ever made. I hope I'm up to it."

"Don't think about the whole quilt. That's too daunting. Take it one stitch at a time. You can do one stitch, right? Then do another, and then another, and eventually you'll have a quilt."

"Well said." Bonnie smiled as she carefully folded the beautiful pattern and tucked it into her carry-on for safekeeping. "Maybe you should teach at Aloha Quilt Camp."

"Maybe I already have enough to do."

Bonnie laughed and hugged him, but the hour had grown late and she had to get to her plane. "I'll miss you," she murmured close to his ear.

"I'll see you in September, snowbird." He kissed her and reluctantly let her go. "Aloha, Bonnie. Come home soon."

"I will, Hinano. Aloha."

And then she had to leave.

❖

Tears came as she sat awaiting takeoff, but she pulled the scratchy blanket up to her chin and closed her eyes, feigning sleep. She was sad to leave, but full of joy and anticipation for the path she had finally chosen. Half the year in Pennsylvania with cherished friends, the manor, and Elm Creek Quilts; the other half in Maui with Aloha Quilt Camp, Claire, Eric, Midori, and Hinano. Only months before she had thought she had lost everything, but she had emerged with a new business partnership, new friends, a new understanding and respect for Claire—and new love. And a new quilt to look forward to creating, from choosing the fabric to cutting out the appliqué to reminiscing about her Hawaiian adventure as she took one careful stitch after another. She remembered what Midori had told her so many weeks before, that all true Hawaiian quilt patterns were unique, made for a particular person, purpose, or occasion. "An original quilt pattern is a precious gift and a sign of great friendship," Midori had said, "because of the prayers and good wishes—part of the very spirit of the designer—that go into its creation."

She knew this was true of the quilt Hinano had designed

for her, and that, perhaps without realizing it, he had captured the meaning and purpose of her journey and all the blessings it had bestowed upon her in every bird of paradise blossom he had drawn, in every graceful curve and elegant point of his pattern. She knew then that she would always think of it as the Aloha Quilt, for it conveyed the spirit of aloha as beautifully and perfectly as any creation of human hands ever could.

She slept restlessly on the plane, awakened by the clattering of flight attendants' carts and the conversation of other passengers. It was six o'clock when they landed, the skies over Phoenix barely pink with dawn. She felt strangely only half-present, as if she were not heading home but had left her real life behind in Lahaina.

Though she had little appetite, she bought a raisin bagel with cream cheese and a small coffee in the terminal but ended up tossing most of her breakfast in the trash before boarding her flight to Philadelphia. She slept better on the second leg of her trip, dozing off shortly after the plane reached its cruising altitude and not waking until the flight attendant came by to remind her to raise her seat back in preparation for landing.

On the ground in Philadelphia, she checked her voicemail and found messages waiting from Claire, who wanted Bonnie to let her know when she had arrived safely, and all three of her children, who welcomed her home and wanted to make plans to see her. Matt McClure had left the last message, reminding her that he and Sylvia would pick her up at the Elm Creek Valley Regional Airport and bring her home to the manor, where Sarah would be waiting to introduce her to their newborn twins, whom Bonnie had seen only in emailed photographs.

The last flight was the shortest of the three, the tiny plane reminiscent of the one she and Hinano had taken to Oahu. As the propellers roared to life, Bonnie found herself suddenly eager to complete her journey and reunite with Sylvia, Sarah, and the others. Even though they had not stood up for her against Craig the way Claire had boldly driven him off from the Hale Kapa Kuiki, they were still some of her dearest friends in the world, and she missed them.

As the plane soared away from the city and above the rolling Appalachians, light green with the first verdant rush of spring, images of Elm Creek Manor flooded Bonnie's thoughts—Candlelight ceremonies on the cornerstone patio, quilters' scavenger hunts on the moonlit grounds of the estate, plucking the first apples of the season in the orchard, collaborating on new quilt designs or classes with friends, sharing good times and bad, happiness and tears. Although she was no longer a part-owner of Elm Creek Quilts, she was and would always be an Elm Creek Quilter. She knew her friends would be delighted for her that she had become part-owner of Aloha Quilt Camp, even though it meant she would be spending half of the year far away.

She smiled as the tiny plane touched down on the single runway of Elm Creek Valley Regional, imagining her friends' reactions when they heard her good news. Yes, they would miss her, but they would be delighted to know they each had a standing invitation to visit her at the Hale Kapa Kuiki.

Bonnie forgot her fatigue as she made her way to baggage claim. She spotted Matt first, his blond curly head standing above the crowd. He caught sight of her, grinned and waved, and as Bonnie emerged from the opposite side of the security barrier, she saw Sylvia. Clad in a lavender cardigan, her silver-gray hair worn straight except for the slightest curl just above her shoulders, Sylvia beamed at Bonnie and held out her arms. Bonnie hurried to embrace her, so overwhelmed that tears filled her eyes. She hugged Matt, too, and asked about the babies. He and Sarah weren't getting much sleep, he told her, but they had never been happier.

Sylvia peppered Bonnie with questions as they waited for her luggage and loaded it into the Elm Creek Quilts minivan. The route to the manor seemed so wonderfully familiar and yet entirely new, adorned with the freshness of spring. Even the narrow, bumpy gravel road that wound through the woods and over Elm Creek made her nearly laugh aloud with delight.

As the early evening sunlight broke through the boughs above, they emerged from the leafy wood and came upon the apple orchard, gracefully adorned with buds that would soon become fragrant blossoms. The road wound past a red barn, climbed a low hill, and rambled across the bridge over Elm Creek. All at once the manor came into view—three stories of gray stone and dark wood, elegant and charming, and suddenly Bonnie felt as if she had come home.

On the other side of the creek, the road broadened and became a parking lot circling two towering elms. "Anna's preparing a special welcome home supper for you," Sylvia promised as Matt parked the van.

"Sounds wonderful," said Bonnie, although she felt unsettled at the thought of facing Anna for the first time since she had purchased Bonnie's share of Elm Creek Quilts. "I'm famished."

Matt helped her carry her luggage, overstuffed with gifts and souvenirs, up the back stairs, but before he could open the door it burst open and suddenly Bonnie was surrounded by welcoming friends—Andrew, Sylvia's husband; Anna, clad in an apron with her dark brown hair in a long French braid; Gretchen, one of the newest Elm Creek Quilters who had joined them only weeks before Bonnie's departure; and another woman who, although she looked only vaguely familiar, welcomed Bonnie like a long-lost friend.

"I'm sure you remember Maggie Flynn," said Sylvia, coming to her rescue.

"Of course," said Bonnie. Maggie was the second of their new hires and had moved into the manor from Sacramento just in time for the start of the new camp season. Bonnie had liked her during the interview process and looked forward to getting to know her better in the months to come.

"We have more friends waiting inside," said Andrew, taking the suitcase Bonnie carried.

Bonnie, assuming he meant the newborn twins, let herself be swept along by her friends into the manor. She stopped short in the kitchen doorway, transfixed by her first glimpse of the newly remodeled room—twice the size she remembered, with gleaming new cabinets, countertops, appliances, and seating. "I barely recognize the place," she marveled, and then stopped short again at the sight of two women seated in a charming breakfast nook. Sarah, cradling one of the twins, rose to meet her, as did her companion, who held the other baby and beamed with pleasure at Bonnie's surprise.

"Judy?" Bonnie exclaimed. She rushed forward to embrace her, was quickly distracted by the adorable babies, and hugged Sarah in congratulations before embracing Judy again. She had missed all of her friends, but it was an unexpected delight to find Judy among them.

"What are you doing here?" she asked. "Dare I hope that you've moved back permanently?"

Judy laughed. "No, I love my new job at Penn too much

to give it up. This is just a weekend visit. I couldn't miss your homecoming and wouldn't dream of spending National Quilting Day anywhere but here."

"Even if it's only for the weekend, I'm glad you came. I've missed you." Bonnie hugged one friend after another. She had missed them so much, more than she had realized. "I've missed you all."

"Judy also came to conduct a bit of business," remarked Sylvia. "Perhaps we can discuss it after supper."

"The chicken needs another twenty minutes," said Anna, with an eager glance at Bonnie. "Why don't you go ahead?"

"First," said Sarah, passing one of the babies to Bonnie, who drew back the edge of the swaddling quilt to offer the little one a fingertip to grasp, "let's make sure Bonnie's divorce is absolutely, completely, and irrevocably final."

"It's about as final as you can get," said Bonnie. "Why? Has Craig been coming around bothering you again? I can call the authorities on him, thanks to that protection from abuse order."

"We haven't seen hide nor hair of him," Sylvia assured her, gesturing to one of the tables. "Why don't you sit down?"

Bonnie had been sitting down for most of the previous twenty-four hours, but Sylvia clearly had something on her mind, so Bonnie slid into the comfortable booth. Judy, Sarah, and Sylvia joined them, while Anna returned to the stove, where she stirred a large copper pot simmering with something that smelled so delicious Bonnie could almost taste it.

"We know how distressed you were to sell your share of Elm Creek Quilts." Sylvia reached across the table to pat Bonnie's hand sympathetically.

"Oh, it's all right now," said Bonnie, eager to share her good news. "I understand. It was a necessary precaution, and it worked. It kept Elm Creek Quilts safely out of Craig's reach. If I had to do it all over again, I'd make the same choice."

Sarah frowned and shook her head. "It was a choice you never should have been forced to make."

"What's done is done. I'm at peace with it." Bonnie caught Anna's eye. "And I hope all of you are too. I don't want there to be any awkwardness. I know what Sylvia says is true: Once an Elm Creek Quilter, always an Elm Creek Quilter."

"I agree completely," declared Judy. "Ownership doesn't make us more or less an integral part of our circle of quilters, and yet ownership should belong first to those of us who are still actively involved in the quilt camp."

"Especially when that person is a founding member," said Gretchen, who was not.

Bonnie glanced around at the smiling, expectant faces of her friends. "What's going on? I haven't been away so long that I've forgotten what you look like when you're plotting something."

"I want to sell you my share of Elm Creek Quilts," said Judy. "You still work here; I don't. I wanted to make a career change; you didn't. It's not fair that Craig forced you to sacrifice something you loved and had worked so hard for."

"We know that you sold your share out of selfless concern for us," said Sylvia. "We believe such generosity deserves a reward. We would have acted earlier, but we had to wait until it was safe, until Craig couldn't claim one single thread of Elm Creek Quilts."

"We didn't think it would be safe even to mention it," added Sarah, "just in case later Craig accused you of holding out on him."

Bonnie looked from one friend to another as their voices tumbled over one another's in their eagerness to speak. "You want to sell me your share of the business?" Bonnie asked Judy, trying to conceal her dismay. Even if she could have chosen between the partnership in Elm Creek Quilts or in Aloha Quilt Camp, it was too late. She had already spent most of her insurance settlement and auction proceeds buying into the Hale Kapa Kuiki. Now her friends were presenting her with the chance to regain all she had lost, and she must refuse them.

"That's exactly what I intend to do," said Judy.

"You're so generous," Bonnie stammered. "All of you. But I'm afraid I can't accept your offer." A chorus of surprise and dismay went up from her friends, and Bonnie raised her hands to silence them. "My circumstances have changed, and I couldn't afford to pay you what it's worth. I'm sorry, Judy. Thank you, but I can't manage it."

Anna set down her long-handled wooden spoon on the counter with a clatter and shot Bonnie a look of pure astonishment. "You mean you've already spent that five thousand I paid you?"

"We thought you'd put it aside for a rainy day," exclaimed Sarah, "not go on a shopping spree."

"Wait," said Bonnie. "Five thousand?"

Everyone nodded. "I understand that's the going rate for ten percent shares of Elm Creek Quilts," said Judy, feigning innocence.

"You know it's worth much more than that," said Bonnie. "I accepted Anna's offer only because it was an emergency, and because it was Anna."

"You were more than generous," said Anna, "and what goes around comes around."

"If that's what you were willing to sell your share for in order to save Elm Creek Quilts for the rest of us, then it's the most you should have to pay in order to restore what you sacrificed." Judy regarded her with fond amusement. "I want to sell, and I've named my price. If you don't want it, I suppose I could see if Craig's still interested—"

"Absolutely not," declared Sylvia. "Bonnie, I'm afraid there's no stopping Judy once she makes up her mind. She's going to sell one way or another. It's up to you to save us from her reckless behavior."

Everyone laughed, and as Bonnie gazed around the room at the faces of her beloved friends, her heart felt full to overflowing.

"I'd love to buy your share of Elm Creek Quilts," she said, blinking away tears of joy. "It just so happens I have enough left over to meet your price."

As Judy smiled and took a folder of paperwork from the satchel on the floor beside her chair, Bonnie gratefully accepted the congratulations and fond hugs of her friends and colleagues. "Aloha," she said to each friend as they embraced, not out of habit but from true feeling. She couldn't wait to share the rest of her happiness with them, to tell them that she was both an Elm Creek Quilter and an Aloha Quilter, that she had left them broken and dispirited but had returned whole. She would no longer define herself by her losses, for she had discovered that when inspired by the aloha spirit she could create her own unique pattern for her life—seamless, beautiful, and enriching—full of love to give and to receive.

"Aloha," she told her friends, both near and far, knowing they would understand it in the warmest and most loving of its definitions.